36 DAYS

Kamlesh Sutar is a broadcast journalist based out of Mumbai. For over 19 years, Kamlesh has worked with leading TV channels like the national broadcaster Doordarshan, Times Now, and News X. Currently, he works with the TV Today network as a Deputy Editor, covering politics in Maharashtra and Goa. A bilingual journalist with India Today TV and Aaj Tak, he has solid experience in covering the state and general elections of Maharashtra since 2004, the state elections of Gujarat and Goa since 2007, and those of Karnataka since 2013. He has an excellent understanding of the socio-political nuances of Maharashtra, and has covered caste conflicts and agrarian issues in the state with great sensitivity. He was awarded the prestigious Red Ink Award (Special Mention) 2019 by the Mumbai Press Club for his work on Dalit music and movement.

36 DAYS

A Political Chronicle of **AMBITION, DECEPTION, TRUST** and **BETRAYAL**

KAMLESH SUTAR

RUPA

Published by
Rupa Publications India Pvt. Ltd 2020
7/16, Ansari Road, Daryaganj
New Delhi 110002

Sales Centres:
Allahabad Bengaluru Chennai
Hyderabad Jaipur Kathmandu
Kolkata Mumbai

Copyright © Kamlesh Sutar 2020

The views and opinions expressed in this book are the author's own and the facts are as reported by him which have been verified to the extent possible, and the publishers are not in any way liable for the same.

All rights reserved.
No part of this publication may be reproduced, transmitted, or stored in a retrieval system, in any form or by any means, electronic, mechanical, photocopying, recording or otherwise, without the prior permission of the publisher.

ISBN: 978-93-89967-65-4

2nd impression 2020

10 9 8 7 6 5 4 3 2

Printed in India by Replika Press Pvt. Ltd.

The moral right of the author has been asserted.

This book is sold subject to the condition that it shall not, by way of trade or otherwise, be lent, resold, hired out, or otherwise circulated, without the publisher's prior consent, in any form of binding or cover other than that in which it is published.

To my parents,
Leelawati Sutar and Damodar Sutar

Dear Tai and Nana,
this is dedicated to all the hardships you faced and sacrifices you made...
I know somewhere in the heavens you are very happy for this book!

CONTENTS

Author's Note / ix

Prologue / xi

Precursor to the 36-day Drama / 1

The Bugle / 4

The 36-day Drama / 17

Acknowledgements / 223

Index / 226

AUTHOR'S NOTE

The 2019 elections have now become an integral part of Maharashtra's political history. I feel fortunate to have witnessed its politics so closely over the last two decades. The only thought behind the book was to document the most riveting phase of the state's politics. The 2019 assembly elections indeed were the turning point in the state's politics. There were many firsts, many twists, many surprises that one saw. All this needed to be documented and told. I don't want to make sensational claims in the book. I stick to facts, most of which are in the public domain and are corroborated. I have been a witness to most of the rapid developments during the period. At some point or the other, I have directly or indirectly communicated with almost all of the players in the narrative. The only liberty I have taken is in the style of writing and presenting, to add to the dramatic style of narration. There is no hero or villain in the story. Everyone had his or her shade of grey. These shades clashed with each other to make a grey rainbow—yes, a grey rainbow—a rainbow of ambition, deceit, trust and betrayal that shone over an unprecedented labyrinth, a political game of brinkmanship, a game of thrones that would leave its impact on the state's politics for years to come. This book is hence my ode to the politics of Maharashtra.

PROLOGUE

24 October 2019; BJP State Headquarters, Nariman Point, Mumbai

Amid the deafening sounds of crackers and dhols, 49-year-old Devendra Fadnavis arrived at the Bharatiya Janata Party (BJP) State Headquarters at Nariman Point. Wearing his usual smile, he walked into the Party office to address the media. More than two dozen cameras stared at the man of the moment in a jam-packed hall.

In spite of the BJP emerging as the single largest party, Fadnavis, the incumbent Chief Minister, wasn't looking ecstatic. As he focused on statistics, his press conference came across as academic and dry. It didn't have the vibe of the press conference of a victor.

In contrast, Sharad Pawar, the 78-year-old leader of the Nationalist Congress Party (NCP), was looking elated even though his party was at number three. At 54 seats, the NCP's tally in the Maharashtra assembly had gone up by 12 against the 2014 elections. The cause of Fadnavis's anxiety was that his party's tally had come down from 122 to 105.

And then there was this other man sitting in his suburban Bandra residence, whose position was slightly mystifying. His numbers had gone down compared to the 2014 elections, and yet he was delighted. With constant phone calls informing him of the latest trends, his mind was busy doing calculations. With 56 seats, Uddhav Balasaheb Thackeray, President of the Shiv Sena, was happy because he was holding the keys to the next government of Maharashtra. With BJP's tally coming down, it had given more muscles to Uddhav for bargaining—an opportunity his party hadn't had in the last five years.

Shiv Sena undoubtedly held the keys to the next government. That afternoon, perhaps even Uddhav Thackeray may have thought that he would emerge as the kingmaker.

PRECURSOR TO THE 36-DAY DRAMA

18 February 2019; Blue Sea Banquets, Worli Sea Face, Mumbai

After an hour-long meeting at the Thackeray residence, 'Matoshri', in suburban Bandra, BJP National President Amit Shah, Shiv Sena President Uddhav Thackeray and his son Aditya, along with Chief Minister Devendra Fadnavis, left for Blue Sea Banquets, Worli in the same car. They were going to address a press conference.

For journalists present in large numbers at the Worli venue, the day was full of speculation about the alliance between the saffron siblings. The décor in the hall perhaps gave broader hints of what was in store. On the left side of the dais were statues of Shivaji Maharaj and Shiv Sena Supremo Late Balasaheb Thackeray, and a photo frame of Late Atal Bihari Vajpayee. But in spite of the obvious, there were still reasons to expect the unexpected.

◆

Barely 13 months ago, on 23 January 2018, at the Shiv Sena's National Executive Committee meeting held at the NSC dome in Worli, two resolutions had been proposed: the first was for the elevation of Yuva Sena Chief Aditya Thackeray as Party Neta (Leader); the second for ending the party's alliance with BJP.

Shiv Sena had decided to pull the plug with several months still to go for the assembly elections, and the decision had received thunderous applause in the meeting. Slogans like *'Jai Bhawani, Jai Shivaji'* and *'Uddhav Saheb, tum aage badho, hum tumhare saath hain'* could be heard all around. At that time, Fadnavis was in Davos to attend the World Economic Forum. Despite the speculations regarding whether his government would be able to complete its full term, he was unperturbed.

◆

On 18 February 2019, at the press conference in Blue Sea Banquets, Worli, Devendra Fadnavis took charge of the mic with the same confidence he had displayed a year earlier. 'The Shiv Sena and BJP have been the longest of allies for more than 25 years. We have the same ideology of Hindutva and that is why we have decided that we will be contesting the forthcoming Lok Sabha and Assembly elections together,' he said, announcing the alliance.

'Shiv Sena has put forth certain demands including the construction of Ram temple, complete loan waiver for farmers and exempting houses less than 500 sq. metres from property tax. While we too are in favour of the Ram Mandir in Ayodhya, the matter is in court and in the final stages. We will look into the farmers who were left out of the loan waiver package and will exempt houses less than 500 sq. metres from taxation,' Fadnavis read out the conditions.

It was announced that for the ensuing Lok Sabha polls, the BJP would contest on 25 seats of the 48, while Shiv Sena would contest on the remaining 23 seats. When asked about the alliance formula, Fadnavis had said, 'We (BJP and Shiv Sena) have decided on having a 50–50 per cent sharing of positions and responsibilities.' His response wasn't highlighted in the headlines of the day, and no one then had the slightest idea that in six months the statement would not just resonate in the state's politics, but would also leave it gobsmacked!

23 May 2019

Poll pundits were divided over the possible outcome of the 2019 Lok Sabha elections. Some had predicted a strong anti-incumbency wave working against the Modi government, while others felt that the Pulwarma attack and the subsequent Balakot strikes would serve as the game changers. The final outcome of the elections proved the latter group to be correct. The BJP returned to power with a thumping majority, winning 303 seats on its own, while the National Democratic Alliance (NDA), led by the party, ended up with 353 seats. Shiv Sena emerged as the second largest party in the NDA fold.

The BJP–Shiv Sena alliance put up an impressive show in Maharashtra, winning 41 of the 48 seats—the BJP won on 23 seats out of the 25 it contested, while Shiv Sena won 18 out of the 23 it fought on. The Nationalist Congress Party (NCP) managed to retain four of its seats and the Congress managed to win only one seat in the state.

30 May 2019

In the presence of important leaders from Asia and the who's who of the business, industry and entertainment sectors, Modi 2.0—as the new Narendra Modi government is popularly referred to—took oath. Of the ministers who took oath that day, 54 belonged to the BJP, one (Harsimrat Kaur Badal) to Shiromani Akali Dal (SAD), one (Ram Vilas Paswan) to Lok Janshakti Party (LJP), and one (Ramdas Athawale) to Republican Party of India (Athawale) (RPI [A]). Shiv Sena too got only one ministerial berth—Arvind Sawant was sworn in as the Minister for Heavy Industries and Public Enterprise. This was despite the fact that Shiv Sena was the second largest constituent of the NDA and had won 18 seats. Moreover, it had been a long-term ally of the BJP in Maharashtra and its partner in Hindutva ideology.

In 2014, too, the Shiv Sena had got only one berth in the Modi cabinet—in fact, it was the same portfolio of Heavy Industries—and the party leaders had felt humiliated. Five years later, things looked no different. Did Shiv Sena swallow its pride in the aftermath of Modi's swearing-in ceremony, choosing to lie in wait for an opportune moment to strike back?

THE BUGLE

6 August 2019

After a nearly five-hour-long debate, the Lok Sabha passed a bill for the abrogation of Article 370 of the Indian Constitution, which gave special status to Jammu and Kashmir (J&K). The resolution was passed in the Rajya Sabha as well. In addition, the state was also bifurcated into two separate union territories: Ladakh, without a Legislative Assembly, and J&K, which would have a Legislative Assembly with curtailed powers.

The abrogation of Article 370 had been a long-cherished dream of the BJP—a dream that its founder Shyama Prasad Mukherjee had fought for. In fact, the special status accorded to J&K was not only opposed by the BJP but also the Rashtriya Swayamsevak Sangh (RSS) on the grounds that *'Ek desh mein do Vidhan, do Pradhan aur do Nishan nahi chalenge* (There cannot be two Constitutions, two Prime Ministers and two flags in one nation).'[1]

Not only the BJP, but its political and ideological ally, the Shiv Sena too had a strong stand on the issue. Shiv Sena founder and supremo, the late Bal Thackeray, had always been vocal against Article 370.[2] So, it came as no surpise that in the aftermath of the decision, Uddhav Thackeray lauded the Modi-led government's move at a press conference in Matoshri. Sweets were distributed at the press meet and Uddhav said that the move on Article 370 fulfilled the dream of the late Bal Thackeray and Atal Bihari

---

[1] The slogan was first coined by Shyama Prasad Mukherjee in the Jan Sangh Convention held in Kanpur in 1952.
[2] Thackeray's political speeches, interviews and cartoons published in *Marmik* attest to this fact.

Vajpayee. 'Today, our country has become fully independent,' he said.

Was BJP fulfilling its idealogical promise with the abrogation of Section 370, or was there more to it than met the eye? After all, the Modi–Shah duo has been known to hit many birds with one shot. Political observers considered it to be a political move—for two important BJP-ruled states, Maharashtra and Haryana, were going to polls.

2 July 2019

It was the last day of the last session of the Maharashtra legislature assembly. Usually known for his firebrand and aggressive speeches, Chief Minister Devendra Fadnavis concluded his speech with a piece of poetry he had written, as the lower house keenly listened.

'*Mee punha yein...* (I will come back...)'

This first line recited by him was met with the thumping of benches in applause. He then went to recite:

> I will come back
> with the same determination,
> in the same role, at the same place,
> for the creation of a new Maharashtra,
> I will come back...!

♦

Even as Fadnavis was confident of making a comeback, the Yuva Sena President Aditya Thackeray, who had been anointed as 'Neta' and implicitly as the party's heir apparent to Uddhav, was gearing up to make an impactful debut. Aditya announced a state-wide tour from 18 July. Called the Jan Ashirwad Yatra, the tour was to start from Jalgaon in north Maharashtra and, according to Aditya's cousin and close confidante Varun Sardesai, the Shiv Sena scion would be visiting all Lok Sabha seats in the state from where the party's candidates were contesting. According to Varun, it was a way of thanking the Shiv Sena's loyal voters and an attempt to win the hearts of those who normally wouldn't vote for the party.

For some, the Jan Ashirwad Yatra was on the same lines as the Praja Sankalpa Padayatra launched by Andhra Pradesh Chief Minister Y.S. Jaganmohan Reddy (YSR) before the state assembly polls in his state. YSR had managed to trounce a formidable Chandrababu Naidu to emerge as the Chief Minister of Andhra Pradesh. The Indian Political Action Committee (I-PAC), led by the noted political strategist Prashant Kishor (PK)—who had planned a successful election strategy for YSR earlier—was now managing the election strategy for Aditya. *Aditya Sanvad*, a two-way communication platform between Aditya and the voters, was launched. Was Aditya being moulded for the role of the Maharashtra CM?

1 August 2019

The state assembly elections were yet to be announced, but Fadnavis had already made big plans for his return. His grand pre-election campaign included a state-wide tour—the Maha Janadesh Yatra—starting 1 August 2019. The yatra was on the lines of those by other BJP Chief Ministers Shivraj Singh Chouhan, Vasundhara Raje Scindia and Fadnavis's mentor, Narendra Modi. Fadnavis's team, which included corporate brains alongside party young guns, charted out a 25-day yatra wherein he would cover a distance of more than 4,000 km, going to 152 assembly constituencies across 30 of the 36 districts in the state. It was to be a packed schedule for him, as he was to hold 104 rallies, 228 Swagat Sabhas and 20 press conferences.

Fadnavis's anointment in 2014 was almost accidental. Following the death of the senior state party leader Gopinath Munde immediately after the 2014 Lok Sabha elections, there was a void in the state leadership. Modi put his faith in Fadnavis, a young leader who was also the then State President of the party. An articulate speaker, he had made his mark in the Maharashtra assembly. His claim to fame was the ₹70,000 crore irrigation scam, which Fadnavis had been vociferous about not just on the floor of the house but also on prime time television debates. The scam had compelled the then Deputy Chief Minister and state irrigation minister Ajit Pawar to resign. It had impacted the political lives of two individuals—putting a question mark on Ajit Pawar's political career while giving a fillip to Devendra Fadnavis's. Little did they know then that their paths would also cross in a dramatic way a few years later...

♦

The Maha Janadesh Yatra, which was not just an outreach programme or an election campaign but a brand-building exercise for Fadnavis, was receiving excellent response. In the last five years as CM, Fadnavis had not just successfully carved a niche for himself in the state's politics, but had also emerged as a prominent personality in the national political arena.

No Maharashtra Chief Minister after Vasantrao Naik (1962–72) had managed to complete a full five-year term till Devendra Fadnavis—a mean feat to achieve. Having weathered political storms that ranged from rivals within his own party to mammoth Maratha Morchas demanding reservations for the politically most dominant community, to the Bhima Koregaon violence and battling the questions over his upper-caste credentials as a Brahmin—Fadnavis had weathered all controversies successfully. Moreover, he had also managed to create an impressionable image through his flagship Jal Yukta Shivar scheme, a water conservation programme aimed at achieving a drought-free Maharashtra. Through a well-managed campaign and equally meticulous planning, Fadnavis more or less turned it into a people's movement.

It was imperative for Fadnavis, who was now eyeing a second term, to become a mass leader like his predecessors. His biggest hurdle was his caste, for the state had only had two Brahmin Chief Ministers in its 70-year history, the other being Shiv Sena's Manohar Joshi (1995–99).

The Maha Janadesh Yatra was to serve as the platform for upgrading Fadnavis's image from that of an administrator to a lok neta—a mass leader. With his strong oratory skills, Fadnavis managed to make all the right noises in his yatra. As he travelled across districts in his specially designed chariot, he was often asked about the seat-sharing formula with Shiv Sena—a question he cleverly dodged, like some others.

Fadnavis and his team had recently made a strong dent into the NCP led by Sharad Pawar. Several NCP leaders joined the BJP during the Maha Janadesh Yatra. But when you are making political speeches in apolitical rallies, you have to pick your target. Fadnavis had chosen his. On his radar was none other than the grand old man of Maharashtra politics—Pawar himself.

In an interview to *India Today* in Gondia during the yatra, Fadnavis had attacked Pawar, who had criticized the BJP for the movement of leaders to the party. 'I wonder how some people [Sharad Pawar] who have built their political careers by splitting parties, are complaining today. I urge them to introspect why people are leaving them and accepting Modiji's leadership,' he had said in the interview.[3] In his interaction with Rajdeep Sardesai at the India Today Conclave held in Mumbai in September 2019, he had further stated, 'The era of Sharad Pawar's politics is over!' This was considered a bold statement by political observers. Some believed that Fadnavis had gone overboard in taking Pawar head-on. Had Fadnavis bitten off more than he could chew?

◆

At the BJP's head office at Nariman Point in Mumbai, a portrait of the late Sushma Swaraj was kept for party workers and leaders to pay homage to. A senior BJP functionary sitting in the media room of the office was fondly remembering the firebrand leader, who had passed away on 6 August 2019 after a massive cardiac arrest. Known as a powerful orator, Swaraj had worked closely with BJP stalwarts like Atal Bihari Vajpayee and Lal Krishna Advani, but had taken a backseat with the rise of Modi and Amit Shah, even

---

[3] The author interviewed Devendra Fadnavis in his capacity as Deputy Editor, India Today TV.

though she served as the Minister of External Affairs in Modi's cabinet in his first tenure.

The leader, while remembering Swaraj, informed that the Maha Janadesh Yatra would be suspended for some days. This, however, was not going to be the only temporary halt to Fadnavis's yatra. Heavy rains had started lashing western Maharashtra, with Pune, Satara, Sangli and Kolhapur witnessing unprecedented flooding. The situation was only growing from bad to worse, and close to 1,50,000 people had to be evacuated to safer places. Fadnavis had already faced criticism for continuing with his yatra despite the havoc caused by the rains. His close aide Girish Mahajan was assigned the task of overseeing the flood relief situation, but soon a controversy erupted around his selfie video during the relief tour. Fadnavis was again forced to take a break from his yatra. And then, when party senior leader and former Finance Minister Arun Jaitley passed away on 24 August, the yatra was halted yet again for a day.

A superstitious leader sitting in the media room of the BJP office called this series of breaks a bad omen. Was it?

18 October 2019

Challenged by a young turk like Devendra Fadnavis, NCP President Sharad Pawar was readying for his rally in Satara. This rally in the Maratha fiefdom was for the assembly as well as Lok Sabha bypolls. Once very close to Pawar, the Bhosale cousins, Shivendra Raje Bhosale and Udayanraje Bhosale—the descendants of Chhatrapati Shivaji Maharaj—had deserted him to join the BJP. Shivendra, the former NCP MLA from Satara, was contesting for the assembly as per the routine while Udayanraje, who had been one of the NCP's four MPs from the state, had resigned, leading to bypolls for the Lok Sabha seat.

The Bhosales were not the only ones who had quit the party—NCP was facing a mass exodus. The crisis had reached Pawar's doorsteps, with his close relative Rana Jagjit Singh Patil[4] joining the BJP. Old guards like Madhukar Pichad, founding member and

---

[4] Rana Jagjit Singh Patil is the son of Ajit Pawar's brother-in-law Padmasinh Patil.

former State President of the party; Navi Mumbai strongman Ganesh Naik, who controlled the cash-rich Navi Mumbai Municipal Corporation; and Women's Wing President Chitra Wagh, too, bid adieu to the party. Some others like Beed strongman Jaidutt Kshirsagar, Mumbai strongman Sachin Ahir and former State Party President Bhaskar Jadhav had joined the Shiv Sena. And if this wasn't enough, speculations of NCP's OBC strongman Chhagan Bhujbal being in touch with Shiv Sena were rife. It was this mass exodus that had prompted Devendra Fadnavis to claim that the Pawar era of Politics was over in Maharashtra.

While many in the NCP believed that the party was in the middle of a shipwreck, the 78-year-old Pawar was leading the campaign from the front. Though the party had already launched its Shiv Sampark Yatra with young faces like Amol Kolhe and Dhananjay Munde taking the lead, it was ultimately the tumultuous electioneering by the Party's founder that was going to matter. After being named by the Enforcement Directorate (ED) in the ₹25,000 crore Maharashtra State Co-operative Bank scam, Pawar had taken the agency head-on. Questioning the timing of the ED's move right ahead of the assembly elections, Pawar had said he would voluntarily visit the ED office in South Mumbai's Ballard Pier area at 2 p.m. on 27 September to put forward his side of the story in connection with the case.

Two days earlier, addressing a press conference at the Y.B. Chavan Centre, Pawar had perhaps given a broad hint of what was on his mind. 'Maharashtra believes in the ideology of Chhatrapati Shivaji Maharaj. We don't know bowing down before the Delhi takht (throne),' Pawar had roared.

On 27 September, party workers staged large-scale protests near the ED office since morning. The entire area leading to the office was cordoned off. The protests were not restricted to Mumbai; they happened in several parts of the state. Owing to law and order problems, Mumbai Police Commissioner Sanjay Barve himself went to Sharad Pawar's house—Silver Oak Estate—requesting him to call off his plans to visit the ED Office, a request that Pawar obliged.

The decision was welcomed with loud cheers at the party office, which was a stone's throw away from the ED Office, as it was perceived as a victory for Pawar and for a party that had started to look frail. By evening, TV channels had already planned prime time debates on how Pawar turned the challenge into an opportunity. However, a catastrophe hit the party within hours, with Pawar's nephew and former Deputy Chief Minister Ajit Pawar resigning as a legislator. Ajit submitted his resignation to Assembly Speaker Haribhau Bagde in Mumbai in a very stealthy manner and within hours, the headlines had gone from being all about Sharad Pawar's victory to Ajit Pawar's resignation.

There had been speculation since 2004 about Ajit Pawar rising in rebellion against his uncle. And it seemed now that this was finally unfolding in reality. What was going on in Ajit's mind? Why did he take away the sheen from the party workers' moment of glory?

Pawar addressed media at his Pune residence soon after, saying he wasn't aware of Ajit's decision and that Ajit had never discussed his plans of resigning with him. After resigning, Ajit Pawar went incommunicado.

The rebellion, however, was short-lived. Next day, Ajit Pawar met his uncle at Silver Oak and addressed the media, saying that he took the decision as he was pained to see his uncle go through the torture that followed him being named by the ED in the alleged Maharashtra State Co-operative Bank scam. Breaking down in tears, Ajit said, 'After all, we all are human beings.'

Was Ajit Pawar painting a genuine picture of his pain at Sharad Pawar being named in the scam? Regardless, he had now raised suspicion in the minds of some top party leaders. A senior leader, anguished, went on to say, 'Party workers were charged after the ED protests... Dada [as Ajit Pawar is referred in the party circles] has thrown cold waters on the party's hopes.' This feeling was to haunt them again soon...

On Friday, 18 October 2019, Pawar took the mic to address a large gathering in Satara. His friend of many years from his college days and the NCP candidate for the Satara Lok Sabha bypolls,

Shriniwas Patil, sat by his side. It was a cloudy evening with forecasts of showers.

Suddenly it started raining heavily. Pawar's guards and some leaders on the stage offered him an umbrella, but Pawar refused. He continued to speak for 25 minutes even as he got drenched in heavy rains. The sight froze the audience. No one moved an inch. It was not just the speech, but Pawar's fortitude and grit that won their hearts. The images of Pawar weathering heavy rains and addressing the rally went viral on social media.

Every election has its defining moments. It could be a simple statement that changes the tide, as was the case with Mani Shankar Aiyar's 'chaiwala' comments, or how Narendra Modi turned the tables over comments like 'Maut ka Saudagar' by Sonia Gandhi during the 2007 Gujarat elections or the 'neech' remarks by Priyanka Gandhi Vadra during an election campaign speech in Amethi in May 2014.[5] In this case, perhaps the image of a rain-drenched Sharad Pawar was going to become the defining moment of the 2019 Maharashtra assembly elections.

◆

In the entire scheme of things, Congress was missing from the action. Plagued by large-scale defections and intra-party rivalry, the party didn't look poll-ready. On 26 August, the Maharashtra Congress kicked off its Pol Khol Yatra or Maha Pardafash Yatra from Amravati in Vidarbha. The yatra was to cover several parts of the state, including north Maharashtra, Marathwada and Konkan, over the next few days. The Congress was also facing a mass exodus like the NCP. Radhakrishna Vikhe Patil, who was the party's face in the assembly as Leader of the Opposition, quit the party to join the BJP. Another senior leader, Harshavardhan Patil from Indapur in Pune district, too joined the BJP and so did MLAs like Nitesh Rane, Kalidas Kolambkar and Jaikumar Gore, while Nirmala Gawit

---

[5] http://www.ptinews.com/news/9721261_Cong-used-most-abusive-language-against-Modi--BJP.html; last accessed 16 March 2020.

and Abdul Sattar joined the Shiv Sena.

In spite of this mass exodus, the party didn't adopt an aggressive approach to winning the elections. While Narendra Modi and Amit Shah were addressing back-to-back election rallies for the BJP, the Congress's national leadership showed little interest. Rahul Gandhi addressed only three election rallies—one in Latur and two in Mumbai.

In spite of these glitches, the party managed to form an alliance with the NCP. The two parties had a 15-year alliance before they went their separate ways in the 2014 elections. Keeping their egos aside, the allies agreed on a formula of 144 seats for the Congress and 117 for the NCP, leaving 17 seats for other smaller allies.

The lines were now drawn. In what still appeared to be a one-sided fight, the Congress–NCP alliance was pitched against a formidable looking BJP–Shiv Sena alliance.

21 September 2019

The Election Commission of India (ECI) held a press conference on Saturday, 21 September 2019, and made the much-awaited announcement of the Maharashtra and Haryana assembly elections. With 8,95,62,706 registered voters for the 288 seats of the Maharashtra assembly, single-phase voting was declared for the state. The elections were to take place on 21 October and the counting of votes was to take place on 24 October.

◆

Even as the Congress and the NCP announced their seat-sharing formula, the Shiv Sena and BJP were yet to arrive at one. In 2014, the seat-sharing talks between the two parties had gone sour and led to them parting ways. Having had a bitter experience in the past, both parties were taking it slow and the seat-sharing formula was still under wraps.

On 1 October, with just three days left for the filing of nominations, BJP and Shiv Sena released their first list of candidates. In the BJP's list of 125 candidates, while Devendra Fadnavis was given the ticket from his turf, Nagpur South west, some big names were missing from the list. In Shiv Sena's list of 70 candidates, Aditya Thackeray was named as the party's candidate from Worli constituency in South Central Mumbai, as had been announced earlier. With this, Aditya became the first in the Thackeray clan to ever contest any election, which resulted in suspense building around his future role.

On 3 October, Aditya filed his nominations for the Worli seat in a grand show of strength. Interestingly, posters in Gujarati, Urdu and Tamil were put up in the area, which is an ideal blend of chawls and high-rises and boasts of a perfect mix of cosmopolitan voters. In fact, Aditya wore a veshti—South Indian dhoti—for an election rally in his constituency. His photo went viral and many criticized the Thackeray scion for compromising on the party's core ideology.[6] However, the party wasn't bothered. For the likes of Aditya Thackeray, this was the new Shiv Sena—one that was willing to change. Was this indeed the beginning of an ideological change in the party that was once not beyond rabble-rousing for the rights of the Marathi manoos?

◆

On 4 October, after filing his nominations in Nagpur, Devendra Fadnavis headed for Mumbai straightaway. He was scheduled to address a joint press conference with Shiv Sena President Uddhav Thackeray. At the press conference, it was announced that BJP would contest on 150 seats and its allies would contest via its lotus symbol on 14 seats, while Shiv Sena would be contesting on the remaining 124 seats. This announcement raised several eyebrows in

---

[6] When the Shiv Sena was launched in 1966, it had taken up the hard-line Marathi agenda alleging that South Indians were snatching away jobs from the locals. The agitation had turned violent with Shiv Sena workers attacking several South Indian Udupi restaurants. The war cry the Sena gave then was: *'Bajao Pungi, Hatao Lungi',* as seen in Bal Thackeray cartoons in *Marmik*, and the film *Thackeray* (2019) by Sanjay Raut. Fifty-three years later, the slogan was now haunting the new face of the party.

the jam-packed hall at Nariman Point where the press conference was held. The Shiv Sena had always been the senior partner in any alliance in the state for assembly elections;[7] this time, however, it had accepted the junior role.

'It's not about who is the big brother and who is the small brother. It's about the relation, and we have decided to maintain our relationship,' Uddhav had said in response to a query about whether the roles of 'big' and 'small' brother had finally been resolved between the two parties.

But in spite of what Uddhav had said, the question haunting everyone's mind was: What had compelled the Shiv Sena to agree to this? Had it accepted that 'BJP had arrived'? Was there another trade-off that had taken place between the two parties? Or was there something else going on in Shiv Sena President Uddhav Thackeray's mind? The wait for the answer wasn't going to be too long...

21 October 2019

Maharashtra witnessed lower voter enthusiasm compared to the 2014 assembly elections, when it had witnessed a multi-cornered fight. The final voter percentage in 2019 was 60.46 per cent, 3 per cent lower than in 2014 (63.13 per cent).

While the highest turnout was registered at Karvir assembly constituency in Kolhapur district at 83.20 per cent, South Mumbai's Colaba seat recorded the lowest at 40.20 per cent.

The overall turnout in the state capital, Mumbai, was a dismal 46.93 per cent.

The flood-affected western Maharashtra, especially Kolhapur district, which was worst affected, saw voters turning up in huge numbers. Of the top five highest voter-turnout constituencies, four were from the Kolhapur region.

The Karvir and Shahuwadi seats registered 80.19 per cent

---

[7] As a norm in their alliance, the Shiv Sena always contested on more seats in the state assembly elections while the BJP would get the bigger pie in the seat-sharing in the state for Lok Sabha elections.

turnout, Kagal 80.13 per cent, Radhanagari 75.59 per cent, while Shirala constituency in neighbouring Sangli district witnessed 76.78 per cent voter turnout.[8]

The exit polls were out by the evening. Most of them predicted a win for the BJP not only in Maharashtra but also in Haryana, the other state that had gone to polls.

The counting of votes was still a few hours away. With the pre-poll alliance firmly in place in Maharashtra, the game was appearing more or less set.

But another story was slowly unfolding. The voter turnout had perhaps sent a message, one that was about to be revealed in a few hours...

Maharashtra waited with bated breath for the morning of 24 October, a day that was about to not only throw some numbers, but also launch an unprecedented 36-day saga full of surprises and deceit—and politics.

---

[8] Data taken from the Maharashtra State Election Commission release.

THE 36-DAY DRAMA

DAY 1: THURSDAY, 24 OCTOBER 2019

Maharashtrian voters were barely interested in the election results. Almost all exit polls had predicted a clean sweep for the BJP–Shiv Sena alliance. There was reason enough for the agencies to arrive at the conclusion. The Maha Yuti (grand alliance), led by BJP and Shiv Sena, was looking formidable.[9] They even had as their war cry, '*Ab ki baar, 220 paar*'—they were confident of winning more than 220 of the 288 seats.

Since 5.30 a.m., crews from all TV news channels were stationed outside the BJP headquarters in South Mumbai's Nariman Point area. Reporters from every other channel were deployed at the BJP office, which was already wearing a festive look. With Diwali just a couple of days away, a huge lantern with bright lights was hung near the gate. Flower decor and a huge beautiful rangoli at the entrance caught everyone's attention. The party's state headquarters was undoubtedly the epicentre of activities, at least in the first half of the day.

By 6 a.m., most channels had hit their first bulletin and by 8 a.m., the counting of votes had begun. As trends started coming in, the crowd and enthusiasm around the BJP state headquarters started gaining momentum. Laddoos had already been prepared the previous evening. Dhol players and colourfully dressed dancers started preparing for performances as two huge LED screens live-streamed news channels with graphic-heavy content. By noon, however, the enthusiasm started fading. The results were not

---

[9] Several smaller parties like RPI (A), Rashtriya Samaj Paksha (RSP), Shiv Sangram and Rayat Kranti Sanghatana (RKS) were also part of this alliance.

something that the BJP could cheer about. By the time the picture became clear, the BJP had barely crossed the 100 mark...

While the results were in favour of Maha Yuti, the Congress and NCP hadn't fared badly either. Together, they were close to the 100 mark. The NCP led by Sharad Pawar had come up as a surprise player.

While early trends in Maharashtra had given BJP a comfortable lead, with the emergence of the real picture, there was nervousness in the party. Their plan hadn't worked. The plan wasn't just for their alliance to win maximum seats. 'The BJP had also worked on another plan; while they wanted to win big on their own, they also wanted to bring down our numbers. They wanted the benefit of alliance to win maximum seats, but on the other hand they were plotting to bring down our number of seats,' a senior Shiv Sena leader said during the campaign, adding that, 'At local levels, they encouraged rebel candidates against Shiv Sena's candidate. Some rebels were provided with all needful "resources".'[10]

The Shiv Sena, however, had similar plans. While the BJP manipulated the rebel factor, the Shiv Sena too did the same. 'Trust dies but mistrust blossoms'—these words from the Greek playwright Sophocles held true for Shiv Sena and BJP. After their split in 2014, the allies had fought a bitter battle in the ensuing assembly elections. Even though Shiv Sena later joined the BJP-led government in Maharashtra as a junior partner, it was more a marriage of convenience. The Shiv Sena's mouthpiece *Saamana* never let go of a single opportunity to target the Centre or the Modi–Shah duo.

Many had thought that things had changed for the better between the two when they announced their alliance for both the Lok Sabha and assembly polls, before the general elections. Even after being snubbed at the Centre by being allotted a lesser ministry, Shiv Sena had continued with the alliance. But clearly, as the assembly elections approached, the allies had their own plans.

---

[10] Author's sources on condition of anonymity during ground reports.

Both parties fielded rebels against one another. At some places the candidates officially used party flags or even pictures of the likes of Bal Thackeray or Narendra Modi and Devendra Fadnavis. Around 43 assembly constituencies saw strong candidates as rebels. In at least 31 seats, the BJP and Shiv Sena rebels were pitched against each other. Four Shiv Sena rebels won, while three from the BJP secured victory. On seven to 10 seats, the rebellion factor between the allies went on to directly benefit the Congress, NCP or other candidates.

But in spite of the rebellion, the two parties were seen campaigning together in the state, with the only exception being the Kankavli seat in Konkan region, where the two parties fought a bitter war. The BJP candidate Nitesh Rane, son of Narayan Rane who was formerly with the Shiv Sena and is now the bête noire of the Thackerays, defeated Shiv Sena's Satish Sawant to win the seat. While the Kankavli seat was an open fight between the Ranes and Thackerays, several constituencies witnessed a hidden but direct war between the two parties. BJP veteran Eknath Khadse was denied a party ticket for the Muktainagar seat in Jalgaon district; the party fielded his daughter Rohini instead. Shiv Sena sensed the opportunity and provided all possible help to its rebel, Chandrakant Patil. With Khadse himself not in fray, things were already looking difficult for the BJP's official candidate. Chandrakant Patil also received support from the NCP and Congress, and the NCP even withdrew its official candidate. In a way, Muktainagar saw a unique battle between BJP and the combined forces of Shiv Sena, Congress and NCP. This was just one instance; there were several others.

But the rebel factor turned out to be counterproductive for both the BJP and Shiv Sena—more so for the BJP. The final tally for the BJP stood at 105, which was 17 less than in its 2014 tally. The Shiv Sena's tally too came down by seven seats to 56. The allies, however, were still comfortably ahead of the magic figure of 145.

It wasn't just the rebel factor that damaged the final tally. NCP

Supremo Sharad Pawar's frenzied campaign had helped his party improve its tally in Maharashtra by 13 seats against the 2014 elections. They now stood at 54 seats—and this despite large-scale defections. The surprise pack was the Congress. Despite a lacklustre campaign, apathy by national leadership and a divided house, the party managed a slightly better show as compared to 2014. The grand old party stood at 44, which was two seats more than its 2014 tally.

While the rebel factor affected the numbers of BJP and Shiv Sena, it had also resulted in the election of 13 independents and 16 candidates from smaller parties.

A message from top party bosses in Maharashtra reached the BJP State Headquarters in Nariman Point. The celebrations that were on hold were to begin after that message. Devendra Fadnavis arrived amidst the bursting of crackers and declared at the press meet that BJP and Shiv Sena would be forming the next government. He tried to play with numbers—highlighting how the percentage of votes had gone up—but somewhere the conviction was missing in his statements. While talking about the alliance with Shiv Sena, something else was on Fadnavis's mind. He, however, did mention that he had seen Uddhav Thackeray's press conference and had spoken to him a while back... So, was it the Shiv Sena President's press conference that was bothering Fadnavis?

An hour earlier, Uddhav had said that several options of government formation were open before him. It was perhaps an indication of the political storm that was going to rock the state's politics over the next 36 days!

1.30 p.m., Silver Oak Estate

After the impressive show by the NCP against all odds, Silver Oak was now the epicentre of media attention. The superlative performance by the NCP, led by the Maratha strongman, was directly responsible for halting BJP's juggernaut. The man who knew every nook and corner of the state like the back of his hand, toured the state like a hurricane. As he addressed 66 election rallies, the gusto of the 79-year-old would have made any young leader stare in awe.

The results, till now, were a mixed bag and hence, the media had numerous questions for the man who had perhaps changed the tide of what had been seen as a one-sided fight. With Praful Patel by his side, Sharad Pawar addressed the media. 'The trends do not show any signs of *"ab ki baar 220 paar"*!' quipped Pawar. 'What I can see is that people have not taken the arrogance of power kindly.' Pawar was perhaps referring to the jibes that Fadnavis had taken at Pawar during the poll campaign—from claiming that the Pawar era was over to comparing him with veteran comic actor Asrani's character in the movie *Sholay*.[11]

But more than Pawar's analysis, some were keen to know whether there was a possibility of a new permutation in the state. With fewer than expected seats in BJP's kitty, the Shiv Sena was in a stronger position to bargain. Possibilities of the NCP and Shiv Sena joining hands had already started doing the rounds.

'We have got a mandate to sit in the opposition, and we respect that,' Pawar said.

When asked if the NCP would consider a proposal from Shiv Sena, he had categorically replied, '*Proposal aaye na aaye, hum jaane wale nahi hai* (Whether or not a proposal comes, there is no question of us going with the Shiv Sena).'

In Maharashtra politics, it is widely believed that there are always several layers to what Sharad Pawar says—that one has to read between the lines, because sometimes he doesn't do what he says or apparently means.

BJP leaders perhaps would have heaved a sigh of relief hearing him say that his party had received a mandate to sit in the opposition.

---

[11] Devendra Fadnavis's speech at an election rally in Vikramgarh, Palghar on 19 October 2019.

4.15 p.m., Shiv Sena Bhawan Dadar, Uddhav Thackeray, Press Conference

As celebrations were on at Shiv Sena Bhawan in Central Mumbai's Dadar, Party President Uddhav Thackeray was set to address a press conference. Shiv Sena Bhawan welcomed its Party President with loud cheers of *'Kon aala re kon aala? Shivsenecha Wagh aala!* (Look who has arrived—the Tiger of Shiv Sena has arrived!)' The biggest reason for the celebrations was that 29-year-old Aditya Uddhav Thackeray had comfortably won from the Worli assembly seat, becoming the first from the Thackeray clan to enter the assembly.

Dhols played outside the Sena Bhawan building, and a photo of its Supremo Bal Thackeray was overlooking the iconic Shivaji Park where, just a few days ago, Uddhav had addressed his annual Dussera rally, heaping praises on the Modi government for the abrogation of Article 370.

The numbers were not something that the party could cheer about and yet Uddhav appreared confident as he entered to address the media. An aggressive-looking Uddhav surpised many in that packed hall, saying, 'I want to remind the BJP of its 50:50 per cent power sharing. We need to discuss that first and then talks of government formation can happen later... I can't adjust the BJP every time, I too have to run my party.' The belligerence in his statement was not usual. 'The mandate clearly indicates that people have seen to it that democracy stays alive. The mandate is an eye-opener,' he added.

What Uddhav said later in his address to reporters was a loaded message. 'When we announced the alliance before the Lok Sabha polls, the formula that was decided for assembly elections seat sharing was that of 50:50. We should have contested on equal number of seats then. But Chandrakant Patil (then State President of the Party) requested me to understand his party's position and I obliged. But I can't be accommodating every time. I too have a party to run. First the 50:50 power-sharing formula should be discussed. Only then further talks of government formation can take place.' Uddhav sounded like he was in no mood for compromise.

In November 2018, Uddhav had visited Ayodhya to demand speedy construction of the Ram temple at the disputed sight. During the much-hyped visit, he had demanded a concrete assurance from the Centre on the temple construction. He had even floated a new slogan *'Pehle mandir, phir sarkar* (first the temple, then government).'[12] What he said in this press conference about *'pehle formula, phir sarkar* (first the power-sharing formula then government formation)' had the same tone. 'I have all the options open... This is not a warning, just a reminder,' he said. In BJP's loss, Uddhav had sniffed his gain.

4.35 p.m., BJP State Headquarters, Nariman Point, Mumbai

Fadnavis arrived with his trademark smile and his allies Ramdas Athawale of the RPI(A) and Sadabhau Khot of Rayat Kranti Sanghatana (RKS). Fadnavis's smile was as unreadable as Sharad Pawar's statements—confusing and deceptive at times. This time, though, one could see that the smile was a bit strained.

Riding on the success of his five-year term, Fadnavis had gone to the elections announcing that there was no real opposition to challenge him. 'There is no wrestler left in the ring' had been his catchphrase in election rallies. The final outcome, though, meant that despite the BJP winning the most seats, they were heavily relying on the Shiv Sena as they had failed at a clean sweep. Moreover, the BJP had received a drubbing in Fadnavis's home turf Vidarbha, with the party's tally in the region going down from 44 in 2014 to 29. TV debates had already started putting the blame on him for denying tickets to the likes to Chandrashekhar Bawankule, who belongs to the dominant Teli Other Backward Caste (OBC) community that

---

[12] https://www.indiatoday.in/elections/story/shiv-sena-clarion-call-for-ram-mandir-pehle-mandir-phir-sarkar-1395210-2018-11-24; last accessed 16 March 2020.

has sizeable presence in the Vidarbha region. The setback of the Teli community's withdrawal was felt on six seats.

Before Fadnavis spoke, BJP State President Chandrakant Patil took a dig at the Opposition saying that they should stop daydreaming about forming the government in Maharashtra as the BJP–Shiv Sena led alliance was going to form the next government.

Fadnavis started his address by thanking allies, including Uddhav Thackeray. He said he had seen the press conference by Uddhav, and yet claimed that he was sure that the Maha Yuti would form the next government in Maharashtra.

Continuing with his confidence of 'I will come back', Fadnavis in his thanksgiving address talked about what 'his' next government was going to do. 'I assure the people of Maharashtra that our government will fulfil their aspirations. We will work better than last time.'

Going by Fadnavis's speech, anyone would have thought that he had yet again convinced the Shiv Sena to tag along. There was reason enough to believe that, as in the preceding term, Fadnavis had once again managed to bell the tiger into playing second fiddle.

Meanwhile, Prime Minister Narendra Modi had already taken to social media to congratulate Fadnavis for the victory. Back in Mumbai, however, Fadnavis knew well that it wasn't going to be easy to get the Shiv Sena on board this time.

DAY 2: FRIDAY, 25 OCTOBER 2019

One could not miss the headline in *Saamana* that morning. It read: 'MAHA JANADESH FOR MAHAYUTI'. Yes, the word 'MAHA' had been struck off. What's interesting here is that Maha Janadesh was the tag line for Devendra Fadnavis's state-wide yatra. By striking it off, the Shiv Sena was likely taking a veiled dig at BJP's dwindled numbers, despite being an ally.

'Chief Minister Devendra Fadnavis was expecting that only lotuses would blossom out of the electronic voting machines (EVMs). But out of 164 seats, it didn't blossom at 63 places. Shiv Sena–BJP have got the mandate but democracy is about the game of numbers', the editorial read. 'People have given a loud and clear message that they do not like arrogance of power. They have busted the myth that victory can be achieved by breaking parties'—it was a scathing attack targeted at the BJP. 'Chhatrapati Shivaji Maharaj was known for keeping his word; this state would run on this inspiration'—the Shiv Sena mouthpiece yet again reminded BJP of its 50:50 promise.

◆

Journalists covering the post-poll developments were expecting Devendra Fadnavis to call upon Shiv Sena President Uddhav Thackeray. But there was no message or sign of the meeting between the duo. Fadnavis had gone to Nagpur earlier in the evening but had returned immediately, fuelling speculations of a late night meeting between Uddhav and him.

11 a.m., Matoshri

The newly elected Shiv Sena MLAs started calling on Party President Uddhav Thackeray at his residence with great fervour. After meeting Uddhav, they came and spoke to the media. Going by the way Aditya was pitched as the party's face during the poll campaign, many MLAs and leaders had come to express their wish to see Aditya as the next Chief Minister of Maharashtra.

Prakash Surve, the MLA from Magathane in North Mumbai, was one of the first MLAs to come out of Matoshri and pitch for Aditya. 'Maharashtra wants to see Aditya as the Chief Minister of Maharashtra. But Uddhavji will take the call,' Surve told the large gathering of reporters and camerapersons. He was not the only one. Pratap Sarnaik, MLA from Owala-Majiwada constituency from Thane, too spoke to the media. 'Adityaji has done remarkable work during the campaign and he will continue to do the good work. Every Shivsainik[13] wants to see him as the Chief Minister. But top leaders like Uddhavji and Amit Shah will take the final call,' he said.

◆

---

[13] A Shiv Sena worker is referred to as a sainik or a soldier.

As MLAs and leaders were gathering at Matoshri, Sanjay Raut, the party's Rajya Sabha MP and Executive Editor of *Saamana*, tweeted a cartoon depicting a tiger (symbolic of Shiv Sena), wearing a pendant of clock (NCP's election symbol), with an open paw that resembled a human hand (Congress's election symbol) and sniffing a lotus (BJP's symbol). The text of the cartoon read: 'Look at the creativity of the cartoonist... *Bura na mano, Diwali hai* (Don't mind, it's Diwali time).' Was this just a cartoon shared in a lighter vein, or was it a cryptic message aimed by the Shiv Sena at its ally, the BJP?

DAY 3: SATURDAY, 26 OCTOBER 2019 CHANDIGARH

Like Maharashtra, the Haryana poll results too had returned not-so-great results for the BJP. Like Maharashtra, it failed to reach the majority mark on its own. Debutant Jananayak Janata Party (JJP) led by Dushyant Chautala had emerged as the kingmaker. Initially the Congress, through its ally the Shiromani Akali Dal, tried to reach out to Dushyant, but the BJP central leadership immediately swung into action. The swift move was to not let go of the opportunity to form the government in the state. The party had shown the same speediness in forming the government in Goa. BJP National President Amit Shah, known for his acumen in forming governments in special scenarios like this, played a key role in getting Dushyant Chautala on their side. During the election campaign, Dushyant had been vociferously critical of the BJP. The young and articulate great grandson of former Deputy Prime Minister Devi Lal had even gone on to tag the BJP as liars and even raked up the issue of the Gujarat riots during his fierce poll campaign.

But politics makes strange bedfellows. The alliance between the BJP and JJP was one such example. Letting bygones be bygones, Amit Shah sealed the deal for incumbent Chief Minister Manoharlal Khattar. While winning over Dushyant Chautala, the BJP offered him the Deputy Chief Minister's post. Dushyant's father Ajay Chautala, who was in Tihar jail after being convicted of corruption in a teacher recruitment scam, was granted a furlough of 14 days.[14] This also meant that he would be attending the swearing-in of his son on Sunday.

Amit Shah told reporters in Delhi that the Haryana government with JJP as an ally would work for the next five years for the betterment of the state.

The BJP leaders in Maharashtra were eagerly waiting for their man with the magic wand to work wonders in the party's favour. After all, he was the one who had come down all the way to Matoshri in February 2019 to seal the deal for the Lok Sabha elections. Many thought that Amit Shah would fly down after the Diwali weekend.

There was, however, someone in the state BJP who knew that Shah may not show the same ardour here that he showed in states likes Goa and Haryana.

Noon, Matoshri

Uddhav Thackeray had convened a meeting of his newly elected party MLAs. As the Thackeray residence wore a festive look ahead of Diwali, Uddhav's wife Rashmi Thackeray took the lead in welcoming the guests. She performed *aukshan*[15] of all the party MLAs who were present there. Uddhav's mother Meenatai, or Maa Saheb, also used to do that during Bal Thackeray's days. Rashmi, respectfully referred to as Vahini Saheb, was now stepping into Maa Saheb's shoes.

This was the first gathering of Shiv Sena MLAs since the election results. A majority of them had a series of complaints against the BJP for not following the alliance dharma. Some like Gulabrao Patil from Jalgaon recited instances of how BJP officially helped its rebels during the elections. Uddhav was patiently listening to all the complaints.

Senior party leader Eknath Shinde moved a proposal to give

---

[14] https://economictimes.indiatimes.com/news/politics-and-nation/ajay-chautala-walks-out-of-tihar-on-two-week-furlough/articleshow/71783985.cms?trom=mdr; last accessed 16 March 2020

[15] A ritual performed by the waving of a lit lamp for better luck, or after the achievement of a feat.

Uddhav the right to take a decision on government-formation on the party's behalf. Pratap Sarnaik made a demand for Aditya to be the party's Chief Minister candidate. Party MLAs even demanded that the BJP give a written assurance on the rotational CM, that is, both parties will have their candidate as the Chief Minister for two and a half years each, with Shiv Sena's candidate getting the initial term.

After hearing everyone out, Uddhav rose to speak. His short speech was focused on the pre-poll assurance made by the BJP to the Shiv Sena. 'Our alliance with the BJP is on the ideology of Hindutva. But if they are not going to fulfill the promise of equal power sharing and a rotational Chief Minister's post, then we have our options open,' he told his MLAs. 'However, I will not do that sin,' he added a rider. Many eyebrows were raised when the Thackeray heir spoke of options being open. What options was Uddhav referring to? The numbers that had come up had put up an interesting scenario. But was the Shiv Sena really open to tying up with the Congress and NCP, or was it just a veiled threat?

10 a.m., Govind Baug, Baramati, Sharad Pawar's Residence

Congress's State President Balasaheb Thorat called upon the NCP Supremo at his Baramati residence. It was said to be a courtesy visit. But Shiv Sena's latest statement about there being other options had opened up possibilities of political realignment in the state. Both Thorat and Pawar, however, denied the discussion of a political rearrangement. 'We have got a mandate to sit in the opposition, and we will do a good job as a responsible opposition,' Thorat told reporters after the meeting.

While Pawar too reiterated this, he backed the Shiv Sena's demand for the Chief Minister post. 'I dont think the Shiv Sena is wrong in demanding the CM's post. Shiv Sena has the experience of running the government from 1995–1999,' Pawar said. For those who know Pawar's brand of politics, he wasn't just testing waters or fishing in troubled waters.

While Thorat and Pawar had denied the possibility, former Chief Minister Prithviraj Chavan had added fuel to speculations by telling the reporters that 'No possibility can be ruled out at this moment. Though we haven't thought or discussed anything on those lines.'

Devgiri Bungalow (Official Residence of Finance Minister Sudhir Mungantiwar), Walkeshwar, Mumbai

Shiv Sena's latest stand had ruffled some feathers in the BJP camp. Reporters caught hold of Sudhir Mungantiwar at the entrance to his house. He denied any possibility of the Congress and Shiv Sena joining hands. '*Sher kitna bhi bhookha ho, ghaas nahi khata...* (Howsoever hungry a tiger is, he will not eat grass...),' he said in his trademark style.

10 p.m., Matoshri

Two Shiv Sena rebels who had won as independent MLAs—Ashish Jaiswal from Ramtek assembly seat and Narendra Bhondekar from Bhandara seat in Vidarbha—called upon Uddhav Thackeray and handed him a letter of support to the Shiv Sena.

With the BJP as its ally, why was Shiv Sena garnering support from Independents?

DAY 4: SUNDAY, 27 OCTOBER 2019

It was the day of Diwali. While the swearing-in ceremony had already taken place in Haryana, Manoharlal Khattar took oath as the Chief Minister for the second consecutive term. Dushyant Kumar Chautala was sworn in as his deputy. Burying a vicious campaign, the BJP and JJP had kissed and made up there.

There were still were no signs of government-formation in Maharashtra. With each passing day, Shiv Sena was slowly adding pressure. Two Shiv Sena rebels had already extended their support to the party. Moreover, Prahar Janshakti Party's Bacchu Kadu had met with Uddhav the previous night and extended his support to the Shiv Sena. With this, Shiv Sena's tally now touched 60. On the other end, BJP rebels Geeta Jain and Rajendra Raut extended their support to BJP after meeting Devendra Fadnavis.

◆

The editorial of *Saamana* on the day of Diwali was about the economic slowdown. It pointed out how there was a lull in the markets and Diwali was a damp squib this year. Sanjay Raut, known to always make a political statement, had not stopped at the silence in the markets. 'This Diwali, the situation in the country is not something to cheer about. Markets are empty and online companies are filling the coffers of other countries. The elections that took place in Maharashtra were less of fanfare and more of silence,' the editorial read. '[T]he silence in the country and state is asking one question *"Itna sannataa kyu hai bhai?* (Why so much silence?)", it further said, quoting a dialogue from the blockbuster movie *Sholay*.

◆

While earlier a large section within Shiv Sena had been lying low because the party's tally had gone down against the 2014 elections, Uddhav's posturing, as he referred to the options being open, had struck a chord with the party.

The most common thought in the minds of newly elected Party MLAs was the election campaign tag line of the party—'*Hich ti vel* (this is the moment)'.

Largely focused around party scion Aditya Thackeray, the pre-election party campaign of the Shiv Sena had highlighted him as the party's new face. Discarding the Thackeray tradition of not taking any position of power or contesting any elections, Aditya announced his candidature from the Worli constituency on 30 September 2019. Soon, Shiv Sena posters calling for 'Aditya for CM' were displayed all across the state, especially Mumbai. And thus came the slogan of '*Heech ti vel*'—it was the moment to make a Thackeray the Chief Minister of Maharashtra.

◆

Marine Drive in South Mumbai witnesses spectacular fireworks on Diwali night. Mumbaikars from not only south central Mumbai, but also other parts of the metro gather here and indulge in bursting crackers. The nonstop fireworks on Sunday night had left the sky hazy. After midnight, a convoy zoomed past Girgaum Chowpatty, with the unclear skies resembling the prevailing political situation. He was going to meet the Governor the next morning.

Maharashtra Governor Bhagat Singh Koshyari was still getting a hang of things at the magnificent Raj Bhavan overlooking the Arabian Sea. In office for just over 50 days, the RSS Swayamsevak[16] was still getting acclimatized to Mumbai's humid climate. Always dressed in a simple dhoti, khadi kurta, jacket and black cap, the 78-year-old Koshyari was known for his simple lifestyle. The Pahadi in Koshyari was slightly uncomfortable with the colonial hospitality at the plush Governor's house. A Raj Bhavan staffer once told journalists that Koshyari, an early riser, would sip his first cup of tea before sunrise. The staff—at that point not aware of his routine—was asleep, when one day, he walked into the kitchen before daybreak. His entry woke up a few of the staffers, who were shell-shocked to see 'His Excellency' walk into the kitchen. A very polite Koshyari told them not to worry; he only wanted to know where tea and sugar were kept, so that he could make a cup for tea for himself. The simplicity of the man who had been the Uttarakhand Chief Minister and had an active political career of more than four decades bowled them over.

When Koshiyari was sworn in as the Maharashtra Governor on 5 September 2019—just over a month before the Assembly polls—he perhaps would have thought that life in Mumbai was going to be relatively peaceful. Like many poll pundits and BJP leaders, he too expected the Maharashtra elections to be a one-sided affair. But little did he know that the city of dreams never allows you to sleep. His habit of waking up before the sunrise would soon lead him to see one of the most memorable dawns in his political life...

---

[16] https://indianexpress.com/article/who-is/who-is-bhagat-singh-koshyari-6116168/; last accessed 16 March 2020.

DAY 5: MONDAY, 28 OCTOBER 2019

10.20 a.m., Raj Bhavan, Malabar Hill, Mumbai

Mediapersons had been thronging the gate of Raj Bhavan since morning. There was news of senior Shiv Sena leader and minister Diwakar Raote reaching the Governor's house. With four days of political impasse, there were no signs of the Shiv Sena or the BJP blinking first.

Raote, though a senior Shiv Sena leader, wasn't much involved in the seat-sharing talks. Uddhav Thackeray trusted him as an old guard in the party and as a Bal Thackeray loyalist. But in spite of that, he was not someone who would be assigned such an important task. Raote's convoy entered Raj Bhavan. He went in. On his way out, he cleared all doubts by telling the reporters: 'I come every year to meet and greet the Governor since 1993; no politics was discussed in the meeting.'

◆

But minutes after Raote left, Devendra Fadnavis's convoy was spotted zooming towards the vast white gates of Raj Bhavan. The consecutive meetings alerted the journalists at the gate and conjectures were drawn about the agenda of the meeting.

After spending almost 20 minutes with the Governor, Fadnavis left without speaking to the mediapersons waiting outside. Was Fadnavis's meeting with the Governor more than a simple exchange of pleasantries?

2 p.m., Maitree Bungalow, Friends Colony, Bhandup (Sanjay Raut's Residence)

A few journalists were waiting at Sanjay Raut's residence. The back-to-back meetings with the Governor by both Shiv Sena and BJP leaders were only adding to the anxiety. Was the BJP still in awe of its emerging as the single largest party? Was the Shiv Sena enjoying this flexing of political muscle reminding the BJP of its 50:50 promise? Were these the causes of delay in government formation?

If there is one man who understood Bal Thackeray and his line of thinking, it was undoubtedly Sanjay Raut. His editorials had the same fire-spitting style as that of Bal Thackeray. The similarity between the two was not just restricted to their writing style, but also the approach—direct, piercing and politically incorrect at times. Raut's editorials attacking the BJP and its top leaders had been the bone of contention between the two allies, to the point where Fadnavis had gone on record to say that he didn't read *Saamana* at all.

Over a cup of tea and Diwali-special chakali, Raut told the journalists that his party wasn't responsible for the delay in government formation. 'You all know what happened in the press conference before Lok Sabha elections. The alliance dharma has to be followed. What's wrong in asking for the Chief Minister's post for two and a half years?' This was perhaps the first time a direct demand for rotational Chief Minister post was being made and that too publicly. 'We are not delaying, and who's stopping the BJP from forming the government? They formed a minority government in 2014 with just 122 MLAs. Now if they are able to do that with 105 MLAs, it will be a world record... They should also remember that Atal Bihari Vajpayee's government had fallen for the lack of just one vote...' Raut was daring the BJP.

Was Raut testing waters on the behest of his party boss Uddhav Thackeray? Or was there actually some substance in challenging the BJP and driving it to one corner? When asked if the Shiv Sena was thinking of any other option like NCP, Raut had said: 'There is no Dushyant Chautala in Maharashtra whose father is in jail... Options are always open in politics... Just like what happened in Haryana...'

◆

Every year Sharad Pawar meets his supporters at his Baramati residence 'Govind Baug'. This time the crowd has been exceptional. Pawar, his daughter Supriya and nephew Ajit Pawar were at the centre of attraction. And so was another young man—the newly elected MLA from Karjat Jamkhed constituency and Sharad Pawar's grandnephew, Rohit.

10.15 p.m., Matoshri

Another independent had knocked on the doors of the Thackeray den in Bandra. This man wasn't a Sena rebel, nor was he just another independent. He was Shankarrao Gadakh, who had won from the Nevasa assembly seat in Ahmednagar constituency—the consistuency famous for the Shani Shingnapur pilgrimage. The Gadakh family has a political background spanning more than five decades and a stronghold on the co-operative and educational sectors in the area.

Gadakh's support to Shiv Sena was intriguing for many. The Gadakh family was known to be very close to Sharad Pawar. Shankarrao's father, Yashwantrao had defeated Balasaheb Vikhe Patil in a bitterly fought Lok Sabha election in 1991 for the Ahmednagar seat. The matter went to the courts where Gadakh's election was rendered invalid. Gadakh was supported by none other than Sharad Pawar, who too was dragged into the case by Vikhe Patil. The Pawar vs Vikhe Patil war had reached its peak and Gadakh was Pawar's Man Friday in Ahmednagar.

Three decades later, the Pawar vs Vikhe battle resurfaced yet again when Pawar refused to give up the Ahmednagar seat for its ally, Congress. Radhakrishna Vikhe Patil wanted the seat for his son, Sujay. Though NCP had given political reasons for the decision, everyone knew the real reason was Pawar's feud with the Vikhe Patil family. Left with no choice, Sujay joined the BJP and went on to contest and win the seat. Sujay's father Radhakrishna too soon joined the BJP after the Lok Sabha elections and contested on a BJP ticket.

In the politically dynamic Ahmednagar district, Shankarrao Gadakh, who was close to the Pawars, chose to contest independently. He won, but straightaway went to Matoshri and handed over a letter of support to Shiv Sena.

Why did a man so close to Pawar choose Shiv Sena? Or was it Pawar who had sent him?

♦

On the other hand, at Varsha—the Chief Minister's official residence—two more Independents met Devendra Fadnavis and extended their support to the BJP. Mahesh Baldi, a BJP rebel from the the Uran assembly constituency near Mumbai, and Vinod Agarwal, another party rebel from Gondia in Vidarbha, were back in the party fold.

DAY 6: TUESDAY, 29 OCTOBER 2019

It was Bhau-Beej (or Bhai Dooj) in Maharashtra, the last of the Diwali celebrations. Leaders from BJP had earlier announced that the discussions on government-formation would start after Diwali. It was going to be an important day, with the first round of talks between BJP and Shiv Sena leaders scheduled for that evening. With the Shiv Sena still sticking to its guns over the Chief Minister post, all eyes were on how the discussions would move forward. Senior leaders from both the parties were deputed for the intial round of talks, after which Fadnavis and Uddhav were going to take a final call.

◆

Unlike its tirade against the BJP over the last few days, *Saamana* took a break on Tuesday morning, choosing instead to praise the Modi–Shah duo for the abrogation of Article 370 in its editorial. A delegation of the European Union was in Kashmir to study the situation in the valley after the abrogation of Article 370, and *Saamana* urged the delegation to go back, saying that the abrogation was part of a war against Pakistan-sponsored terror and that the Modi government had won that war. While some may have read it as a sign of a thaw between the warring allies, it was illusory...

12.30 p.m., Varsha

Every year, the Maharashtra Chief Minister hosts a festive lunch for journalists at his official residence. Ever since he became the CM, Fadnavis, who was once known for his frequent media interactions, had cut down on it. A section of media held a grudge against Fadnavis for meeting selective journalists. With no sign of defrosting between the Shiv Sena and BJP even on Day 6, journalists were looking forward to this opportunity to meet and interact with Fadnavis.

In his usual calm, Fadnavis walked into the special canopy erected for the function. The interactions during the CM's annual festive lunch with the journalists are usually off the records, but at a time when the political activity was at its peak, no conversations could be off the record. The man who had already announced on the floor of the house that he 'will' return as the Chief Minister again had a lot to offer, this cloudy afternoon with light showers.

'Contrary to whatever that is being reported in the media, the government will be formed under BJP's leadership and I have no doubt that I will be the Chief Minister again,' Fadnavis confidently reiterated. This has been his stand since the day of the election results. In a mood to hit sixers on all the bouncers that came in, Fadnavis assertively announced that there was no Plan B or Plan C; there was only one Plan A, and it was going to work. As expected, Fadnavis was asked about the recent barbs in *Saamana* about the BJP and the alliance, but he maintained his usual stand on the issue—that they don't take *Saamana* seriously. This had been his stand even when he was the CM; he would say that he only takes whatever Uddhav Thackeray says seriously. Today, however, he hit out at the Sena mouthpiece saying it was derailing talks with its barbs. The anger in the reply was evident. Barely 24 hours ago, Sanjay Raut had dared the BJP to form a minority government, like in 2014. The brazen dare hadn't gone down well with BJP's state leadership. '*Saamana* writes things that even Congress and NCP won't say. They should show the same fortitude while writing against the NCP. You contest together, win together, then why such remarks in *Saamana*?' a visibly irritable Fadnavis told the gathering of journalists.

Fadnavis was unstoppable that afternoon. This wasn't the first time the Shiv Sena had dared the BJP in such a manner. In spite of being part of the government, Uddhav had time and again said that he doesn't care for power. Once he even went on to say that his ministers in the Fadnavis government carry their resignations in their pocket.

Fadnavis's attack on Shiv Sena only got bigger as he was asked about the party demanding the CM's post on rotational basis for first two and a half years. 'Shiv Sena may even demand the CM's post for five years... Wishing for something like this and it actually happening are two different things,' Fadnavis said, clearly turning down the proposal. 'They should first come with whatever demands they have; we will discuss those on merit when we sit for talks,' he added, while also informing that there have been no talks of government formation with the Shiv Sena till now.

But the biggest statement from Fadnavis was yet to come. Though he was always known to say politically correct things, the statement he was about to make was going to leave the Shiv Sena red-faced. The man who was in control of the press conference where the alliance for Lok Sabha and assembly elections was sealed made a revelation: 'There was never any promise on the CM's post in the 50:50 formula,' Fadnavis revealed. Within the next half hour, TV screens were full of breaking news reading Fadnavis denied any promise of a rotational CM's post.

♦

There was anger and anxiety in the Shiv Sena camp after Fadnavis's denial of the deal. The man who was leading the charge for Shiv Sena, Sanjay Raut was thronged by journalists at the *Saamana* office in Prabhadevi. Raut was animatedly holding and waving his mobile phone. He then played a video clip of the 18 February 2019 press conference on the phone in front of TV cameras. In it could be seen Fadnavis announcing that the BJP and Shiv Sena have decided on having a 50:50 per cent sharing of positions and responsibilities.

'Our only expectation is that whatever was decided on power-sharing should be honoured. The definitions of equal distribution haven't changed. If Fadnavis is saying nothing was decided, then he should clarify on what was it that was decided in that meeting,'

Raut said. And then came the bolt from the blue: 'If there was no formula discussed, what is the need for talks? As asked by my Party President Uddhav Thackeray, we are calling off the meeting with BJP scheduled this evening...' Raut announced.

Within an hour, Uddhav's media advisor Harshal Pradhan shot off the same video on several WhatsApp groups with the title, *'Jara Yaad Karo Jabani* (remember the assurance)'.

5 p.m., Karad, District Satara, Prithviraj Chavan's hometown

The knives were out. BJP's denial of the power-sharing promise had angered the Shiv Sena. In Nagpur, Congress leader Vijay Wadettiwar called the fight between Shiv Sena and BJP a cat fight. But in Karad in western Maharashtra, former Chief Minister Prithviraj Chavan had a different view. The man, known to be close to 10, Janpath (residence of the Gandhi family), was asked whether Congress would think of supporting the Shiv Sena if need be. Though initially dubbed as a hypothetical question, what Prithviraj said in response later was certainly going to raise eyebrows: '[I]f Sena wants then they should approach us with a proposal...if they do, we will put it before our party high command and also discuss it with our ally... For now there isn't any such proposal...'

So, was Prithviraj Chavan hinting at extending a 'hand' to Shiv Sena, or was the Congress trying to just fish in troubled waters?

DAY 7: WEDNESDAY, 30 OCTOBER 2019

Vidhan Bhavan, Nariman Point, Mumbai

Newly elected BJP MLAs had started to reach Vidhan Bhavan. Some of them had just returned from their constituencies after celebrating Diwali. Many of them had jumped to the BJP ship just before the elections. Some like Ganesh Naik (former NCP and a strongman from the satellite city of Navi Mumbai) were sure of becoming a minister in the BJP-led government in a few days.

The TV crews stationed in large numbers were almost blocking the entrance of Vidhan Bhavan. Fadnavis's right-hand man, Girish Mahajan's car reached Vidhan Bhavan. Those who had seen his meteoric rise in the last five years knew that Mahajan's words were the words of his boss. The Fadnavis–Mahajan duo was seen like the miniature version of the Modi–Shah duo. The entire focus of TV cameras was now on Mahajan. 'We are sure that the government will be that of Maha Yuti... Today all our allies except Shiv Sena will be attending the Legislative party meeting...we are electing our Legislative Party leader today, however we will not stake the claim to form the government today...' Mahajan told the journalists.

One thing was clear from Mahajan's statement—the deadlock with Shiv Sena was likely to go on for another day at least.

◆

Amidst thunderous sloganeering, Fadnavis entered the Vidhan Bhavan premises. Wearing saffron 'phetas' (Maharashrian turbans), MLAs welcomed the man who they believed will be returning for his second consecutive term as CM. Fadnavis too was made to wear the pheta. The gathering of MLAs then followed him to the statue of Chhatrapati Shivaji Maharaj right opposite the stairs of the Vidhan Bhavan. Fadnavis garlanded the statue and headed towards the central hall of Vidhan Bhavan.

Union Minister Narendra Singh Tomar and BJP National Vice President Avinash Rai Khanna were deputed for the BJP legislative party meeting. BJP State President Chandrakant Patil moved the motion to elect Devendra Fadnavis as the leader of the BJP legislative party, saying that there could undoubtedly be none other than Fadnavis for the post. The motion was seconded by senior party leaders. Those present at the central hall welcomed the motion with the thumping of benches and loud cheers.

Right at the onset of his speech, Fadnavis made a special mention of Shiv Sena President Uddhav Thackeray for their contribution in the Maha Yuti's victory, apart from Prime Minister Narendra Modi, National President Amit Shah and BJP's Working President J.P. Nadda.

'No one should have an iota of doubt about the fact that the next government will be that of Maha Yuti. Do not believe the rumours. Let the gossip mills run, there is no fun without it,' Fadnavis said in his address, downplaying the murmurs of 'alternate formulae'. According to Fadnavis, those were just rumours with entertainment value.

Tilak Bhawan, Maharashtra Pradesh Congress Office, Mumbai

While the BJP had already appointed its legislative party leader and the NCP was about to elect theirs, there was no talk in the Congress about electing its legislative party leader. Top party leaders, including Mallikarjun Kharge, were present for the meeting. The general tone in the meeting was that though the party has fared well in the elections, the performance could have been better had the national leadership been more active in the campaign. Apart from three rallies by Rahul Gandhi, neither Sonia nor Priyanka Gandhi had campaigned in Maharashtra. But in spite of that, the Congress managed to better its performance as compared to the 2014 assembly elections.

Usually, inside details of any Congress meeting are juicy for a journalist. But this time, everyone was interested in knowing whether there was any substance to the speculations that had just started—of Congress being inclined to support the Shiv Sena. But the balloon was soon bursted by Kharge. In response to a question on Prithviraj Chavan's statement on the Shiv Sena, Kharge shot it down completely: 'Whatever Prithviraj Chavan has said is his personal opinion. It does not reflect the opinion of the party. We have fought against the ideology of these parties; we cannot support them. We have the mandate to sit in opposition. We will sit in opposition.'

While Kharge was firm on his party's ideology, Prithviraj Chavan was still maintaining his stand.

5 p.m., Y.B. Chavan Centre, Nariman Point, Mumbai

Barely 100 metres away from the Vidhan Bhavan, where Devendra

Fadnavis was elected as the legislative party leader, the NCP met at the Yashwantrao Chavan Centre to elect its legislative party leader.

Party President Sharad Pawar was himself present for the meeting with daughter and MP Supriya Sule. State President Jayant Patil proposed the name of Ajit Pawar for the post, and Nawab Malik, Jitendra Awhad, Dhananjay Munde and Hasan Mushrif seconded the name.

Ajit Anantrao Pawar was making a comeback as the legislative party leader. The last five years had been a tad difficult for the maverick nephew of Sharad Pawar. The allegations of involvement in the multi-crore irrigation scam had put a question mark on his political future before the 2014 state assembly elections. The erstwhile young and dynamic State President of the BJP, Devendra Fadnavis had become Ajit Pawar's nemesis as he followed up the matter, making it a poll issue. Fadnavis even went on to announce that if the BJP is voted to power, Ajit Pawar would be behind bars. He even quoted a famous dialogue from *Sholay*, saying Ajit Pawar would be seen '*chakki peesing, peesing and peesing...*'[17]

It was a coincidence that the two leaders, who had once crossed swords, were chosen as the legislative party leaders of their respective parties within a gap of a few hours.

Meanwhile, Sanjay Raut, Shiv Sena's pinch hitter at the moment, told mediapersons that the Shiv Sena was in favour of forming the government with the BJP. A segment of media considered the statement as a hint of climbdown by the Shiv Sena. Within hours, Raut took to social media, calling these inferences as planted by BJP. According to him, his party would settle for nothing less than the promised 50:50 power-sharing formula.

Taking a cue from Raut's statement in the afternoon, a senior BJP leader fed some inside dope to journalists standing near the stairs of Vidhan Bhavan. 'Shiv Sena will soon fall in line. The BJP too does not want to play hard ball and will offer the Shiv Sena

---

[17] https://www.freepressjournal.in/mumbai/chakki-peesing-when-devendra-fadnavis-threatened-to-jail-his-deputy-ajit-pawar; last accessed 16 March 2020.

Deputy CM's post,' he said. He also told the group of journalists that a 15:13 ratio of ministries was being worked out. However, important portfolios like Home, Urban Development and Irrigation would stay with the BJP.

◆

Back at the Y.B. Chavan Centre, the NCP's newly elected legislative party leader Ajit Pawar was addressing his party MLAs. In his trademark style, Ajit Dada (as he is popularly addressed by party leaders and workers) underlined the role of the Opposition. 'The condition of farmers is not good. They have faced huge losses due to drought and now unseasonal rains. We will have to take care of the same. The condition of the economy too is poor and we need to work on that as well. People want us to raise their voice as a strong opposition and that is what we have got the mandate for,' Ajit was almost getting into the skin of the leader of Opposition. But when he was stopped on his way out of the venue by TV crews for a reaction on the political impasse, Ajit, much like his uncle, bowled a googly: 'There are no permanent enemies in politics,' he quipped. This statement, as inferred by some, fuelled speculations of talks with Shiv Sena.

DAY 8: THURSDAY, 31 OCTOBER 2019

It was going to be an important day for the Shiv Sena. With the BJP and NCP having chosen their respective legislative party leaders, it was Sena's turn to pick theirs. All eyes were on the Shiv Sena Legislative Party meeting. The much-hyped 'Aditya' factor had raised everyone's curiosity. After all, the young and suave scion of the Thackeray family had been pitched by the party as the chief ministerial face in the run-up to the elections. There was no doubt about Aditya venturing into a territory where no Thackeray had ever entered. He had successfully contested the election from Worli seat and was now set for the bigger role. The insistence by Shiv Sena on the Chief Minister's post, even if on a rotational basis with the BJP, seemed to be for Aditya.

◆

It was the last day of October, and November was going to be witness to political mayhem. If there was one person who was going to be at the centre stage, it was undoubtedly Sanjay Raut. His stance, as reflected in *Saamana*, had led to not only some BJP leaders but even some Shiv Sena leaders wanting him to not be a part of the alliance talks.

The previous day, Raut's statement that Shiv Sena wanted to form the government with the BJP had triggered talks of a climbdown by the Shiv Sena. Raut had, however, quickly refuted the charges of blinking first. It was perhaps for this very reason that his editorial on Thursday morning was even more hard-hitting.

'If everything was pre-decided, why should there be a deadlock? We keep our words and we live by our words... So be it a deadlock, or even a *Chakravyuh*, fighters do not shy away from challenges,' the editorial lead read.

The Shiv Sena had yet again opened up its wound of the BJP snapping its ties with the party in 2014—a wound that still hadn't healed. Alleging a use-and-throw policy by the BJP, the editorial further attacked the ally: 'In 2014 when BJP got a thumping majority in Lok Sabha elections, they dumped the alliance. Then they came back to us when needed, to form the government. In 2019, again when they are the single largest party, they are not ready to meet the commitments of an alliance partner.... Whatever was decided about power sharing, was announced by the chief minister (Devendra Fadnavis) during that press conference before Lok Sabha elections. Sena is not backing out on its commitment. We don't need witnesses to prove what was decided,' it further stated. The editorial had set the tone for the party's legislative party meeting.

12.30 p.m., Shiv Sena Bhawan, Dadar

Uddhav Thackeray arrived at Shiv Sena Bhawan for the Shiv Sena's legislative party meeting. This was Uddhav's second visit to the iconic building after the assembly poll results. Roads leading to

Shiv Sena Bhawan were packed with bumper to bumper traffic. Not just newly elected MLAs from 56 constituencies, but seven independent MLAs who had till now pledged their support to the party, and all top leaders and members of the legislative council too had reached the venue.

Usually known for his calm and composed entry to any party meeting, Uddhav's hurriedness while entering the meeting hall on the fifth floor suggested a sense of unease. 'Fadnavis shouldn't have said that there was no promise of 50:50 per cent power-sharing formula. He is trying to show that we are liars. Do you think I'm lying?' Uddhav began his address with a question for his MLAs. 'No,' was the reply in chorus.

'Is it okay for you, if someone calls our party a party of liars?' he then asked. The response again was in the negative.

'Whatever was decided should be honoured. We are not asking for anything less than what was decided and not anything more than that. There is nothing wrong in asking for the CM's post. NO ONE IS ENTITLED TO THE CM'S POST FOR ETERNITY,' Uddhav hit out at Fadnavis, amid thumping applause. This was one of the first open and most direct attacks by Uddhav on Fadnavis, who till now had been claiming that only he would return as the Chief Minister.

♦

Aditya Thackeray rose to speak. Contrary to the expectations of his big leap, Aditya proposed the name of Eknath Shinde as the Legislative Party leader. The proposal was seconded by party leaders like Pratap Sarnaik, Dada Bhuse, Sada Sarvankar and others. The bearded staunch Shivsainik from the neighbouring Thane city was rewarded for his loyalty. Once an autorickshaw driver, Shinde had grown rapidly in the rank and file of the party. He had quickly picked up the ability to utilize the 'muscle power' in the party after Thane's most dreaded Shiv Sena leader Anand Dighe. With a similar bearded look and almost identical style of functioning, Shinde had not just wielded control over Thane and Navi Mumbai, but also in other parts of the state.

Immediately after being crowned as the Legislative Party leader, Shinde, alongwith Aditya Thackeray and other Shiv Sena leaders, headed for Raj Bhavan, but it wasn't to stake claim. The meeting was to demand relief for farmers affected by unseasonal rains.

Shinde's election had given away certain hints. Being the legislative party leader meant that in case there is a coalition government, Shinde was to be the Sena's choice to play deputy. But that was Plan B. Plan A was possibly something that was only known to a few.

It wasn't just the loyalty that paid off for Shinde; Uddhav Thackeray had perhaps chalked a bigger role for Shinde in days to come...

Silver Oak Estate

Just as the Shiv Sena leaders were meeting at Shiv Sena Bhawan, senior Congress leaders, including State President Balasaheb Thorat, former Chief Ministers Ashok Chavan and Prithviraj Chavan, called upon the NCP Supremo at his residence. Till now there were just speculations about extending a hand to the Shiv Sena. This wasn't the first time that the thought of the NCP tying up with Shiv Sena had come up. After the 2014 elections, a similar proposition was thought of by an NCP leader, which was turned down by the Sena.

A lot of water had flown under the bridge ever since. The situation wasn't the same at the Centre and in the state. The newfound confidence for the Congress and NCP in the recent poll results was seen as an opportunity not just to bounce back, but also a golden chance to isolate the BJP in the second largest state.

But after the meeting, none of the leaders from Congress and NCP admitted about the new proposition. On the contrary, Dhananjay Munde yet again reiterated the oft-repeated 'mandate to sit in Opposition' dialogue.

◆

One thing that did come up while discussing the new permutations and combinations was whether the Congress leadership, especially

Rahul Gandhi, who has always held sharp views against parties like the Shiv Sena,[18] would even agree to a proposal like this. Even though the thought of supporting Shiv Sena was unthinkable, perhaps the larger idea of isolating the BJP and stopping its juggernaut could work. Perhaps it was with that thought that the Congress leaders yet again postponed the appointment of the leader of the Congress Legislative Party and took off to New Delhi to call upon 10, Janpath instead.

◆

Apart from NCP's top leadership, Congress leaders were not the only ones to visit Silver Oak that evening. A grey SUV zoomed past the narrow yet serene lanes leading to Silver Oak. Camerapersons from media houses were surprised to see this person making his way into Silver Oak Estate. He was always known to be close to Sharad Pawar and had never shied away from praising the NCP Supremo in public. He and Pawar had been seen together on many occasions and while in normal circumstances their meeting wouldn't have raised eyebrows, the timing of this meeting was crucial. Their meeting lasted for half an hour. The person, while leaving, called the meeting just a courtesy visit. But this person was none other than Sanjay Raut...

DAY 9: FRIDAY, 1 NOVEMBER 2019

On Friday morning, a team of Congress leaders comprising of Balasaheb Thorat, Ashok Chavan, Prithviraj Chavan, Manikrao Thakre and Vijay Wadettiwar had flown to Delhi to meet Sonia Gandhi. The agenda was to discuss the possibility of a new permutation in Maharashtra, a state that was once the stronghold of Congress. Not very long ago...

Mumbai

Hours after meeting NCP Supremo Sharad Pawar, Sanjay Raut was

---

[18] Rahul Gandhi's speeches at various political rallies in Maharasthra as well as other states attest to this fact.

in a different mood altogether this morning. The meeting had given him more than just confidence. No one can easily judge Pawar and what's going on his mind. But Raut was somewhere firm. Things were no more just restricted to speculations now. Sanjay Raut yet again took to Twitter to make a point. This time, Raut went even further than his cryptic message from earlier.

साहिब... मत पालिए, अहंकार को इतना,
वक्त के सागर में कई, सिकन्दर डूब गए..!

(Do not have so much of ego;
Several Alexanders have drowned in the sea of time.)

The timing of the tweet was not just a coincidence. The media was at Raut's Bhandup residence to understand what his party was up to. The tweets laced with shayari and early morning media briefings at his residence were now going to be the regular feature for times to come.

♦

'The meeting with Sharad Pawar was a courtesy call. One doesn't always meet with political motives,' Raut said in response to media queries on his much-hyped meeting with Pawar. Raut was asked about the movements of Congress leaders and whether there was any possibility of joining hands with the party. All he had to say was: 'Even the Congress does not want a BJP government in Maharashtra.'

But yet again, Raut asserted that the next Chief Minister would be from Shiv Sena. 'If Uddhav Thackeray has said that the next Chief Minister will be from Shiv Sena, take it in writing that it will be from Shiv Sena. We will get two-third majority to form the government,' Raut made a huge claim.

Shiv Sena had 56 MLAs plus support of seven independents; NCP had 54 MLAs—between the two, the total was coming to just 107. Their combined numbers were way short of the magic figure of 145. So, was Raut also counting the Congress in?

New Delhi

Congress state President Balasaheb Thorat was in Delhi along with Ashok Chavan, Prithviraj Chavan and Manikrao Thakre. The younger lot in the Congress—the likes of Yashomati Thakur, Vishwajeet Kadam and Amit Deshmukh—was in favour of a political adventure. They saw no harm in going with the Shiv Sena in a three-way tie-up. The senior leaders, however, were wary. Though the idea sounded fine, the question was how to convince the High Command.

The Maharashtra stalemate was being closely monitored by the Congress High Command. But in spite of this, the leaders were denied a meeting in the earlier half of the day. The group then held talks with All India Congress Committee (AICC) General Secretary K.C. Venugopal who was completely averse to the idea of going with Shiv Sena. Venugopal hailed from the southern state of Kerala. The state has a large-scale Muslim population. Moreover, Rahul Gandhi had contested and won from the Wayanad seat in Kerala. Venugopal clearly told the delegation that going with the Shiv Sena may backfire for Rahul Gandhi in his constituency.

With negative feedback from Venugopal and appointment being denied by the Party President, the proposition could not be taken forward. The state Congress leadership then thought that the idea won't work.

But towards the evening, Balasaheb Thorat got a call from 10, Janpath for a meeting with Sonia Gandhi at 6 p.m. The troupe of state Congress leaders met 'Madam'. The AICC in charge for Maharashtra Mallikarjun Kharge, and K.C. Venupgopal were present for this hour-long meeting. The state Congress leaders, however, did not overtly speak about the possible tie-up with Shiv Sena. Sonia Gandhi was only briefed about the strained relations between the BJP and Shiv Sena over the CM's post. The national leaders present in the meeting also apprised the President that this could also be a tactic by the Shiv Sena to exert pressure on the BJP by its loud suggestions of a possibility of going with the Congress. Sonia Gandhi wasn't much convinced. 'Let's see what happens, we will wait and watch,' was all she told the leaders.

Speaking to reporters in New Delhi, Ashok Chavan told reporters that the party was adopting a wait and watch policy in Maharashtra. 'There is no proposal from the Shiv Sena. We have not made any claim from our side nor we have indulged into any talks with the Shiv Sena,' Chavan said, only to add ambiguity to the Congress's stand in the drama.

Nashik

Back in Maharashtra, Sharad Pawar was back in action. After his heroic performance during the election campaign, he set on a tour to visit farmers in Nashik who had been affected by unseasonal rains. Pawar is often termed a Janata Raja in Maharashtra, a leader who knows and understands the plight of the farmers. At a time when the politics over government-formation was at its peak, Pawar, rather than indulging in politicking, preferred to be on ground zero.

In Nashik, he termed the tug of war between the Shiv Sena and BJP over the CM's post as 'juvenile'. 'At a time when the farmers are facing harrowing time due to unseasonal rains, the Shiv Sena and BJP are not able to arrive at a conclusion over formation of government,' Pawar said. He, however, did not forget to take sides. 'The BJP has little options, I think it should agree to Shiv Sena's demands,' he said.

Mumbai

There was restlessness in the BJP camp. A senior BJP leader suspected that something was cooking between the Congress, NCP and Shiv Sena. NCP and Shiv Sena had flirted with other parties openly many times in the past, but even the thought of Shiv Sena and Congress coming together seemed far-fetched. At a time when leaders were treading cautiously with the Shiv Sena, any statement that would provoke them was being avoided.

But some of them were losing patience. Sudhir Mungantiwar, an old hat in the BJP, said something that gave another opportunity for the Shiv Sena to hit out at the BJP. 'If the government is not formed by 7 November, President's rule in the state is imminent,' he told a regional news channel.

What Mungantiwar said was set to strain the relations between the warring saffron siblings further.

♦

But somewhere down the line, the BJP was confident of forming the government. A senior BJP leader and a close confidante of Devendra Fadnavis met a group of journalists in south Mumbai. 'We are 105 and have gathered support from 15 others... Like 2014, BJP will go ahead and swear in our CM... Shiv Sena will fall in line. There is no question of bowing down to Shiv Sena's pressure,' Fadnavis's Man Friday informed with great optimism.

For the selective gathering of journalists, there was reason enough to believe him. A few hours ago, a team of BJP leaders along with senior police officials had toured the Wankhede stadium and booked it for 5 November.

DAY 10: SATURDAY, 2 NOVEMBER 2019

Sudhir Mungantiwar's 'President's rule' provocation had hit the Shiv Sena hard. The *Saamana* editorial on Saturday morning not just lashed out at Mungantiwar but also tore into the BJP, calling the 'threat' as 'undemocratic' and 'unconstitutional'. The Shiv Sena hadn't taken Mungantiwar's words kindly. 'Since the threats and fear of Central Investigating agencies (like the ED, Income Tax and CBI) haven't worked, Sudhir Mungantiwar has "farted" the new threat of Presiden't rule', attacked the piece. 'This (threat) is an insult to the mandate given by the people of Maharashta. The arrogance of power that thinks only we can form the government regardless of a mandate and that we are born to rule has been defeated. Those threatening of imposing President's rule should first go and stake claim to form government. Let us see what happens next,' the editorial hit back in a Sena style of threat. 'President's is the highest post and he is not in anyone's pocket,' read the editorial, comparing the 'threat' to a Mughal diktat.

Chandrapur, Maharashtra

The war of words had now begun between the BJP and Shiv Sena. In his constituency around 600 km away from the state's capital, Sudhir Mungantiwar hit back at Sanjay Raut. 'Is explaining constitutional procedure a threat?' he said, not forgetting to mention that such statements would only derail the talks.

1.00 p.m., Varsha

Amid the political hustle bustle, Fadnavis called a meeting of the Cabinet Sub-Committee to review the 'wet drought' or the 'unseasonal rains'. But this wasn't just going to be a 'Sarkari' meeting. Senior Shiv Sena leader Eknath Shinde, minister in the outgoing government, was a member of the sub-committee along with another Shiv Sena leader and Minister of State, Vijay Shivtare. In the deadlock, there were no signs of any formal meeting between the allies. This perhaps would have been the first. Early in the morning, all eyes were on Eknath Shinde, the man who was chosen by Uddhav to be the leader of the Shiv Sena's legislative party.

Senior leaders of the BJP and minister members of the sub-committee started arriving for the meeting. By afternoon, journalists who had gathered outside the Chief Minister's residence came to know that the man they were waiting for wasn't in Mumbai. Eknath Shinde had left for Aurangabad early morning, giving the meeting a skip. The only person who attended the meeting from Shiv Sena was Vijay Shivtare, who had recently lost the elections and was not involved in government-formation in any capacity. The meeting ended as Devendra Fadnavis announced a package of ₹10,000 crore for the affected farmers.

3.00 p.m., Silver Oak Estate

NCP's top brass gathered at Sharad Pawar's residence. Mediapersons waiting outside were told that the huddle was to discuss the farmers' issues after the unseasonal rains. But the political agenda was different. A senior leader opined that in any case the BJP should be kept out of power. Most of the leaders agreed. The NCP should take a lead, said another. The consensus in the meeting was that it was imperative to keep the BJP and Devendra Fadnavis at bay.

The grand old man of Maharashtra's politics was carefully listening to all suggestions and opinions. He knew well that all this was easier said than done. After the meeting, a senior NCP leader, on the condition of anonymity, informed the journalists that the NCP was awaiting the Congress's stand on the issue. 'Shiv Sena by now has almost made up its mind to part ways with the BJP. Congress needs to make up its mind now. But the Shiv Sena too has to show seriousness. Mere posturing is not enough,' he said.

Chhagan Bhujbal officially came on record. The former Shivsainik had a piece of advice for his former party. '[I]f there was a promise made by the BJP of 50:50 sharing of power, Sena should stick to their demand,' Bhujbal said, wrapping his Louis Vuitton muffler around his neck.

Saamana Office, Prabhadevi

The NCP was shying away from making a direct statement on a possible tie-up. The Congress too was non-committal. Even though a majority of the leaders were whispering about how good the proposal was to join hands with the Shiv Sena, no one wanted to be quoted officially. As senior leaders buckled, a veteran from the Konkan region took the lead. As the NCP went into a huddle at Pawar's residence, Congress's Rajya Sabha MP and senior leader Husain Dalwai directly headed to meet Sanjay Raut at the *Saamana* office. The duo chatted for an hour. Raut, by now, was not just in touch with Sharad Pawar, but had also opened communication lines with Congress leaders like Ashok Chavan and Prithviraj Chavan.

A prominent Muslim reformist, progressive leader Dalwai's meeting with Raut was significant. Dalwai did not hide anything after coming out the meeting. 'Following the secular principles of Shivaji Maharaj, it's the need of the hour that the Congress, NCP and Shiv Sena should come together to maintain the secular fabric of Maharashtra,' Dalwai straightaway came to the point. Dalwai was then asked the obvious question: 'Wouldn't Shiv Sena's Hindutva ideology be a problem for a secular party like the Congress?'

Dalwai's answer was not just the momentary reply, but it also set the tone for any future replies to that question that were bound to be asked in every press meet to Congress leaders from Delhi to Mumbai. 'Shiv Sena's Hindutva is different from that of the BJP. BJP talks about one nation, one religion and one party; Shiv Sena never does that. Unlike the BJP, it also gives tickets to Muslims.' Dalwai was defending the Shiv Sena to the core.

Dalwai's statement somehow came as the much-needed impetus for some who wanted the alliance and for those who wanted to keep the BJP at bay.

◆

The Shiv Sena's assault on the BJP meanwhile continued on social media. Amid the series of meetings on one hand, the Yuva Sena led by Aditya Thackeray uploaded an old video of Bal Thackeray on social media sites. The video showing party supremo late Bal Thackeray hitting out the BJP went viral. In the video, Bal Thackeray could be heard warning the BJP: 'We tolerate you only for the ideology of Hindutva. But we won't do that every time. Remember, you also have benefitted from the alliance with Shiv Sena.'

◆

While the NCP meeting ended inconclusively, Sharad Pawar and Sonia Gandhi had a telephonic conversation later to discuss the political situation. It was decided that Pawar would meet Sonia Gandhi in a day or two. This was going to be one of the most crucial meetings.

◆

Devendra Fadnavis's core team was starting to get edgy by now. The Shiv Sena was not showing any signs of a climbdown. There were still a few around Fadnavis who believed that the Shiv Sena would soon come to heels. Fadnavis made yet another attempt to reach out to Uddhav in the late afternoon. This time too, Uddhav refused to come on the line to speak. By now, Fadnavis had sensed that this wasn't just brinkmanship. A plan was worked out.

Late in the night, an emissary from Devendra Fadnavis was sent to Uddhav's residence. Contrary to the suggestions by his core team, Fadnavis did the climbdown. The emmisary, a known face in the power-broking circles of Maharashtra, took Fadnavis's message that he has offered a 50:50 per cent sharing of portfolios to the Shiv Sena. Some important portfolios and important corporations would also be shared equally. But the offer had a rider—that the BJP won't part with portfolios like Home and Urban Development. But Uddhav was not at all interested in the portfoilios. His confidante asked the emissary about the CM's post. 'Well that can't be shared...!' was the response. 'Then there can be no talks, *Jai Maharashtra*,' pat came Uddhav's reply.

DAY 11: SUNDAY, 3 NOVEMBER 2019

For Sanjay Raut, convincing his Party President was not an easy task. It was not just about the ideology that was the biggest hurdle. The main barrier lay within the party. Some senior leaders in the party who had served as ministers in the Devendra Fadnavis government initially laughed at the idea of breaking ties with the BJP yet again. But when things started inching towards serious talks, this lot was disturbed. They were firmly of the opinion that the BJP was not just an ideologically viable option, but since the BJP was in power at the Centre, it was only prudent to go with them. According to them, it wasn't wise to go against the might of Narendra Modi and Amit Shah. The mandate too suggested the same. Some of them had no qualms whatsoever in playing second fiddle to the BJP. A senior leader from the Shiv Sena initially thought the aggression from their Party President was just to get a good pound of flesh from the BJP in the form of some big ministries.

Like Pawar, Uddhav too was carefully gathering the opinions of his close aides about the BJP. The common minimum factor that was emerging between these two leaders for now was to keep the BJP at bay, but Shiv Sena was slightly wary. Some said that the time was not right for any adventure.

But after that meeting with Sharad Pawar, Sanjay Raut was even more emboldened. The Executive Editor of *Saamana* writes a weekly column 'Rok-Thok' (roughly translating to 'Upfront') in the party's mouthpiece. That Sunday's piece hammered the BJP, saying that the wheels of the chariot were stuck in the mud of arrogance.

'Fadnavis is not willing to keep his word on giving CM's post to Shiv Sena and instead making moves to form government with the help of agencies like the Police, CBI, ED and Income Tax Department. What type of Democracy is this?' Raut made serious allegations against Fadnavis. 'Had Fadnavis respectfully gone to Matoshri on the first day of results, situation wouldn't have heated up like this. But they were under the impression that, Shiv Sena would come dragging behind, like it did in 2014. But Uddhav Thackeray busted that myth in the first eight hours after the results. In 2014 Shiv Sena went with the BJP, but it won't commit that mistake again. And Uddhav Thackeray has now closed the doors for any unnecessary talks. If you can achieve majority without Shiv Sena, please go ahead and form the government.' Raut was almost giving away intricate details of the Shiv Sena meetings and his talks with Uddhav.

Raut's soliloquy, however, wasn't just restricted to bashing the BJP and Fadnavis. This article by the man who was in the thick of action was one of the most important disclosures of the recent times. The piece also presented five possible scenarios that could emerge in the present political impasse.

According to Raut,

> Scenario One: BJP will exclude Shiv Sena and go ahead to form the government. BJP has 105 MLAs. They will need 40 more. If they don't manage 40 MLAs, their government will fall on the day of trust vote. Getting 40 MLAs seems impossible.
>
> Scenario Two: NCP will support the BJP led government like it did in 2014. NCP will join the NDA. Supriya Sule will

be a Minister at the Centre, while Ajit Pawar will be a minister in the State Government. But Sharad Pawar won't repeat the blunder he committed in 2014. He has got the success against the BJP. He is on the peak of popularity, which will be reduced to ashes if he does that.

Scenario Three: If BJP fails the floor test, Shiv Sena may stake claim to form the government as the second largest party. With the help of NCP (56 MLAs), Congress (44 MLAs) and others, Shiv Sena will be able to achieve the figure of 170 to prove the majority. Shiv Sena will have its Chief Minister, and will have to take the risk of running a government of three ideologically different parties. For that they will have to prepare a common minimum programme (CMP). The way Atal Bihari Vajpayee (the former prime Minister) ran the NDA government with several parties, this government will have to function on similar lines taking everyone along. 'This will be in the interest of Maharashtra'.

Scenario Four: Left with no options, the BJP and Shiv Sena will have to come together to form the government. For that both will have to walk back four steps. BJP will have to consider Shiv Sena's demands and share the CM's post, as it is the only option. But arrogance won't allow that to happen.

Scenario Five: BJP will form the government using agencies like Police, ED, CBI and use money power and threats to break MLAs from other parties. But results have shown what happens to those who jump parties. This will also badly affect the image of Prime Minister Narendra Modi.

Not one, but a mix of the possibilities expressed by Raut were going to come true in the future. Raut was no prophet. For those who had closely monitored the meetings between Raut and Pawar, this was perhaps the summary of the discussions between the two and also an insinuation of what was to come.

♦

The scathing attack in *Saamana* wasn't the only one by Raut. In line with the cryptic messages in his past tweets, Raut complemented his scornful attack with a confrontational sher (couplet) by poet Waseem Barelvi.

> उसूलों पर जहाँ आँच आये, टकराना जरूरी है
> जो जिन्दा हो, तो फिर जिन्दा नजर आना जरूरी है ....
> जय महाराष्ट्र...

(When your principles are endangered, you have to resist. If you are alive, then you should appear that you are alive.)

The press meets at Raut's Bhandup house had by now become a daily feature. For the first time ever since the Shiv Sena spoke of options being open, Raut had given a clear-cut figure of 170. Where was Raut's confidence coming from?

Kannad Tehsil, District Aurangabad

A middle-aged frail-looking farmer in a white kurta pyjama and a white Gandhi cap walked towards Uddhav Thackeray. A couple of years ago, he was battered by drought and now unseasonal rains had taken away ready crop from him. While assuring him, Uddhav said, 'Don't worry, our government is coming soon...' Not just farmers but Sena leaders accompanying him were also relieved for some time, perhaps thinking that Uddhav was talking about a BJP–Shiv Sena government.

'Rains continue to come back. Even farmers are now afraid of the rain's attitude saying *"Mee punha yein* (I will come back)",' Uddhav took a jibe at Fadnavis a few moments later to the amusement of the crowd and the puzzlement of the team of Shiv Sena leaders.

Uddhav Thackeray had completed his day-long tour of Marathwada to visit farmers affected by unseasonal rains. Now call it a coincidence, but the NCP Supremo too had embarked on a similar tour a couple of days earlier. Moreover, Fadnavis too was touring Akola in Vidarbha region, while Aditya Thackeray was meeting farmers and fishermen in the Konkan region.

Uddhav Thackeray went to the fields and engaged in talks with the farmers. Known as a patient listener and a good communicator, Uddhav heard the plight of the farmers. After the series of visits, he demanded that the state government should give a compensation of ₹25,000 per hectare to the affected farmers without any documentation and inquiries.

Y.B. Chavan Centre, Nariman Point, Mumbai

NCP had its eyes on the meeting between its Supremo Sharad Pawar and Congress President Sonia Gandhi. Addressing the media, Ajit Pawar yet again crooned the oft-repeated 'mandate to sit in the Opposition' raga.

Sanjay Raut explained this as a trap by the NCP. The BJP was closely watching the developments in the NCP camp. A section in the party was sure that the NCP would not have the guts to go with the Shiv Sena. So the NCP was keeping the suspense around its actions on one side, and kept flirting with the Shiv Sena on the other.

'Sharad Pawar is going to Delhi and he will hold talks with Sonia Gandhi on the future course of action. Whatever decision has to be taken will be taken together by the Congress and NCP. We have contested the elections together and we will take a decision with each other's consent,' Ajit told the media in his baritone voice. 'I don't know how Sanjay Raut reached the figure of 170. Only he can explain that,' he replied when asked about the number game put forth by Sanjay Raut.

In the middle of the press briefing, Ajit Pawar checked his phone. Always known for his unpredictable ways of reacting to a situation, he read out a message from Sanjay Raut. *'Jai Maharashtra, Mee Sanjay Raut* (Jai Maharashtra, this is Sanjay Raut),' Ajit read the message and kept the phone down, leaving everyone in a tizzy.

Interestingly, the same day, Raut in his piece for *Saamana* had mentioned the possibility of the NCP willing to go with the BJP and of Ajit Pawar being made a minister in Maharashtra. So, what was Ajit Pawar up to when he disclosed the private message from Raut?

♦

Raut's piece in *Saamana* had also mentioned an update that was not only intriguing for the Shiv Sena, NCP and Congress, but equally worrying for someone in the BJP. Even after 10 days, the Central leadership of the BJP was not stepping in to resolve the Maharashtra deadlock. This was strange because Amit Shah had himself taken on the responsibility to resolve the Haryana issue—and resolve he did within two days. Shah was, however, missing from the action in Maharashtra. Why was he not showing any interest in the second largest political state and the financial capital of the country?

The man who was perhaps the most worried because of the apathy of his party's national leadership was Devendra Fadnavis. While Sharad Pawar was in Delhi, Fadnavis too decided to go to Delhi himself. It was high time. The action on Monday was now in the national capital.

DAY 12: MONDAY, 4 NOVEMBER 2019

Sanjay Raut began the day with yet another tweet. *'Laksh tak pahuchne se pehle safar me maza aata hai'* read the mysterious tweet accompanied by a picture of Raut and Uddhav walking together. Roughly translated, it means 'The journey before reaching your aim is more enjoyable.' The journey had begun. Raut was all set to meet the Governor of Maharashtra later in the day.

♦

Sunday night ended on yet another big speculation. In case of a deadlock between the Shiv Sena and the BJP, the NCP, Shiv Sena and Congress would form the government with Sharad Pawar as the Chief Minister and Aditya Thackeray as Deputy CM. The gossip mills were running bizzare at times. The news about Pawar's comeback as Chief Minister was, however, short-lived.

10, Janpath, New Delhi

All eyes were on the much-awaited meeting between Congress President Sonia Gandhi and Sharad Pawar. In spite of the perpetual distrust about Sharad Pawar in the minds of State Congress leaders, a big section of the Congress MLAs wanted Pawar to take lead in changing the political equations of the state. The five-year rule of Devendra Fadnavis was seen as a monolithic rule by the old guard in Congress and NCP. Fadnavis was forming a team of young leaders in the party and while doing that, he was also politically wiping out the satraps in the Congress, NCP and his own party at times. While some had lost political credibility due to the cases against them, some who were fearing cases had surrendered to Fadnavis and BJP by joining the party. The residual ones hence wanted a new government without the BJP. In spite of his saffron credentials, Uddhav was the lesser evil for them. These leaders, who could not muster up the courage to propose the alliance with Shiv Sena to 10, Janpath, wanted Sharad Pawar to bell the cat.

The first thing that the astute Sonia Gandhi wanted to know was how serious was the rift between the Shiv Sena and the BJP. Pawar briefed the Congress President about the chronology of events and the reasons behind the rift, insisting that the Shiv Sena appeared serious about its demands this time. Sonia Gandhi's close aide A.K. Antony was also present in the meeting. Maharashtra as a state was equally important for both the Congress and NCP. The duo had ruled the state for 15 long years from 1999. But now, the BJP was aggressively growing in the state since 2014. The Congress–NCP alliance had been completely decimated in the the 2014 Lok Sabha elections, when the alliance had won just six seats, and the Congress in its one-time bastion had been reduced to just two seats. In 2019, they tried really hard to wrestle back in Maharashtra, but the results were even worse. While the NCP could save its face by maintaining a status quo, Congress went down to winning just one seat. For Pawar and Sonia, this could be an opportunity to sneak back in power. But the risk of joining hands with Shiv Sena was higher.

The hour-long meeting inched things slightly ahead. The one point on which both Sonia Gandhi and Sharad Pawar agreed was the agenda of keeping the BJP out of power. The question was how. The modalities were to be discussed in another round of meeting between the two.

The media was eagerly waiting for Pawar's version on the meeting. 'I briefed Soniaji about the ground situation in Maharashtra. Whatever is happening between the Shiv Sena and BJP doesn't seem to be a bargaining game. This time it appears serious,' Pawar told the media.

Pawar is known to never make direct statements. His statements need to be cleverly deciphered. 'Neither Uddhav Thackeray has spoken to me nor he has given us any proposal. We too haven't given them any proposal. We have got the mandate to sit in the opposition... However I can't say what will happen in the future...'—with that statement he lived up to his reputation, leaving the journalists bewildered.

Raj Bhavan, Malabar Hill

Sanjay Raut and Shiv Sena leader Ramdas Kadam reached Raj Bhavan. This wasn't the first time that a Shiv Sena leader was calling upon the Governor. After an hour-long meeting with Governor Bhagat Singh Koshyari, Raut and Kadam briefed the media outside the Governor's palatial bungalow: 'We also want the government to be formed at the earliest. However, we have made it clear to the Governor that we are not responsible for the delay. We haven't created any hurdle in the government formation procedure,' Raut said.

Devgiri, Sudhir Mungantiwar's Bungalow

While Devendra Fadnavis was in Delhi, some BJP leaders gathered at Sudhir Mungantiwar's residence. The state BJP camp was always a divided house between two strongmen from Nagpur. While a camp of new leaders owed its allegiance to Devendra Fadnavis, another group rallied behind Union Minister Nitin Gadkari. Throughout the drama, these two groups were seen holding separate meetings. While one centre was Fadnavis's Man Friday Girish Mahajan's Shivneri bungalow, right next to Varsha, the other group often met at Sudhir Mungantiwar's Devgiri residence. Mungantiwar was a staunch Gadkari loyalist. Raosaheb Danwe and Ashish Shelar were present here. Leaving after the meeting, Union Minister of State for Food and Civil Supplies, Raosaheb Danve insisted on the 1995 formula.[19] At a point when the Fadnavis camp was slowly preparing for a slight climbdown, the other camp in BJP wanted to play hardball. Internal conflict in approach was making things more difficult for Devendra Fadnavis.

6, Krishna Menon Marg (Amit Shah's Residence)

Devendra Fadnavis reached his party boss's house. This was the first face-to-face meeting between the two after the political drama began.

Shah and Fadnavis's equation were always a topic of discussion in the political circles of Maharashtra. Some believed that Shah was never fond of Fadnavis. More than once, Shah had seriously mulled over replacing Fadnavis with other leaders. During the Maratha reservation agitation, these talks had gathered serious momentum. But the TINA (There Is No Alternative) factor worked in Fadnavis's favour and he was able to weather the storm.

A large chunk of national media had always loved to call Fadnavis the future Prime Minister. Whenever he was asked about his national ambitions, he would laugh it out and say that he was much happier in the state. But this praise for Fadnavis never went down well with some seniors in the party. Some saw a potential competitor in Fadnavis—a contender who had good command over the administration, was articulate in English and Hindi and, moreover, had the blessing of RSS as he came from Nagpur. Add to it that he was seen as the blue-eyed boy of Prime Minister

---

[19] In 1995, the formula that was decided was that the party with the greater number of seats would have the CM's post, while the other would get the Deputy CM's post.

Modi. In all the rallies Modi addressed in Maharashtra, he always showered rich praises on Fadnavis, a rare feat for any BJP leader.

When Fadnavis came to Delhi, many thought he would return with a solution. The national leadership of the party had successfuly worked out solutions in states like Goa, Manipur and, more recently, Karnataka. Maharashtra wasn't looking as difficult as these states. For the BJP leadership, the Maharashtra stalemate was only about addressing the tantrums of its ever-cribbing ally Shiv Sena.

Fadnavis briefed his Party President about the Sena's demands and its aggressive muscle flexing. 'We can only consider the legitimate demands. Whatever extra they want, should be discussed on merits. No question on giving the CM's post. However, continue with the backroom talks,' Shah told Fadnavis.[20] The meeting didn't end with a concrete solution to the deadlock.

Speaking to journalists at the Maharashtra Sadan, Fadnavis yet again asserted that the government will be formed soon and he will take oath as the Chief Minister of Maharashtra.

After meeting Amit Shah, Fadnavis called upon other party leaders in the national capital. He met party Executive President J.P. Nadda and Nitin Gadkari. But more than these meeting, Fadnavis was keen on meeting his mentor Narendra Modi. But even after waiting till late in the night, Fadnavis did not get an appointment with the PM. This hadn't happened on any of his earlier visits to Delhi...

DAY 13: TUESDAY, 5 NOVEMBER 2019

Monday's hectic political activity in the national capital had failed to yield any substantial results. The scene of political manoeuvring had now shifted back to Mumbai.

Sanjay Raut yet again shot his shayari missile on Twitter on Tuesday. Raut's shayaris were as integral to this political drama as songs are to a Hindi potboiler—conveying the situation or the mood

---

[20] Source-based information on condition of anonymity.

of a character when dialogues couldn't. He quoted these famous lines by the poet Dushyant:

> 'Sirf Hungama khada karna mera maqsad nahi,
> Meri Koshish yeh hai ki yeh surat badalni Chahiye
> Mere sine me nahi, tere sine me sahi,
> ho kahi bhi, magar aag jalni chahiye'
>
> (I don't just want to create a ruckus,
> I want to change the scenario
> Be it your heart or mine,
> the fire has to be lit somewhere...)

With Raut's early morning tweets followed by press meets attacking the BJP everyday, the distance between the allies was growing and possibilities of talks resuming between the two were fading rapidly.

Ahmedpur, District Latur

A farmer was complaining that the loan waiver declared by the earlier government was of no use to him. He hadn't received a single penny. Uddhav Thackeray, who was on his second leg of visit to areas affected by unseasonal rains, was patiently listening. For him, the route for the solution to the farmers' issues was through power. He promised the farmer that once 'his' government came to power, the 7/12 extract of farmers would be cleared off all their dues.

Varsha

After his insistence on taking Shiv Sena on board in his meeting with Amit Shah and denial to go with the NCP in that late night meeting, the onus was now on Devendra Fadnavis to bring the Shiv Sena on board.

An emergency meeting of the core committee of the State BJP, comprising Fadnavis, State President Chandrakant Patil, Fadnavis's close aide Girish Mahajan, Sudhir Mungantiwar, Ashish Shelar and Pankaja Munde, was called at the CM's bungalow. As the BJP too was losing its patience, the anti-Fadnavis camp blamed the stalemate with the Shiv Sena on Fadnavis being adamant about the CM's position. Pressure was building up on Fadnavis from all sides.

After the meeting, Chandrakant Patil, Sudhir Mungantiwar and Pankaja Munde briefed the media: 'There is no proposal from the Shiv Sena yet. We are still waiting for it. Party's national leadership has given its nod to the government being formed under Devendra Fadnavis, we firmly stand behind him,' Patil told the media.

Sudhir Mungantiwar was more optimistic. He announced to the media that 'a good news is expected any moment'. 'Whatever their demand is, we are ready for talks, 24x7... But they should come for talks first... It's for the Shiv Sena to take a call,' he added.

The précis of the meeting was to accelerate talks with the Shiv Sena. BJP was now at least willing to discuss the CM's post. A proposal was mooted in the meeting to form a steering commitee for the alliance with Uddhav as the chair. This was a way to give him and the Shiv Sena the confidence that the real remote of power lay with Matoshri.

◆

The growing rift between the Shiv Sena and BJP was closely monitored by Sharad Pawar. The initial die was cast. The rapidly going distrust between the allies would mean Shiv Sena would be left with little options. The keys to power that were currently in the hands of Uddhav Thackeray were slowly getting into Pawar's hand.

Pawar was in no hurry. Politics is a game of patience and Pawar had mastered that. He was playing his cards too close to his chest. He continued to hold parallel talks with Sanjay Raut even as his public posturing was that of receiving the mandate for being the Opposition party.

The smartest in the entire scheme of characters involved in the drama, Pawar's next moves were going to stump one and all.

10.00 p.m., RSS Headquarters, Nagpur

The city of Nagpur retires early. At 10 p.m. a convoy whizzed through the narrow bylanes of Reshim Baug. The RSS Headquarters in the orange city rarely gets visitors so late. But this was urgent. Fadnavis had slowly started to realize that the game could slip out of his hands, if swift steps were not taken. Twenty-four hours after his meeting with Shah, Nadda and Gadkari in Delhi, Fadnavis was here to brief the parent organization.

Mohan Bhagwat, the RSS Chief, as well as the RSS Sar Karyavah (General Secretary) Suresh alias Bhaiyyaji Joshi were present in the meeting room. 'Shiv Sena is our natural ally. And in any case, we have to take them along. It will take some time and more convincing to get them along. NCP, though an option at this point, would be detrimental in the longer run,' Fadnavis explained his point of view.

The meeting lasted for one hour. The RSS too agreed with Fadnavis that the BJP and Shiv Sena were tied with an ideological umbilical cord. The message from the RSS was to put an end to the stalemate as the verdict on Ayodhya was close and not having Shiv Sena on its side wouldn't send a positive message.

◆

The proposal to make Uddhav Thackeray the Chief of the Steering Committee reached Matoshri through yet another emissary, but Uddhav shot it down.

DAY 14: WEDNESDAY, 6 NOVEMBER 2019

New Delhi

Till now, the Congress had almost kept out of heavy political activity. Prithviraj Chavan set the ball rolling. Though the party appeared like a divided house in several camps, there was a new group that was emerging, comprising young turks, some of whom were descendants of regional satraps and influential senior politicians. These young turks, like Amit Deshmukh,[21] Dr Vishwajeet Kadam[22] and Yashomati Thakur, the fiery MLA from Tivasa in Vidarbha and the State Working President of the party, were of the opinion that the BJP should be kept

---

[21] Son of former CM, Late Vilasrao Deshmukh.
[22] Son of senior Congress leader, Late Patangrao Kadam.

away from power in Maharashtra. A few days before the elections, the Marathi daily *Punyanagari* had reported that Amit Deshmukh and Vishwajeet Kadam were in touch with the BJP. The young Congress leaders had vehemently denied the news, with Vishwajeet even going on to threaten legal action against the newspaper.

The young group of MLAs started building a pressure group within the party. They had seen and experienced factionalism in the party and were unsure of the current state seniors being in a position to take some radical decision. The common factor between these younger MLAs was that most of them were close to Rahul Gandhi. Another young leader sitting in Delhi shared the same views as these young MLAs. Being closely associated with Rahul for the last few years, he had already apprised the party leadership of the strong feelings of these MLAs. The senior leadership of the state was quick to gauge that. After Prithviraj Chavhan had gone a step ahead to moot the idea at the very beginning, another senior leader Ashok Chavan was now slowly coming out of the closet. 'There is no proposal from the Shiv Sena, but we cannot say what will happen next... But the larger feeling in the party is that all out efforts should be made to keep the BJP out of power...' Chavan said. His statement, however, came with a rider: 'The Shiv Sena will first have to walk out of the NDA and snap its ties with the BJP, and then only we can think of any such proposal,' Chavan had added.

The Congress, which so far had been operating from behind the curtains and relying solely on Sharad Pawar, had started to come on record. The condition it laid before the Shiv Sena was not going to be easy for the saffron party.

As Chavan gave broader hints, Yashomati Thakur was yet again at Silver Oak. The dissent in the young MLAs has found a voice in the form of Sharad Pawar. This was also exerting pressure on the Congress party.

Silver Oak Estate

After his tweet in the morning, Raut had yet again indulged everyone into guesswork: *'Jo log kuch nahi karte, woh kamal karte hai* (Those who don't do anything, work wonders).' Many thought that the tweet was aimed at the Congress leaders.

Raut met Pawar for over half an hour and left immediately for Matoshri to update his party boss about the meeting.

♦

While Pawar and Raut met in Maharashtra, another meeting in Delhi caught everyone's attention. This was not a usual meeting. Rarely do we see a senior BJP and Congress leader meeting like this. Sonia Gandhi's political advisor, Ahmed Patel, was at Union Minister Nitin Gadkari's bungalow. While the official statement was that Patel had gone to discuss some issues in his constituency, a source close to Gadkari later said that the BJP was keen in knowing how serious the talks between the Congress and Shiv Sena were.

But what intrigued many was the fact that Gadkari had little or no role in the state's politics. He personally had denied any interest in returning to state politics on several occasions. Then why was he holding closed-door talks with the Congress?

Varsha

As things appeared to be moving towards a point of no return, there came a sign of thaw. Fadnavis had called a meeting of his ministers to discuss the issue of unseasonal rains. Earlier last week, Shiv Sena ministers had given a skip to a similar meeting. But most of the senior ministers were present for this meeting. This was perhaps the first in recent times where the top Sena leadership was seen mingling with BJP. Most of them, especially the Sena ministers present there, wanted an alliance with the BJP. A minister requested Fadnavis to end the impasse soon. 'Your statement has hurt Uddhav Saheb. He strongly feels that BJP has made him look like a liar. There has to be a respectable exit out of it... You need to find a way out...' the minister told Fadnavis.

With Uddhav and his party not budging, the BJP Core Committee went into a huddle yet again.

A senior member of the Core Committee wasn't impressed by

the way his party was waiting for the Shiv Sena to tag along. He was aggressively pitching to go ahead and stake claim to form the government. In 2014, when the BJP had formed the government, they were just 122, way short of the majority. NCP had announced unconditional support to the BJP. The floor test was passed amidst pandemonium. Left with no alternative, the Shiv Sena was forced to tag along. Not only did it support the BJP government, it also became a part of the Fadnavis-led BJP government as its junior partner. The Shiv Sena, then, even willingly accepted some junior portfolios. The same Shiv Sena was now flexing muscles.

Saturday was the last day of the 13th Assembly of Maharashtra. A government should have been in place by now. The BJP in its Core Committee decided to meet the Governor the next day. For some, the government-formation drama was nearing an end, but in reality this was just the beginning.

Y.B. Chavan Centre, Nariman Point, Mumbai

Though they were next-to-difficult to decode, Sharad Pawar was making moves that were talking the story forward. The regular meetings between him and Sanjay Raut were hinting that they were discussing government formation. Pawar, however, consistently maintained that his party had got a mandate to sit in the Opposition. But he was also the sole channel between the Shiv Sena and Congress, with the latter stuck in dilemma.

While addressing the media, the first thing Pawar 'clarified' was that his meeting with Raut was routine and no politics was discussed. In times of frantic political activity, there was obviously no scope to take that statement at its face value. However, it's not just difficult but impossible to make Pawar say what you want.

'You require the figure of 144 to prove your majority and form the government in Maharashtra; with 54 MLAs, it will not be wise to stake claim to form the government. We are, however, closely monitoring the situation. I cannot say what will happen tomorrow,' Pawar said, adding to the already raging fire of speculations.

When someone said to Pawar that the deadline of the present

assembly was ending soon, he responded that anything could happen even in the last hour. One thing was clear: from a firm stand of sitting in Opposition, Pawar was gradually opening up and keeping the hopes of an atypical alliance still alive.

A journalist sitting in one corner asked Pawar a question that was haunting political players and journalists alike: 'Amit Shah is known for his knack to form governments in states where the BJP is in trouble… He hasn't visited Maharashtra as yet. Do you think he will able to repeat his magic here?' The entire Rangswar hall in Y.B. Chavan Centre was all ears for Pawar's response.

Those who have seen the Maratha strongman's phenomenal rise in politics know one thing very well—he has always been known as 'Chanakya', a title which is now associated with Amit Shah. Pawar's response hinted that, from now, it's going to be the Battle Royale between two political gaints. 'Even I'm keen to see Amit Shah's skill and how he forms the government in Maharashtra…' Pawar said. Was it a veiled dare or an open challenge?

DAY 15: THURSDAY, 7 NOVEMBER 2019

Two days from now, 9 November, was to be the last day of the present assembly. Things had rapidly shifted beyond just mind games. The action was slated for more acceleration. Behind the curtains as well as on the stage, all four players had now rolled up their sleeves. If no government could be formed by 9 November, the state would soon see President's rule.

For the Shiv Sena, offence was the only defence. And Sanjay Raut was in charge of exasperating the BJP. On Thursday morning, his scathing attack on the BJP got even sharper. The Shiv Sena made serious allegations of poaching against the BJP. The editorial alleged that some 'newly joined money bags' in the party were using the power of money to lure the Shiv Sena. Raut was indirectly referring to BJP's member of the state legislative council Prasad Lad, who had grown very close to Devendra Fadnavis in the recent times. He was seen as his man on mission. Lad ostensibly was the man behind the recent successful poaching of 13 Karnataka MLAs.[23] The majority of the political drama in that state was played out in Mumbai. This Karnataka thriller eventually led to the toppling of the JDU–Congress government and the return of the B.Y. Yediyurappa-led BJP government. Prasad Lad, a businessman with interests in the hospitality and real estate sectors, had quit the NCP to join the BJP a few years ago.

Without naming Lad, the editorial went hammers and tongs against him.

'People will not forgive those who are indulging in horse trading. There are rising complaints that some turncoats are approaching new MLAs offering money. We don't want to state that this has the blessings of the Chief Minister. But this certainly does not suit the State of Shivaji Maharaj,' the editorial slammed.

While attacking the BJP, Raut also took a dig at Sudhir Mungantiwar's 'Good news soon' remark from two days ago. 'If there is any good news that is expected, it will be that of a Shiv Sena Chief Minister', the editorial read.

Matoshri

The allegations of poaching were serious. Uddhav wanted to speak to his party MLAs on an urgent basis. The message was sent across the previous night to MLAs from the rest of Maharashtra. Media contingents were stationed in huge numbers as MLAs and leaders started to arrive. As MLAs entered Matoshri, the farthest bungalow in Kalanagar, the suspicion in the air was evident. The MLAs were asked to leave their mobile phones outside.

Dressed in a brown kurta, Uddhav Thackeray greeted his newly elected MLAs with his trademark 'Jai Maharashtra'. The MLAs, especially those who had come from rural Maharashtra, wanted to know what exactly was going on in their Party Chief's mind. 'You all are aware what is being reported in the media. What do

---

[23] Prasad Lad was also named by the erstwhile Karnataka CM, H.D. Kumaraswamy, on the floor of the house for his role in the Karnataka political crisis.

you think we should do now?' he asked his MLAs. Emotions were running high. Eknath Shinde, Abdul Sattar and other MLAs said that whichever ally he chose—be it BJP or NCP–Congress—they would stay firmly behind the decision. After the reassurance, Uddhav spoke for nearly 15 minutes. 'This is not an exercise to isolate the BJP. If they are not going to keep their word, then I too am firm on my stand. For last several days, "they" are calling me. But they should only call me if they are willing to give the post of Chief Minister to Shiv Sena.' He then added, 'I won't commit the sin of breaking the ties with BJP, they have to take a call now... I don't expect anything more than what was promised before the Lok Sabha elections. If they are trying to prove me a liar, then it's not done. I will declare my decision soon.'

The meeting didn't mark an end of the action on the Shiv Sena's side. Amid the alleged attempts of poaching Shiv Sena MLAs, Uddhav and his core team had planned to shift all their MLAs to a city hotel. Some MLAs were given an idea about it, but most of them had come unprepared for a stay. The MLAs were herded to Hotel Rangsharda in Bandra East, barely 4 km from the Thackeray residence.

This was slightly unusual for the Shiv Sena, a party that was known to work on 'aadesh (orders)'. Shivsainiks were known as staunch soldiers of the party who would never betray the party. But the situation was volatile, and trust, the costliest commodity. Uddhav was in no mood to take any chances.

And it wasn't Shiv Sena alone, but even the Congress levelled similar allegations against the BJP. The Congress was specific in its allegations. Vijay Wadettiwar, senior leader of the party, alleged that their MLA from Igatpuri (Nashik district) got a phone call from a close aide of a senior BJP minister, offering 25–50 crore,[24] an allegation that was outrightly refuted by the BJP. From a war of words to backchannelling, things were now taking an ugly turn.

---

[24] https://timesofindia.indiatimes.com/city/nagpur/bjp-offered-rs25-50cr-to-cong-sena-mlas-wadettiwar/articleshow/71976445.cms; last accessed 16 March 2020.

Raj Bhavan, Malabar Hill

As decided in the Core Committee, a delegation of senior leaders from the BJP visited Raj Bhavan. The situation was still logjammed and the tenure of assembly was ending soon. Uddhav's statement of no plans of snapping ties with BJP came somewhat as a breather for the party. As cars of BJP leaders crossed the ivory gate of Raj Bhavan, one person was missing from the delegation—Devendra Fadnavis. The possibility of BJP staking claim was thus written off—at least for the day. The delegation included the party's State President Chandrakant Patil, Girish Mahajan, Sudhir Mungantiwar and Ashish Shelar. After the meeting, Patil informed the media waiting outside Raj Bhavan that the meeting was to apprise the Governor about the present stalemate. 'We have told the Governor about the situation and the reasons behind the stalemate. We, BJP and Shiv Sena, contested the elections together, and have got a mandate to form the government together. But the Shiv Sena is not willing to join the exercise to form the government. We have requested the Governor to take these factors into consideration before taking any further step,' he said.

♦

Minutes after the delegation left, the Governor summoned the Advocate General of Maharashtra to discuss the snarl-up. The situation was classic and needed opinions of constitutional experts. A few possible options were discussed with Advocate General Ashutosh Kumbhakoni. The discussion was largely centred around the the Sarkaria Commission report on inter-state relations. According to the report, the following order of preference was suggested for Governors to follow:

1. An alliance formed prior to the election (In this case, it was Shiv Sena–BJP and Congress–NCP, where the BJP and Shiv Sena, in spite of a clear mandate, were almost on the verge of calling off the alliance).
2. The largest single party staking claim with the support of

others, including independents (In this case, the BJP. Apart from backchannel talks with the Shiv Sena, it was also wooing independents on its side. So was Shiv Sena).
3. A post-electoral coalition, with all partners joining the government (There was still no clarity on post-poll alliance between other players).
4. A post-poll coalition, with some joining the government and others extending support from outside.

A large section of the BJP was also of the opinion that the Governor would invite the single largest party to form the government. As the process would take a few more days, it would give leeway to the BJP to continue talks with the Shiv Sena. All eyes were now on the Governor, Bhagat Singh Koshyari.

7.30 p.m., Matoshri

A frail-looking old man wearing a crumpled kurta and dhoti with a Gandhi cap was waiting outside the security gates at Matoshri. Sporting a white stubble and walrus moustache, this unkempt old man told the security guards that he wanted to meet Uddhav Thackeray. One of the people on duty immediately recognized him and he was escorted inside.

The octogenarian was no simple man. The prime minister called him his guru. Sambaji Bhide aka Bhide Guruji was known as a hard-line icon of Hindutva. Just a year ago, the Hindutva flag-bearer, who runs an organization called Shiv Pratishthan Hindustan, was in the eye of a storm for his alleged role in the Koregaon Bhima riots.[25] In spite of all the controversies around the name, Uddhav had firmly stood behind Bhide[26].

Incidentally, earlier this morning, Nitin Gadkari had met the

---

[25] https://www.timesnownews.com/india/article/exclusive-bhima-koregaon-violence-secret-state-documents-pune-police-maharashtra-government-accuse-sambhaji-bhide-milind-ekbote-for-clashes-hindutva/278017; last accessed 16 March 2020.

[26] *Saamana* Editorial, 12 June 2018.

RSS Chief in Nagpur. There were speculations that the latter may step in to end the stalemate, as the Shiv Sena had been the BJP's natural ally because of their shared Hindutva ideology. But, here we had another extreme Right-wing icon who had come with a message. Bhide wanted to meet Uddhav and tell him that under no condition should Hindutva be compromised. In any other situation, Uddhav would have accorded a red carpet welcome to this man, who had a great following in western Maharashtra and also in parts of Karnataka, but at this point he was in no mood to relent.

Bhide was told that Uddhav Thackeray was not at Matoshri. Instead, Uddhav's close aide and member of the legislative council, Advocate Anil Parab met Bhide Guruji and assured him that he will convey his message to Uddhav. Parab also assured him that he will arrange for a meeting between the two at the earliest. But the ragged-looking Hindutva leader was not the only one who Uddhav had refused to speak to. A top industrialist had also offered to mediate, but Uddhav had politely declined.

Midnight, Hotel Rangsharda, Bandra

Aditya Thackeray himself drove his car to Hotel Rangsharda. Almost all the MLAs were still awake. Though Raut had clarified in the afternoon that there were no restrictions on the MLAs, a team of Yuva Sena members was keeping a close eye on every movement inside and outside the hotel premises. Aditya knew that while he could guard his own MLAs, the same couldn't be said about the Congress and NCP.

◆

NCP Supremo Sharad Pawar was in Satara for the whole day, meeting farmers affected by unseasonal rains. According to Pawar's tour itinerary, he was to visit the Konkan area the next day.

Pawar's phone rang. He appeared serious while talking to someone on the other side. He then cancelled his Konkan tour and headed for Mumbai the same night. Friday was going to be a long day...

DAY 16: FRIDAY, 8 NOVEMBER 2019

10, Janpath, New Delhi

The young MLAs from Congress called upon Party President Sonia Gandhi. While the leadership was in favour of keeping the BJP out of power, the thought of going with Shiv Sena was scary. The party was stuck between the devil and the deep sea. A poaching attempt of its MLA the previous day had shook the party. On one hand, there was an imminent danger of a split in the party; on the other, the pressure to join hands with Shiv Sena and NCP was increasing from within the party. The Central leadership, however, felt an alliance with Shiv Sena would affect the party's secular credentials. But there was also a reward for it—the party could regain the important state of Maharashtra from the BJP.

Maharashtra was an opportunity. Kumar Ketkar, a senior Congress MP and a noted journalist from Maharashtra, had submitted a two-page note to the Party High Command, which mentioned the open and tacit understandings between the Congress and Shiv Sena since 1966—the most prominent being Bal Thackeray's open support to the National Emergency declared by Indira Gandhi. Moreover, the Shiv Sena had openly gone against the BJP while supporting Pratibha Patil for the post of President and similarly voted for Pranab Mukherjee, when he was the President's nominee. It has been a successful experiment of the Shiv Sena, Congress and NCP coming together. The situation was conducive for the Congress to take a call.

The Congress's Interim President kept her decision on hold. Her top priority was to keep her flock together. After the meeting with the young MLAs on Friday morning, all MLAs were summoned to Mumbai. Within 24 hours of the Shiv Sena shifting its MLAs to a Mumbai hotel, the Congress too decided to shift its MLAs to a resort in Jaipur.

◆

आग्नेय परीक्षा की इस घड़ी में–आइए, अर्जुन की तरह उद्घोष करें:
'न दैन्यं न पलायन।' –अटल बिहारी वाजपेयी

(In these trying times, let's give a war cry like Arjuna:
No begging for pity and no running away –Atal Bihari Vajpayee)

Sanjay Raut, as part of his morning ritual of tweeting, quoted the late Atal Bihari Vajpayee to announce that the Shiv Sena was now gearing for a heads-on battle.

Eknath Shinde was summoned by Uddhav Thackeray along with district presidents of the Shiv Sena at the party's Dadar headquarters. Shinde was assigned the duty to see to it that no MLAs were approached by the BJP. The duty was not just to keep the MLAs in Mumbai under one roof, but to also assure their family members of their safety and well-being. Moreover, the district presidents were asked to provide a discreet security cover to the family members of the MLAs in their respective districts. They were also asked to monitor the movements in and around the houses of the MLAs without disturbing their families.

◆

Nitin Gadkari boarded the flight for Mumbai. Speculations were rife about him calling upon Uddhav Thackeray later in the day as a last-ditch effort to mend fences with the Shiv Sena. But this was hard to digest for two reasons. One, Gadkari was never a favourite at Matoshri. Second, he had already clarified that he wouldn't interfere in the party's state affairs.

By noon, Gadkari reached his residence in the Sukhada Housing Society in Worli. Speaking to India Today there, he hardened his party's stand, assertively denying any 50:50 power-sharing formula with the Shiv Sena. 'Shiv Sena has demanded the Chief Minister's post. As far as my knowledge is concerned, there was no promise of rotational Chief Minister to the Shiv Sena. Whenever there has been such a situation in the past, even when Balasaheb Thackeray was alive, the formula was whichever party has more MLAs will get the CM's post. We are ready for discussions; it's for the Shiv Sena to positively think now,' Gadkari said, once again bringing back things to square one.

12.15 p.m., Varsha

Hours after making an unsuccessful attempt to mediate between the warring saffron siblings, Sambhaji Bhide called upon Devendra Fadnavis at his official residence. Unlike in Matoshri, Bhide got an appointment at Varsha. Bhide and Fadnavis spoke for 20 minutes, where the former briefed him about the incident at Matoshri. Earlier in the day, Sanjay Raut had already announced that no one should try to mediate between the two parties.

Fadnavis understood that he was racing against time, and that Uddhav was in no mood to open the blocked doors of communication.

2.30 p.m., Vijay Wadettiwar's residence

Congress MLAs had started to reach Wadettiwar's residence opposite the Mantralay. A bus was parked in front of the bungalow, which was to take the MLAs to the airport. 'Attempts are being made to lure away MLAs with offers of ₹25 to ₹50 crore to switch sides. We have told our MLAs to record such calls so that people of the state know about them,' Wadettiwar told the media.[27] Some leaders were to join them in Jaipur from Delhi.

4:00 p.m., Raj Bhavan, Malabar Hill

There was sudden activity outside the gates of Raj Bhavan. Media vans started to arrive amid frantic activity. As cameras focused on the route leading to the Governor's official residence, Fadnavis's convoy reached Raj Bhavan. With no headway in talks with the Shiv Sena to form the next government and less than a day left for the tenure of the present assembly to end, Fadnavis had come

---

[27] https://www.indiatoday.in/india/story/rs-25-cr-rs-50-cr-being-offered-to-mlas-to-switch-sides-congress-1616981-2019-11-08; last accessed 16 March 2020.

with senior party colleagues in toto to submit his resignation as the Chief Minister of Maharashtra to Governor B.S. Koshyari. The Governor accepted the resignation and requested Fadnavis to continue as the caretaker Chief Minister till further arrangements were in place.

Fadnavis, usually known for his composure, looked visibly irritated. He straightaway headed to Sahyadri Guest House, where he had invited the media for an interaction. More than 100 journalists and over two dozen TV cameras were eagerly waiting for this first-ever interaction with Fadnavis since the political drama had turned bitter. Fadnavis's body language was indicating that things were going from bad to worse...

4.40 p.m., Sahyadri Guest House

'I am here to give a good news...' The jam-packed hall broke into laughter with that opening remark by Fadnavis. This was the only light moment in the press conference. Fadnavis then went all out against the Shiv Sena President. 'While the elections were fought by the two parties as allies, Sena's sudden change of stand after the results came as a shocker,' he began. 'Maharashtra gave us a great mandate during Lok Sabh elections and even in assembly we faced the elections as allies. Maha Yuti got a clear mandate. We won more than 160 seats and BJP emerged as the single largest party with 105 seats,' he continued. 'But Uddhav Thackeray on the day of results made it clear that they have their options open and this was a shock for us... People gave mandate for the Maha Yuti. In such a situation, why would he say that options are open is a big question for us,' he added.

Fadnavis also addressed the issue of the rotational CM: 'Once it was discussed, and over the same issue our talks had fizzled. And that is why during my casual interaction with the media I made it clear that it wasn't decided in my presence. It may have been discussed between Amit Shah and Uddhav Thackeray. I asked Amit Shah and he said he never gave any assurance to Shiv Sena on this front.' He added, 'All the misunderstandings that took place over this issue could have been resolved through discussions but they never wanted to talk.'

Fadnavis concluded by saying that doors were still open for talks, but someone watching the press conference live on their TV was not pleased with his attack on the Shiv Sena. Uddhav asked his men to call for a counter press conference.

5.50 p.m., Matoshri

Uddhav Thackeray took the remote and switched off the TV as Fadnavis's press conference ended. He called someone and instructed the person on the other side: 'Call the press and I want "those" video clips to be played during the press meet, arrange for it ASAP.' Uddhav was agitated.

At 5.50 p.m., Uddhav and his son Aditya left Matoshri and headed for Shiv Sena Bhawan. His mood suggested that he was going to hit back...

6.20 p.m., Shiv Sena Bhawan, Dadar

Uddhav stared blankly for a moment before starting his press briefing.

'After listening to Devendra Fadnavis, I thought I must reply... For the [first] time someone has accused Shiv Sena of lying. I am following my father's footstep to stand for the truth...' Uddhav's hostility was evident. 'I had very clearly discussed with Amit Shah about the 50:50 formula and rotational Chief Minister post. We talked of equal cabinet seats and equal responsibility. They sweet-talked us into this alliance. I supported Devendra Fadnavis through and through last time. I never expected this from him. Shiv Sena is not a party of liars; I am not a BJP person who would lie,' Uddhav went on.

He didn't spare the BJP leadership either. 'Fadnavis said he was shocked when I spoke about options, I was more shocked when the caretaker Chief Minister said that he will form the government. How are they going to do it? Like they did in Karnataka and Manipur?' Uddhav Thackeray asked. 'I have travelled in Maharashtra... The love and respect that people of Maharashtra have for Shiv Sena...it is the opposite for Amit Shah and company. More trust people of Maharashtra have on Shiv Sena and Balasaheb, the more distrust they have on Amit Shah and company.' Uddhav was going all out. 'I do not see the BJP as enemy party but they must stop telling lies. See who lied about note ban. People know who lied... From "achhe din" to "give me 50 days" after demonetisation everyone knows who lied.'

Uddhav then asked his men to play a video clip of JJP leader and newly sworn-in Deputy Chief Minister of Haryana, Dushyant Chautala. This was in response to the allegation made by Fadnavis that Shiv Sena often uses uncalled-for language against the Party's leadership. In the clip, Dushyant Chautala was allegedly seen saying that Gujaratis cannot teach him and his workers nationalism. 'Unlike Chautala, Modi has twice called me his younger brother, I have never targeted him,' Uddhav added.

Rejecting the claims that the Shiv Sena and NCP would be unnatural allies, Uddhav said that if the BJP could form an alliance with PDP in J&K, then the Sena could do so with NCP in Maharashtra.

'I had promised Balasaheb that one day I will make a Shiv Sena CM. I will do that and for that, I don't need any blessings from Amit Shah,' Uddhav said. He further warned the BJP, 'Unless you admit you lied about the 50:50 agreement there will be no talks with you.'

Once known to be good friends beyond politics, it now seemed that irreparable damage had been caused to the bond between Fadnavis and Uddhav.

Silver Oak Estate

After Uddhav's press conference, Sanjay Raut headed to Pawar's residence. This was his second meeting with Pawar in the day. Earlier that day, Pawar had held separate talks with Congress leaders Ashok Chavan and Prithviraj Chavan.

With not much time left to stake claim for the next government, there were both behind-the-curtain movements and on the ground.

Hotel Rangsharda, Bandra

Shiv Sena MLAs started boarding the bus. They were now being moved to The Retreat Hotel in Malad, as the next few hours were going to be crucial.

Nearly 1,200 km away from Mumbai, Congress MLAs reached the Beuna Vista resort on the Delhi–Jaipur Highway. The Congress government in Rajasthan had issued strict instructions to the cops to ensure that security at the resort was not compromised. Senior leaders were to join soon.

But as everyone was gearing up for the next political action, a sudden newsbreak sent everyone into a tizzy. The Supreme Court was set to pronounce its prolonged verdict in Ayodhya's Ram Janmabhoomi–Babri Masjid title suit on Saturday. The five-judge bench of the Supreme Court were going to pronounce the judgment at 10:30 a.m.

At a time when the Congress, NCP and Shiv Sena were inching closer, this verdict was going to be an acid test, particularly for the Shiv Sena.

DAY 17: SATURDAY, 9 NOVEMBER 2019

Amidst hectic political activity in Maharashtra, the day of the Ayodhya verdict was going to be the biggest day for the country. The dispute over the piece of land had divided the Hindus and Muslims of the country since 1853, when the first communal riot over the site was recorded. Over the years, the Hindus had been claiming that the spot where the mosque now stood was originally the birthplace of Lord Rama or Ram Janmabhoomi, and that Emperor Babur had demolished a temple to build the Babri Masjid. There were a few instances when events had taken controversial turns—in 1984 and in 1989—but the biggest turn of events happened on 6 December 1992 when a mob of thousands demolished the Babri Masjid. It was followed by large-scale communal riots across the country. Mumbai bore the biggest brunt. Even before the culpability of the demolition could be fixed, one man unabashedly, and unapologetically too, upped the onus: 'If my party men have done it... I'm proud of them,' Shiv Sena Chief Bal Thackeray had then said.[28] The popularity of Bal Thackeray had suddenly multiplied manyfold all across the nation. The man who championed the cause of the sons of the soil or Marathi manoos was now the Hindu Hriday Samrat—the Emperor of Hindu Hearts. In the present political context, the Shiv Sena was standing at awkward crossroads. Once known for its hardline Hindutva agenda that directed its political vent against the Congress for what it termed as politics of appeasement, the Shiv Sena was now slowly inching towards the possibility of its joining hands with the same party.

10.32 a.m., Supreme Court of India, New Delhi

The five-member bench arrived in the packed courtroom to deliver its verdict on the dispute. In a 1,024-page verdict taken unanimously by the judges, the Supreme Court paved the way for the construction of the Ram Temple at the disputed site. The verdict further said that the mosque should be constructed at a 'prominent site' and a trust should be formed within three months for the construction of the temple at the site where many Hindus believe Lord Ram was born.

Usually known for their over-the-top comments on the issue, Right-wing politicians showed unprecedented composure while reacting to the verdict. But all eyes were on Shiv Sena and its present leader Uddhav Thackeray, on what he had to say on the verdict of a movement that his father had once aggressively pursued.

Matoshri

Uddhav had visited Ayodhya in November 2018 to flare up the issue. Amidst sadhus on the banks of Sarayu river, he had raised the slogan

---

[28] Bal Thackeray's views published in *Saamana* in the aftermath of the demolition. He also repeated this in his interview with Rajat Sharma on the latter's show *Aap ki Adalat*.

of *'Pehle Mandir Phir Sarkar* (Temple first, then Government)'.[29] His stand after the verdict was now keenly watched.

The NCP and Congress, specially 10, Janpath, was watching the stand taken by Uddhav very closely. The road of future politics in Maharashtra would depend on it.

'This day will be written in golden words in the history of the country. I will go to Ayodhya soon to seek blessings of Lord Ram,' Uddhav announced, cautiously reacting to the verdict. He did not mention Narendra Modi at all, while remembering the likes of Atal Bihari Vajpayee, L.K. Advani, Pramod Mahajan and Gopinath Munde. The caution was further underlined when Uddhav appealed to his Shiv Sena workers to not indulge in celebrations or any act that will hurt the sentiments of 'others'. His appeal was in stark contrast to Bal Thackeray owning up the demolition of the mosque and bragging about it. Was this tectonic shift a sign of the party's new political compulsion?

◆

Shiv Sena's reaction disappointed a few of its leaders and also a section of the BJP. Had the Shiv Sena taken a more aggressive stand, it could have eased the party's stalemate with the BJP. The more balanced reaction seemed tilted towards a secular line.

Raj Bhavan, Malabar Hill

Just as the reactions over the historic verdict were settling down, Governor Bhagat Singh Koshyari stepped in. With no single party or alliance coming forward to form the government even after 15 days, Koshyari followed the textbook after consulting legal experts and the Advocate General of the state. He asked Devendra Fadnavis, the leader of the single largest party, to 'indicate the willingness and ability of his party to form the government' in Maharashtra.

---

[29] https://www.indiatoday.in/elections/story/shiv-sena-clarion-call-for-ram-mandir-pehle-mandir-phir-sarkar-1395210-2018-11-24; last accessed 16 March 2020.

Fadnavis was still hopeful of working out some deal with the Shiv Sena. A meeting of the party's Core Committee was called on Sunday to discuss the probabilities.

Buena Vista Resort, Jaipur

A young Congress MLA appeared furious in a meeting held at the resort. His anger was directed at the Centre. Just a day ago, the Narendra Modi-led NDA government had downgraded the Gandhi family's security cover from Special Protection Group (SPG) cover to Central Reserve Police Force (CRPF) Z-plus security. 'The BJP is vindictive. This decision has been taken deliberately,' he said as several MLAs and other leaders carefully listened. 'The BJP needs to be taught a lesson. We should start that from Maharashtra. If they lose Maharashtra, they lose confidence. Even if it means joining hands with the Shiv Sena. If Modi and Shah can take such an extreme decision, why can't we? The Shiv Sena is a lesser evil,' he said.

Even though party leaders K.C. Venugopal and Mallikarjun Kharge, who were patiently listening, knew this view will not find any sympathies with the party high command, in the aggression of the MLAs they saw a vulnerable group that may slip out of its hands in the future. A decision had to be taken at the earliest...

DAY 18: SUNDAY, 10 NOVEMBER 2019

After being approached by the Governor, the BJP camp had to get its act together. All efforts done to woo back the Sena so far had not yielded any results. The emissary who had gone to Matoshri with the 'message' was also not able to break the ice. The distance between the two allies was only growing. On the other hand, the Shiv Sena was steadily going ahead with the plans of joining hands with the NCP and the Congress.

The late night casual meetings between Shiv Sena MLAs at the Retreat Hotel had just one agenda—*Aagey kya hoga?* (What will happen next?) What they were witnessing in the resort rooms were only movements of Party Supremo Uddhav Thackeray and other top leaders like Eknath Shinde, Anil Desai and Anil Parab.

Uddhav and Aditya spent maximum time interacting with these MLAs. It was not just about keeping the flock together but also about infusing confidence in them. Inching towards a decision like forging an alliance with the Congress and the NCP was not going to be an easy task to explain. After all, they have all fought against each other for years. The MLAs who had recently shifted from NCP and Congress were the most worried.

Whenever Uddhav Thackeray visited the hotel, he always delivered a small pep talk. The one statement that was always common in these talks was that the BJP had gone back on its words and he was being portrayed as a liar. These pep talks, however, always came with an indirect rider—that the alliance wasn't still officially called off.

Varsha

There were going to be a series of meetings on Sunday. The BJP had to take a call. Its ally, the Shiv Sena, was adamant over the CM's post. The tenure of the assembly had ended and the possibility of President's rule being imposed was slowly inching closer to reality. But for now Governor Koshyari had invited the BJP to form the government.

BJP leaders started arriving in the morning for an urgent meeting at Varsha. Top on the agenda was how to respond to the Governor's invite. BJP was still stuck at 105 with the support of a few independents—still far away from the magic figure of 145. In 2014, the BJP had gone ahead to form a minority government with just 122 MLAs. Till the Shiv Sena joined the government a few months later, Fadnavis had received unconditional support from the NCP. This time, that too looked unlikely. With no feasible option in sight, the BJP leaders decided to meet again in the afternoon.

The Retreat Hotel, Malad

Uddhav Thackeray left Matoshri and headed straightaway towards Malad. His convoy crossed an interesting banner at the Bandra Junction. The huge poster demanded that Uddhav Thackeray should be the Chief Minister of Maharashtra. In the course of Aditya for CM, this was setting a new narrative. But this wasn't just an attempt at pleasing the party bosses. In silent whispers doing the rounds at the late night meetings of the MLAs, the question of who would be the Chief Minister if Shiv Sena came to power had come up. Though Aditya was made the face of the party, most knew that he wouldn't be taking on the crown of thorns, at least at this stage. Eknath Shinde had already been chosen as the Legislative Party Leader. But Shinde's sudden rise had made some other senior leaders in the party insecure. And then Sanjay Rajaram Raut's name had started doing the rounds for the CM's post in some circles within the party. There were reasons enough to believe it, as Raut was also known to be in Sharad Pawar's good books and was the one coordinating the talks between the Shiv Sena and NCP.

However, considering the volatile situation, any of these options, when pitched, would have met with resistance. The posters for Uddhav were not just a coincidence.

Aditya was stationed at the Retreat Hotel since Saturday. With the Governor asking the BJP to show willingness to form government, there was some anxiety in the Sena MLA camp. Uddhav, clad in a sky blue kurta, and his leaders gathered at their meeting point in the resort for another round of tactical talks.

'We will no more become the carriers of a palanquin for the BJP. The person who will sit in the CM's palanquin will be from the Shiv Sena,' Uddhav said, infusing confidence in his men. But then he said something that raised hopes in the BJP camp. 'The alliance with BJP is still intact.' With this statement, not only the BJP, but some MLAs in the Sena camp too heaved a sigh of relief. On the other hand, it made the Congress and NCP restless...

12.30 p.m., Buena Vista Resort, Jaipur

In the middle of the meeting, a Congress MLA read out the message he had received on his phone about Uddhav's statement on his party's alliance with the BJP being still intact. It took things a few steps back. But the group of young MLAs attending a meeting with

Mallikarjun Kharge were of the opinion that President's rule was imminent. It was decided that Sonia Gandhi would be apprised of the situation the next day and a decision on the way forward taken after that meeting.

Back here in Mumbai, Congress leader Sanjay Nirupam went public with his strong opinion against tying up with the Shiv Sena. Nirupam, a former journalist and a counterpart of Sanjay Raut, had once headed the Hindi version of Shiv Sena mouthpiece *Saamana*—an eveninger called *Dopahar Ka Saamana*. Nirupam had quit the Shiv Sena on bitter terms. Expressing strong reservations about tying up with his erstwhile party, Nirupam said, 'If the BJP fails to form the government, and if Congress and NCP are invited to form the government, they should politely reject it because given the numbers they have, they will not be in a position to form it on their own. And if they take help from the Shiv Sena to do that, it will be disastrous for the Congress...'

Nirupam's voice, however, had no takers in the big picture.

Varsha

The second meeting in the afternoon too had ended inconclusively. A third round of meeting was called again at 4 p.m. Apart from Fadnavis, the party's top brass, including Chandrakant Patil, Girish Mahajan, Pankaja Munde, Vinod Tawde and Ashish Shelar, attended the meeting. The cobbling up of numbers wasn't looking easy. The decision was taken.

Raj Bhavan, Malabar Hill

The convoy of cars left from Varsha and headed to Raj Bhavan. Interestingly, Fadnavis wasn't present. His absence made it clear that the BJP had shown unwillingness to form the government. 'The mandate of the people was for the Maha Yuti. And since the Shiv Sena is not ready to support, we have told the Governor that we are not in a position to form the government. Shiv Sena has disrespected the mandate, and now they want to form the government with Congress and NCP...our best wishes to them....'

Chandrakant Patil said, squarely blaming the Shiv Sena for the situation. The convoy left for Varsha for another round of meeting.

With his first option exhausted, the Governor was now preparing to look at the second option.

Silver Oak Estate

Sharad Pawar's key aide and senior leader Praful Patel rushed to Silver Oak Estate. Uddhav's statement of the alliance with the BJP still being intact had slightly affected the confidence of the Congress. Now, BJP too had expressed unwillingness to form the government. The NCP, which had firmly maintained that it had received the mandate to sit in Opposition, was now seen making swift moves to stitch together an unlikely alliance. Other leaders from the party too started arriving at Silver Oak.

Pawar spoke to senior Congress leaders in Delhi and Jaipur. The Congress and NCP agreed on one point that the Shiv Sena had to take a clear call on its ties with the BJP. A group in the Congress was sceptical about the Sena's stand and felt that the party may use its talks with the Congress and NCP as a tool for bargaining with the BJP. At least, Uddhav's statement in the afternoon suggested so.

Both the parties decided to draw the line.

For the first time since the speculations about a possible alliance between the three parties had emerged, the Congress and NCP publically put a condition for the Shiv Sena, if the alliance has to happen. 'If the Shiv Sena comes up with a proposal, we will think over it... But for that the Shiv Sena will have to snap all its ties with the National Democratic Alliance or the NDA,' NCP leader Nawab Malik announced after the meeting.

Raj Bhavan, Malabar Hill

Within hours after his meeting with the BJP delegation, Governor Koshyari called upon the Shiv Sena, the second largest bloc with 56 seats in the elected assembly, to show willingness to form the government.

Matoshri

Eknath Shinde and Sanjay Raut rushed to Matoshri. If stitching together the figure of 145 was difficult for the BJP, it wasn't going to be easy for Shiv Sena either, with only 56 seats of their own in the kitty. Plus the condition laid down by the Congress and NCP was another stumbling block within the party, for it would mean letting go of the ministry held by the Sena leader Arvind Sawant in the Modi-led government at the Centre. Uddhav and other leaders left for the Retreat Hotel immediately.

DAY 19: MONDAY, 11 NOVEMBER 2019

The momentum was catching up. In a late night meeting on Sunday, Shiv Sena had discussed the 'Stringent Condition' laid down by its probable allies. The day began with an early morning tweet by Arvind Sawant, setting the tone for yet another day of frenzied political drama.

'The formula for seat sharing and power sharing was sealed before the Lok Sabha elections... This was agreed upon by both the parties... BJP's denial is a shocking attempt to prove that the Shiv Sena is lying and is also a blot on the self respect of Maharashtra... Shiv Sena's stand is that of truth... What is the point of staying with the Government? And that is why I have decided to resign as the Minister,' Sawant dropped the resignation bomb.

Later in the day, Arvind Sawant submitted his resignation in New Delhi, addressing a press conference at the Maharashtra Sadan.

With the severance of its ties with the BJP, the Shiv Sena had fulfilled the first and most important condition laid down by its would-be allies.

◆

All the four players were now going into a huddle. The NCP leaders met at Yashwantrao Chavan Centre in South Mumbai, Uddhav Thackeray and his key aides met at Matoshri, Sonia Gandhi herself went into action mode as she met Congress Working Committee

(CWC)and State Congress leaders at 10, Janpath, and BJP's core committee met at Varsha.

NCP leader Nawab Malik emerged out of the meeting, giving out positive indications regarding the provision of support to Shiv Sena for the government. Malik said that with the Shiv Sena breaking away from the NDA, they were now waiting for a proposal from the Shiv Sena to form the next Maharashtra government.

As the meeting at Yashwantrao Chavan Centre got over, Sharad Pawar and his daughter Supriya Sule drove in his black car out of the media frenzy. The day was full of action and the media couldn't afford to miss even a single movement of the key players. Pawar's car, followed by other NCP leaders like Ajit Pawar, Dilip Walse Patil and Sunil Tatkare, headed towards suburban Mumbai.

Uddhav's convoy too started from Maatoshri a few minutes later.

Media vans continued to chase both the convoys. As expected, both convoys headed in the same direction. After a series of discreet meetings between key players and behind-the-curtain talks, Sharad Pawar and Uddhav Thackeray were meeting in public for the first time at Taj Lands End in Bandra. Uddhav was accompanied by his son Aditya, Sanjay Raut and his personal assistant Milind Narwekar.

Uddhav submitted a proposal to the Congress and NCP, according to which the Shiv Sena was willing to offer two posts of Deputy Chief Minister, one each to the Congress and NCP. It was also decided that the allies would formulate a CMP to ensure smooth functioning.

As Uddhav and Sharad Pawar discussed intricacies, a restless Sanjay Raut walked out of the room. He returned in a few minutes, only to repeat this movement a couple of times. He then went up to Uddhav and whispered something in his ear. Uddhav excused himself and made a couple of urgent phone calls.

Pawar and the Thackerays had shared cordial equations beyond politics for years, but this was perhaps the first time that their parties were discussing a political tie-up in the public eye. However, Sharad Pawar didn't announce the NCP's support, choosing to wait instead for the Congress to announce its stand later in the evening. But the only announcement made after the CWC meet at 10, Janpath that afternoon was about another round of meetings and consultation with the party's Maharashtra leaders at 4 p.m.

But the big news that came out of Taj Lands End after the hour-long meeting wasn't that of any government formation.

Sanjay Raut, who was seen restless during the meeting, was experiencing discomfort in his chest. He had told his Party President, who had promptly alerted the doctors at Leelawati Hospital. Suspecting blockage in the arteries, he was advised to undergo an urgent angiography.

When the political action was set to thunder, Shiv Sena's man of the moment was going to miss the action.

◆

It wasn't just Sharad Pawar that Uddhav had had a word with that day. He had also called Sonia Gandhi from Matoshri. The proposal that was discussed with the NCP was also shared with the Congress. The Congress had some serious discomfort over the idea of supporting the Shiv Sena due to their sharp ideological differences. While a majority of Congress MLAs were in favour of forming government with Shiv Sena, the Kerala unit especially had strong reservations. A.K. Antony and K.C. Venugopal, whom Rahul Gandhi trusted, were vocal in their opposition of the proposal. The Congress decided to hold yet another meeting at 4 p.m.

◆

After having Arvind Sawant resign from the government at the Centre, and his meeting with Sharad Pawar and phone call with Sonia Gandhi, Uddhav by now had played all his cards. The reason why he was moving steadfastly was the deadline given by Governor Koshyari. As it waited for letters of support from the Congress and the NCP, Shiv Sena was still not sure if those letters would come, taking their tally beyond the magic figure of 145.

◆

All four parties went into meeting mode yet again.

Congress President Sonia Gandhi was constantly seeking clarity on the various pros and cons of possible support to the Shiv Sena. On the ideological front, the recent Ram Mandir verdict was the most bothering factor. In the meanwhile, Sharad Pawar also had a word with Sonia Gandhi over the phone. Politics is an interesting game of exchange. The Congress leadership was keen to know what it was getting in return for supporting the Sena-led government. The answer was given by Pawar. The biggest gain would be coming soon in the form of zilla parishad elections. The Congress, once having strong roots in local self-government bodies, was keen to restore that. The party has always believed in the idea of being upwardly mobile from Gram Panchayats to the state and national level. The deal wasn't bad—the Sena would be helping the Congress in the zilla parishad elections.

Rajeev Satav, a leader from Maharashtra, was one of the key people giving inputs to Sonia Gandhi. He too was of the opinion that a new experiment in Maharashtra would help the party grow at the grassroots level.

But before the 4 p.m. meeting, the Congress released a press statement that the party was closely watching the situation in Maharashtra and that a decision would be taken soon after discussing matters with the party's pre-poll ally, the NCP, and its leader Sharad Pawar.

Another Congress meeting was slated for 10 a.m. the next day.

The Congress President was close to making a decision, and those in the corridors of power in Delhi know well that at such crucial junctures, she falls back on one man—Ahmed Patel. Patel, who had been missing in action so far, was set to travel to Mumbai soon.

Raj Bhavan, Malabar Hill

Uddhav Thackeray's meeting with Pawar had been positive and so were his talks with Sonia Gandhi. The deadline of 7.30 p.m. set by the Governor to show willingness was fast approaching. At 6.45 p.m., Aditya Thackeray accompanied by Eknath Shinde and Subhash Desai reached Raj Bhavan. The Shiv Sena was now set to stake claim. Advocate Anil Parab, the man known as the legal eagle of the party, was in touch with the Congress Office in Delhi for a letter of support.

Before meeting the Governor, a seemingly uneasy Aditya was constantly in touch with his team on the letter. Shinde too was busy on his phone.

As mediapersons were constantly asking for updates, Aditya and his men were on the edge. With the Sena team here to stake claim, but no signs of the letters of support arriving anytime soon, the situation was turning out to be embarrassing for the Shiv Sena scion. Aditya's close aide Rahul Kanal was waiting outside Raj Bhavan with his laptop and a printer. With every phone call, he was refreshing his mailbox to check whether the letter of support had reached his inbox. Priyanka Chaturvedi, on the other line, was hesitantly assuring that the letter would be ready in five to 10 minutes.

As the deadline passed, Aditya and the other leaders awkwardly met the Governor to stake claim. With no letters of support in their hands, the delegation requested the Governor for three more days to 'arrange the letter of support'. The Governor turned down the request. Embarrassed and red-faced, the Shiv Sena delegation left Raj Bhavan wondering why the letters of support from the Congress and NCP hadn't arrived.

Putting the blame for the faux pas squarely on the NCP, a senior Congress leader said, 'Our letter of support with signs of all our MLAs was ready with the signature of MPCC President Balasaheb Thorat. But when Sharad Pawar called Sonia Gandhi this afternoon, he was the one who asked Sonia Gandhi to wait as he still needs to fix up a few loose ends with the Shiv Sena. Contrary to the perception, it's not us, but Pawar saheb who is taking time.'

◆

At the Y.B. Chavan Centre where the NCP leaders were still in a huddle, Ajit Pawar suddenly walked out of the building, briefly halting in front of media cameras. 'We have been called by the Governor and our delegation is meeting him now. I have no idea whatsoever why has he invited us... I will only come to know when I reach there,' Ajit said, as he immediately zoomed in his car towards Walkeshwar.

After the Shiv Sena failed to submit the requisite letters of support to stake claim, Governor Koshyari had gone ahead with the third option. He had now invited the NCP, the third largest party, to stake claim at government formation. The NCP delegation was led by its legislative party leader Ajit Pawar, who was accompanied by Jayant Patil, Chhagan Bhujbal and Dhananjay Munde.

◆

At Matoshri, Uddhav was left wondering who had delayed the letter and, most importantly, why. It would take some more time before everyone figured out the real reason behind the delay...

DAY 20: TUESDAY, 12 NOVEMBER 2019

Annoyed by the Governor's denial of extending the time, the Shiv Sena decided to move to the Supreme Court against the decision, which it considered arbitrary, unconstitutional and malafide. The Sena also alleged that the Governor's decision was violative of articles 14 and 21 of the Constitution. Sena leaders alleged that the Governor had given 48 hours to the BJP to prove majority, but only 24 hours to the Shiv Sena.

◆

From the Special Room of the Leelawati Hospital, Sanjay Raut tweeted lines of a famous poem:

> 'Lehron se darkar, nauka paar nahi hoti
> Koshish karne walo ki haar nahi hoti'
>
> (The boat that fears the waves, never gets across;
> The ones who never give up, never lose.)

Through the day, his room was flooded with VVIP visitors—from Sharad Pawar to Uddhav Thackeray and from top Congress leaders to those from the BJP. On a lighter note, BJP leader Ashish Shelar had quipped, 'Doctors have asked Raut to speak less.' Raut has been speaking since day one, and the BJP had constantly been on his radar. No wonder then that Shelar wanted him to speak less...

Y.B. Chavan Centre, Nariman Point, Mumbai

On Tuesday morning, after the invite from the Governor, NCP MLAs gathered to discuss the way ahead. Ajit Pawar, known to be an early bird, was the first to reach the meeting venue. The unanimous view at the meeting was that the deadline set by the Governor was very stiff for the NCP.

Hours before 7.30 p.m., the deadline set by Koshyari, the NCP informed the Governor that they weren't in a position to show willingness to form government. The fact that the NCP had got back to the Governor before the deadline had lapsed got everyone wondering: What's the hurry?

1.50 p.m.

A news flash on the national broadcaster said that the Maharashtra Governor had submitted a proposal to impose President's rule in the state. Landline phones at the Raj Bhavan office were constantly ringing. Raj Bhavan officials, however, clarified that no such appeal had been sent till now.

New Delhi

Just as the three parties—the Shiv Sena, the NCP and the Congress—were headed towards finality in the power-sharing talks in Maharashtra, in the national capital, Prime Minister Narendra Modi was chairing an urgent Cabinet meet, minutes before he left for Brazil to attend the BRICS summit. At the top of the agenda of the Cabinet meet was to give a green signal to Koshyari's recommendation to impose President's rule in Maharashtra. Koshyari had stated in his report to the Prime Minister that after giving an opportunity by inviting all the key parties, he had arrived at the conclusion that it was not possible to constitute a stable government in the state.

At 3.15 p.m., Governor Koshyari announced his recommendation on Twitter and at 3.30 pm., the Union Cabinet approved his recommendation and immediately forwarded it to the President of India. At 5.30 p.m., President Ramnath Kovind signed the appeal and President's rule was imposed in Maharashtra. The imposition of President's rule put brakes on the ongoing power-sharing talks between the Shiv Sena, NCP and Congress.

The NCP's swiftness at conveying its unwillingness to form government to the Governor when there was still some time left for the Governor's deadline to lapse had raised eyebrows in the Congress and Shiv Sena camps. Had the NCP taken longer to decide, the Prime Minister would have had left for Brazil. The Shiv Sena and Congress were left wondering if the NCP's quick decision was 'coincidently' coordinated with the Union Cabinet.

Y.B. Chavan Centre, Nariman Point, Mumbai

Sharad Pawar has a knack of finding gains in any situation. The imposition of President's rule gave more time for the talks to formalize. After a series of meetings chaired by Mallikarjun Kharge, Sonia Gandhi had sent Ahmed Patel to finalize the modalities of the alliance. So far, most of the communication of the alliance was between the Shiv Sena and NCP. The former was in touch with the Congress leadership only through Sharad Pawar. With Ahmed Patel reaching the epicentre of the activity, the group of young MLAs who were keen on joining the government in Maharashtra felt relieved.

At 6 p.m., Patel reached the Yashwantrao Chavan Centre with Kharge and Venugopal in tow. The talks were now moving from an impasse towards a concrete solution. The meeting between Pawar and Patel centred on one point: It wasn't obviously the ideology that was bringing the three parties together; so, it was important to have a CMP to come together and run a government smoothly.

At the Rangswar auditorium of the Y.B. Chavan Centre, Pawar and Patel addressed a joint press conference. 'On Monday the Shiv Sena approached us for the first time. We are in a pre-poll alliance with the NCP. So before taking any decision we are discussing it with our ally. Before we decide on Shiv Sena, there are some more issues that we need to discuss. Once we arrive on unanimity on these issues, we can think of supporting the Shiv Sena-led government,' Patel said. 'We and Congress had a common manifesto before the election, we need to understand some issues related to the Shiv Sena as well before moving ahead. The Governor has given us ample time now,' Pawar said, pointing at the six-month tenure of the President's rule.

The Retreat Hotel, Malad

At 5.30 p.m., Uddhav, Aditya and other leaders left for the Retreat Hotel. Though the Shiv Sena had moved the apex court for not being allotted the extra time it demanded, it felt the President's rule had come as a blessing in disguise. On the way to the hotel, Uddhav dialled Sharad Pawar, who was in a meeting with Ahmed Patel and other Congress leaders. After a short exchange, Pawar handed over the phone to Patel. In an assuring tone, Patel said, 'We are here with a message from Madam...we will be together, don't worry... Only reason why it is taking so long is that we have to finalize a good CMP... Once it is decided, it will be done...don't worry.'[30]

It had been five days since the MLAs were kept in the hotel. As he reached, Uddhav had a smile on his face. With a firm assurance from the Congress, he spoke to the media. 'I had approached the Congress and NCP with a proposal of a new beginning. The politics of the state is headed in a new direction. We will sit and some discuss some points. I have some points; even they have theirs...' he explained his stand.

'For the first time we have had such a generous Governor. We had asked for three days, he gave us six months to discuss and formalize our alliance,' Uddhav quipped, taking potshots at the imposition of President's rule. He also took a dig at the BJP, saying that he

---

[30] Source-based information on condition of anonymity.

is studying the model of how BJP joined hands with ideologically different parties like the PDP in J&K or with the JDU in Bihar.

Uddhav left, but not before taking stock of what the MLAs were upto. Aditya Thackeray stayed back in the hotel overnight and held a meeting with the MLAs and the party's top brass.

◆

The imposition of President's rule was seen by the NCP, Congress and Shiv Sena as additional time to continue with their power-sharing talks. But a senior Congress leader who has seen such political deadlocks resulting in the President's rule had some dreadful thoughts about the move. He was drawing parallels between the situation in Maharashtra now and the situation in Bihar in 2005 where, when the BJP and JDU had staked claim to forming the government a month and half after the imposition of the President's Rule in the state, Governor Buta Singh had turned it down, citing attempts of horse-trading and had written a letter to President A.P.J. Abdul Kalam. Barely a month later, he had recommended the dissolution of the Bihar Assembly. The President has approved the recommendation and fresh elections were held in Bihar in October 2005. While the BJP–JDU alliance won the elections, the decision to dissolve the Bihar Assembly was termed as unconstitutional by the Supreme Court.

Could the three parties end up with a feeling of déjà vu in Maharashtra?

Varsha

A meeting of BJP leaders was held at Fadnavis's official residence. With the imposition of the President's rule, Fadnavis was no longer the caretaker CM. His Twitter handle reflected this change—the words 'Chief Minister of Maharashtra' had been replaced with 'Maharashtra Sevak (Servant of Maharashtra)'.

Fadnavis, who till now was holding meetings with his close aides, had invited to this meeting someone who, so far, had not been a part of the developments. This man not only loved to hate the Shiv

Sena, but he also had a grudge against Ahmed Patel. He could prove crucial for wrecking the ship of the Shiv Sena–Congress–NCP alliance that was taking shape. This man was Narayan Rane. A charged-up Rane, after coming out of Varsha, told the media, 'Shiv Sena does not understand how Congress leaders are, they are being taken for a ride...we will soon meet the Governor with a list of 145 MLAs... I will do whatever it takes to form a new BJP government...be it *saam daam dand bhed* (an idiom that denotes by hook or by crook).'

Minutes later, Rane's maverick MLA son Nitesh Rane tweeted '*Ab aayega maza* (now we'll have fun)*!!*'

DAY 21: WEDNESDAY, 13 NOVEMBER 2019

Post midnight, Uddhav Thackeray and Ahmed Patel met in a five star hotel. After Uddhav's initial talks with Sonia Gandhi over the phone, this was his first tête-à-tête with any Congress top brass. This was all a new game for Uddhav. He, like his father, had kept an eye over political developments in the past but more like a remote control (a term his father Bal Thackeray often used). This time he himself had to lead from the front.

The situation wasn't like the ones he had seen earlier in his political career. Whatever the skirmishes he had had with the BJP in the past, there was a comfort level he shared with the BJP leaders. Pawar and Ahmed were no ordinary players. A political barter was going to be a tough row to hoe.

In politics, people appear too friendly but they are not. Just as Uddhav Thackeray was thinking of the Congress and NCP as one unit that night, he realized that the Congress's demands weren't going to be the same as the NCP's. Patel and the Congress leadership knew that with 42 seats in its kitty, the party wasn't going to get a big pie of the cake. Yet, they also knew that forming a government wasn't possible without them. Patel's first meeting with Uddhav was to send across the message that the Congress had its separate list of demands. The Deputy CM's post wasn't something that was going to please the Congress; it was eyeing something more powerful that will keep its importance alive in the government. After the 'positive' talks between Patel and Uddhav, Congress decided to call its MLAs back from the Jaipur resort.

Sofitel Hotel, Bandra Kurla Complex

After Ahmed Patel drove across his message to the Sena President, it was now time for the state leaders to hold discussions with Uddhav. Ashok Chavan, Balasaheb Thorat and Manikrao Thakre met Uddhav at the Sofitel Hotel in Bandra Kurla Compex. The Congress leaders asked for the Speaker's post for the Congress instead of the Deputy CM's post.

The meeting ended inconclusively. Uddhav wanted to discuss the proposal with NCP before any commitment. For the next few days this was going to be the standard operating procedure till all three parties came together on one table. After coming out of the meeting, Ashok Chavan informed the media that the talks were going in the right direction.

♦

13 November is the birth anniversary of former Maharashtra Chief Minister Vasantdada Patil, against whom a young Sharad Pawar had led a coup to become the youngest Chief Minister of the state at the age of thirty-eight. Pawar and his party leaders headed to Vasantdada's statue in the Vidhan Bhavan grounds to offer tributes.

Earlier in the day, Pawar had met his party MLAs and informed them not to worry about midterm polls or re-elections. Pawar's confidence was a clear message about a leap forward. In the same meeting, Pawar appointed a panel comprising Ajit Pawar, Jayant Patil, Chhagan Bhujbal, Nawab Malik and Dhananjay Munde, which was to work on the CMP along with the Congress.

Jaipur, Rajasthan

The formal rounds of talks between the Congress and Shiv Sena had started now and with this, the vulnerability of poaching had been reduced. It was now time to get the MLAs back in Mumbai.

Just as the bus carrying the Congress MLAs started to move towards Jaipur Airport, the sounds of 'Jai Bhawani, Jai Shivaji' reverberated from the bus.[31] Even though Maharashtra politics centres on Shivaji Maharaj, usually the slogan of Jai Shivaji is associated with the Shiv Sena. The sloganeering by Congress MLAs was blurring the broad lines that divided the two parties.

◆

On reaching Mumbai, all Congress MLAs assembled for a meeting. A joint meeting of the Congress and NCP was planned later in the evening at Prithviraj Chavan's Nariman Point office.

Meanwhile, the NCP leaders were meeting at Sharad Pawar's residence. As mediapersons waited outside for details of the meeting, Ajit Pawar rushed out of the meeting with an unmissable expression. When asked about the meeting with the Congress, he said he was not attending it. He was heading to Baramati...

Knowing the history of Ajit Pawar's tendency to take abrupt decisions, this sudden walkout from the meeting set the rumour mills running. Was everything well in the Pawar camp?

The news wheel angered Sharad Pawar so much so that he came out of his house and blasted the media, warning them that they will not be allowed to stand outside his house from the next day...

◆

At Prithviraj Chavan's office, senior Congress leaders like Sushilkumar Shinde, Manikrao Thakre, Vijay Wadettiwar and Ashok Chavan had already arrived. By now, news of Ajit Pawar leaving the NCP meet had reached the Congress and Wadettiwar came down to inform the media that the joint meeting was called off.

◆

Within a few minutes, all the leaders secretly headed to Oberoi Hotel. Top guns from both the Congress and NCP reached the

---

[31] An India Today TV correspondent in Jaipur was reporting live from the bus.

Belvedere meeting room. NCP coordination committee members Jayant Patil, Chhagan Bhujbal, Dhananjay Munde, Nawab Malik and Ajit Pawar along with Congress coordination committee members Balasaheb Thorat, Ashok Chavan, Prithviraj Chavhan, Manikrao Thakrey, Sushilkumar Shinde and Vijay Vedettiwaar went into a huddle with their respective manifestos.

While everything was being done surreptitiously, an India Today TV crew reached the location and reported live on the developments. The leak upset the Congress and NCP, as they had wanted to keep the meeting away from media glares.

At a time when all the meetings were taking place in full public view, what had prompted the Congress and NCP to go behind closed doors?

The Retreat Hotel, Malad

Congress MLAs were back in Mumbai. With tensions easing, the Shiv Sena too decided to call back its MLAs from the resort where they had been stationed since 9 November. The MLAs were asked to return to their respective constituencies, but to come back to Mumbai on 17 November, the death anniversary of Shiv Sena Supremo Bal Thackeray. This was an indication that the talks between their party and the NCP and Congress were going to continue for another few days.

Leelawati Hospital, Bandra

The afternoon brought with it some good news for the Shiv Sena. Sanjay Raut was discharged from the Leelawati Hospital after undergoing angioplasty. Raut's mission of breaking away from the BJP had been successful so far, but for him the story wasn't over yet.

While coming out of the hospital, Raut gave a cracking byte to the media: 'The next Chief Minister will be from the Shiv Sena,' he said as his car drove out of the hospital.

◆

While NCP's Sharad Pawar and Congress's Sonia Gandhi were by now completely involved in the process of government-formation in Maharashtra, the BJP's central leadership was still missing in action. Amit Shah's absence was especially baffling as he is the man for such situations, as evident from the cases of Goa, Manipur and Haryana. The BJP state leaders had been holding the fort in Mumbai since the day the results were announced.

Maharashtra was a big gamble. Any party would want under its wings the state that has as its capital the financial capital of the country. It wasn't that Shah hadn't taken any interest in the state earlier. In fact, it was he who had stitched his party's alliance with the Shiv Sena prior to the Lok Sabha elections. Why then was he now staying away from Maharashtra? Why wasn't the BJP's Chanakya playing his cards as yet?

♦

Over the last few years, the Delhi political circles had been abuzz about the uneasy relations between Devendra Fadnavis and Amit Shah. The former's rise within the BJP had been phenomenal. From a young MLA to the state president, he had rapidly climbed the ladder to become the first BJP Chief Minister of Maharashtra. In his initial days, many of Fadnavis's opponents from both within the party and outside had thought that the young Brahmin would not be able to sustain the pressure for a long time, but he had proved them all wrong. Behind that ever-smiling face of his was a ruthless political operator. Not only did he excel as an administrator, many saw the decimation of his detractors within the party as something that was not just coincidental. His major opponent in the party, Eknath Khadse, had to resign following allegations of a scam in a land purchase deal. Pankaja Munde, Vinod Tawde and Prakash Mehta were all surrounded by some or the other controversy. Outside the party, Fadnavis engineered defections in the Congress and NCP, netting big names. The troublesome ally Shiv Sena was always kept in check. Within a couple of years after taking charge as the Maharashtra CM, Fadnavis emerged as a strong leader in the state. Many started drawing parallels between his style of politics and that of Sharad Pawar.

After Vasantrao Naik, Fadnavis became the first-ever Chief Minister of Maharashtra in 50 years to complete a five-year term. Delhi journalists now expected an even bigger role for him. On national platforms he was always asked one question—was he Modi's successor? His great understanding of subjects, command over English and Hindi, administrative skills and, most importantly, his proximity to the RSS made him look like the right candidate. In Delhi's political circles he was known as Prime Minister Modi's blue-eyed boy. Fadnavis, however, always politely brushed away the question about his being Modi's successor, saying that he was happy in Maharashtra.

Fadnavis's sharp rise had made some leaders in the state and at the Centre insecure. His portrayal as Modi's successor had changed the equations between him and Shah. Fadnavis's close aides linked Shah's silence on the situation in Maharashtra to this history.

♦

On Day 21 of the ensuing drama, Amit Shah finally broke his silence. In an interview specially given to news agency ANI, he clarified the rotational Chief Minister promise to Shiv Sena. 'During the election campaigns, myself and and Prime Minister said this in several public meetings that if our alliance comes to power, then Devendra Fadnavis will be the CM; the Shiv Sena never objected back then. Now they have come up with new demands that are not acceptable to us,' Shah said. He also clarified that allegations against Governor Koshyari were baseless: 'Even today if any political party has the required numbers in the assembly then they can approach the Governor.'

Shah's intervention had come at a time when things between the Shiv Sena, Congress and NCP had gone far too ahead. Was it a mere lip service by Shah to discredit the speculations of rift between him and Fadnavis? Or had Shah designed some new plan with his entry into the game?

DAY 22: THURSDAY, 14 NOVEMBER 2019

Some may remember the spectacular innings by Sachin Tendulkar against Australia in Sharjah in 1998. How Tendulkar had brought India back into the series against Australia and New Zealand, chasing an almost impossible run rate amidst a sandstorm, and winning with his sheer grit and determination.

Sanjay Raut had always been a consistent player for Shiv Sena, and was known for playing 'square cuts' and 'straight drives' in *Saamana*. However, the formidable innings that he had been playing for his party over the last 21 days could be likened to Tendulkar's Sharjah innings. Not only had the *Saamana* editorials continued to lambast the BJP, Raut had also been working closely with Sharad Pawar to put together an unlikely political alliance. This is why his sudden absence from the scene of political drama was sorely felt in the last two days.

He announced his return to action after undergoing an angioplasty with a poetic tweet that translated to: 'You lose when you accept defeat, and win when you have resolved to.' It was accompanied by the line, '*Ab darna aur haarna mana hai...*' (now it is forbidden to lose or be afraid...)

Raut began his day with a press conference. Taking a leaf out of Amit Shah's interview, he went into attack mode. 'In every public meeting, Narendra Modi said Fadnavis will be CM. But in every public meeting, Uddhav also said the Chief Minister will be from Shiv Sena. Why was Amit Shah silent at that time?' Raut said, countering Shah's claim in the ANI interview.

He further alleged that Amit Shah had kept Prime Minister Modi in the dark over BJP's 50:50 agreement with Uddhav Thackeray. 'We respect Prime Minister Narendra Modi. However, what happened in the meeting between Amit Shah and Uddhav Thackeray was not informed to him... Had Shah given the right information to Prime Minister Narendra Modi about this decision of "50:50 formula" in time, we would not have been facing this situation today,' he said.

'It was the drawing room of late Balasaheb Thackeray, but for us it is a temple. The talks were held in the temple. If someone says no promises were made, it is an insult of the temple, Balasaheb Thackeray and Maharashtra,' Raut continued with his attack. 'Now Amit Shah says that information of closed-door meetings cannot be divulged. We would like to tell him...don't fool the people of Maharashtra,' Raut ended in his trademark style. With this, he was back in action after a brief hiatus.

Undisclosed location, New Delhi

There was reason for Uddhav Thackeray to turn down the BJP's proposal. His phone call with Sonia Gandhi had opened the communication lines with the Congress leadership in Delhi. The Congress, wary of Sharad Pawar, also wanted to have a 'hotline' with Thackeray. On Wednesday, two of Uddhav's close men discreetly flew to Delhi and held talks with 'key Congressmen'. This meeting set the ball rolling for the Shiv Sena–Congress tie-up.

MET Campus, Bandra East, Mumbai

Two days had passed after the imposition of President's Rule in Maharashtra. It was now time for the parties to officially come together and draft the broader lines of the alliance. Leaders from the Shiv Sena, NCP and Congress decided to meet in order to speed up the process of government formation.

The venue was MET Campus, an educational institute run by Chhagan Bhujbal. What a comeback it had been for this man! Having spent more than two years in jail for his alleged involvement in a money-laundering scam,[32] political pundits had written off Bhujbal from the political ring.

While the *ghar wapsi* didn't take place, Bhujbal, now in NCP, was hosting the joint meeting on the MET campus. This was the first time that leaders of the three parties of the unlikely alliance

---

[32] https://www.ndtv.com/india-news/chhagan-bhujbal-former-maharashtra-minister-jailed-in-money-laundering-case-gets-bail-1847221; last accessed 16 March 2020.

were sitting down together to discuss the intricate details of their coalition. Eknath Shinde and Subhash Desai from the Shiv Sena; Prithviraj Chavan, Vijay Wadettiwar and Manikrao Thakre from the Congress and Jayant Patil, Chhagan Bhujbal and Nawab Malik from the NCP closed in ranks for discussing the draft.

Yet again election manifestos of all three parties were compared, and a draft was prepared. In a joint press conference that followed the long-drawn meeting, journalists were informed that the signed draft will be now sent to Sonia Gandhi, Sharad Pawar and Uddhav Thackeray for the final approval. For the record, key issues in the CMP were discussed. These issues included farm loan waiver, review of crop insurance scheme, unemployment, increasing MSP, and the Chhatrapati Shivaji Maharaj and Dr Ambedkar memorials, among other things.

The three parties wanted to avoid a Karnataka-like situation, where the deal between the Congress and Janata Dal (Secular) was sealed hurriedly without working out complex details, leading to regular skirmishes in the alliance. The discussion in the meeting was not restricted to the manifestos. Majority of the time was spent on the power-sharing formula. A list of key departments, to be equally distributed, was drawn up. NCP's Jayant Patil suggested a distribution of 15 ministerial berths each for the Shiv Sena and NCP, leaving 12 for the Congress. The Congress firmly disagreed, with its leader Prithviraj Chavan wanting an equal distribution of 14 each.

Sharing of the most coveted post of Chief Minister was also discussed. A senior NCP leader mooted the idea of rotational Chief Ministers, with the Sena and NCP getting the post for two and a half years each. After deliberations, everyone agreed that since the Shiv Sena had shown enough courage to break ties with its long-time ally and joined hands with the Congress and NCP, its claim for the Chief Minister post should be respected. The NCP, however, demanded significant departments like Home and Finance. It was also proposed to have one Deputy Chief Minister each from NCP and Congress. However, 10, Janpath had not given a complete go-ahead for the Congress participating in the government. It was suggested that the party would stake claim for the Assembly Speaker's post instead.

With the talks now moving firmly ahead, various names for the proposed alliance started doing the rounds; the most popular that went viral on social media was 'Maha-Shiv-Aghadi'!

DAY 23: 15 NOVEMBER 2019

Since the first draft was formulated between the three parties and the copy sent to the respective party chiefs, the state leaders were at ease. The talks of government-formation for many were on the right track. With their common agenda of farmers, both Uddhav Thackeray and Sharad Pawar embarked upon tours to meet farmers. While Uddhav toured Sangli, Pawar went to Nagpur.

Vasant Smruti, BJP Office, Dadar

The BJP camp wasn't yet willing to give up. The party called a 'Chintan Baithak' (brainstorming session) to discuss the poll results and the current situation.

♦

The Maharashtra state unit of the BJP had become a one-umbrella organization. Even though the party boasted of a democratic setup, the voices of dissent never came up openly. Whenever Fadnavis's detractors within the party met journalists in private, they would read out a list of what they called 'Mistakes of Devendra Fadnavis' that, according to them, were responsible for the party's debacle. The haphazard manner of ticket distribution and Fadnavis's pick-and-choose approach were part of this list. Fadnavis's detractors believed that he had played a role in cutting down to size leaders like Vinod Tawde, Prakash Mehta and Chandrashekhar Bawankule, who were denied tickets. They were no ordinary leaders after all. Vinod Tawde was the leader of Opposition during the previous government. Coming from the politically dominant Maratha caste and rising from the Akhil Bharatiya Vidyarthi Parishad, he was seen as the next big leader among the second-rung leaders in the party. His fortunes, however, dwindled after he became a minister in the Fadnavis cabinet in 2014. Tawde, who was expecting an important ministry like Home or Finance, had to settle for Higher and Technical, Medical and School Education, Sports and Youth Welfare departments. In the subsequent years, Tawde's wings were clipped. First, the Medical Education department was taken away from him and was awarded to Fadnavis's close aide Girish Mahajan and towards the end of the tenure, School Education was taken away from him and given to Ashish Shelar.

Prakash Mehta, the party's Gujarati face from Mumbai, had initially openly expressed his grudge on being denied a ticket, but slowly fell in line, accepting the party's decision. Mehta, former Minister of Housing, had to resign after he was named in a housing scam. Party insiders always tell an anecdote about Mehta: he had once said in an official meeting that Fadnavis was young and inexperienced and that the Party President Amit Shah has asked him to guide him. This juicy story, though always denied by the BJP camp, corroborated the uneasy equation between Fadnavis and Mehta. After Mehta was denied the ticket, many saw it as a confirmation of the troubled relationship.

The third person who was denied a party ticket was Chandrashekhar Bawankule. The low-profile MLA from Kamptee in Nagpur was a staunch supporter of Nitin Gadkari, as were others like Sudhir Mungantiwar and Subhash Deshmukh. Ever since Fadnavis became the CM, the state BJP was divided into two camps. It was most likely his allegiance to Gadkari that had costed Bawankule a ticket.

One of the most shocking results in the assembly polls for the BJP had come from the Parli assembly seat. The party's tall leader and daughter of late Gopinath Munde, Pankaja had lost to her estranged cousin Dhananjay Munde of the NCP. Her supporters had put the blame on 'party insiders' of sabotaging Pankaja's chances in the last few years by giving the 'resources and strength' to Dhananjay Munde. During the election campaign, a cryptic slogan in Beed had become a topic of discussion in the state's politics: *'Yeh andar ki baat hai, CM, DM ke saath hai* (It's a secret deal, the Chief Minister is with the DM [Dhananjay Munde]).³³ Pankaja had never shied away from her chief ministerial ambitions. Her high-handed ways of announcing herself as a mass leader and the Chief Minister in the people's mind put her in direct confrontation with Fadnavis. Pankaja's name was embroiled in the Chikki Scam in the first year of the Fadnavis government and the controversy put brakes on her ambitions.

In July 2016, the differences between Fadnavis and Pankaja had peaked when two key portfolios were taken away from the latter. Following this, Pankaja refused to attend the Water Summit in Singapore, tweeting that though she had reached the city, she would not be attending the event as she was no longer the state Water Conservation Minister. Fadnavis had also taken to Twitter and directed her to attend the event. Pankaja's supporters even went on to burn an effigy of Fadnavis in Pathardi (Ahmednagar district). Even in Pankaja's defeat, her supporters saw the history of her political ambitions clashing with that of Fadnavis playing an important role.

◆

The murmurs of dissent, however, didn't reach the brainstorming meeting. What the party called discipline was, however, considered by a section as the fear instilled by the Fadnavis regime. No one wanted to brush him the wrong way. Even after the political stalemate, Fadnavis continued to instill fear in the minds of his detractors within the party.

In the brainstorming session, Fadnavis went on to claim that even if an alternative government was formed in Maharashtra, it wouldn't last for six months. On the other hand, a section of the BJP had become almost complacent after the imposition of the President's Rule. For them, the possibility of an alternative government had almost ceased. Chandrakant Patil firmly believed

---

³³ Author's own ground reports from the time.

that at that juncture, no party could form a government without the BJP. He announced this in the media briefing along with Ashish Shelar. In the same briefing, the latter went on to blame Shiv Sena leader Sanjay Raut for creating a rift between Uddhav Thackeray and Prime Minister Modi.

Press Club, Nagpur

NCP Supremo Sharad Pawar was in Nagpur and the media in Nagpur, Fadnavis's hometown, was keen to hear it from the Maratha strongman on the present political situation. After the CMP draft was formulated, Pawar expressed confidence that the Shiv Sena, NCP and Congress would form the government and the government would complete its term of five years. 'There is no possibility of mid-term polls. This government will be formed and it will complete five years. We all will ensure this government runs for five years,' Pawar told the reporters.

Pawar was in Fadnavis's hometown and he hadn't forgotten the fact that the same Fadnavis had announced that Pawar's era in politics was over. More than anything else, he was seen taking jibes at Fadnavis in this press conference. Hitting back at Fadnavis over his remark that the government of three parties will not even last for six months, Pawar quipped, 'I know him (Devendra Fadnavis) for a long time now... But I never knew that he is a student of astrology as well...' Rubbing it in further, Pawar said, 'All I knew was that he only kept saying, I will come again, I will come again, I will come again.' He was taking a dig at Fadnavis's poem *'Mee punha yein'*.

Sangli, Western Maharashtra

This was certainly the day of raising the farmers' issue. Devendra Fadnavis met the Maharashtra Governor at Raj Bhavan, seeking more help for the farmers. NCP Supremo Sharad Pawar was in Vidarbha, while Uddhav Thackeray too toured the Sangli and Satara districts in western Maharashtra to take stock of the crop loss due to unseasonal rains. A significant sight that was not to be missed by anyone was a person who accompanied Thackeray—local Congress

MLA and state working president Vishwajit Kadam, who along with some other young fellow MLAs, had been vocal in pursuing the party leadership to think of a possible tie-up with Shiv Sena. 'I had assured farmers that I would free them from debt. I will honour that commitment,' Uddhav announced. In an apparent swipe at the BJP, he added, 'The Shiv Sena honours commitments and does not break it.'

◆

The farmers' issue was going to be the core area of focus in the CMP. In a sudden development, it was decided that all three parties of the proposed alliance will go and meet the Governor of Maharashtra and demand more compensation for farmers. The Shiv Sena was elated about the meeting, but it had no idea that its new allies had something else on their minds...

DAY 24: SATURDAY, 16 NOVEMBER 2019

The Shiv Sena had, by now, accepted the fact that it was forming an uneasy alliance with the Congress and NCP. Sanjay Raut, through his poetic messages, was creating the sort of atmosphere that was required in the situation—be it confrontation or egging on! Poking the BJP yet again, his poetic tweet quoted the noted shayar Bashir Badr:

> '*Yaaron naye mausam ne yeh ehsaas kiya hai,
> yaad mujhe purane dard ab nahi aate*'
>
> (Friends, the new season has made me realize that I have forgotten all old pains)

Vasant Smruti, BJP Office, Dadar

BJP's Chintan Baithak continued. The agenda of the day was to take stock of the seats that the BJP had lost. Apart from the much-hyped defeat of Pankaja Munde from Parli, yet another high-profile minister, Ram Shinde, had lost in his bastion of Karjat Jamkhed, with Rohit Pawar, Sharad Pawar's grandnephew, making his electoral debut from here. Another close aide of Nitin Gadkari, Madan Yerawar, who was MoS for Energy and Tourism, lost from the Yavatmal seat. Agriculture minister Anil Bonde lost from the Morshi seat in the Amravati district of Vidarbha region to a political greenhorn, Devendra Bhuyar, the youthful peasants' leader of Raju Shetty's Swabhimani Shetkari Sanghatana. Coming from a very humble background, Bhuyar defeated Bonde in the Vidarbha region, which is known to be the BJP's turf. Bala Bhegde, another Minister of State, lost by close to one lakh votes in the Maval assembly seat.

But more than the ministers, it was the defeat of the party's candidate at Muktainagar in the Jalgaon seat that was the talk of the town. Former Minister Eknath Khadse was denied a party ticket and instead his daughter Rohini, a political novice, was fielded from the seat. In Khadse's absence, it was going to be a difficult seat for the party. Making things worse for Khadse and the BJP, the Shiv Sena District President Chandrakant Patil too came up as an independent challenger. His candidature was openly supported by the NCP and Congress, while Shiv Sena workers and office bearers too openly canvassed for him. As expected, Rohini Khadse lost and Chandrakant Patil returned to his party fold after the elections.

The pattern of defeat was at the centre of discussion in the brainstorming meeting. After hearing out the grievances of the candidates who had lost, a few conclusions were drawn. Next on the agenda was how the 79-year-old Sharad Pawar had managed to create a great wave of sympathy with his whirlwind tour, especially his speech, as he stood drenched in rain. But most important was the grumble against its ally Shiv Sena. Most of the BJP leaders who lost put the blame on Shiv Sena, saying that the non-cooperation from their ally at some places and a complete hostile stand taken by it in some was the reason why BJP lost where it would have won.

The inter-party rivalry was discussed, but intra-party differences weren't. However, the cracks that had started to form in the state BJP were evident, as Pankaja Munde gave the meeting a skip.

◆

The winter session of the Parliament was going to commence on Monday. In the wake of the changing political situation in Maharashtra, all eyes were on the meetings and rendezvous that would tale place in the national capital.

Prior to the session, the ruling parties and the Opposition usually hold a meeting to strategize and discuss issues. A meeting of the BJP-led NDA was also convened on Sunday. The Shiv Sena had been a founding member of the NDA since 1998 and the BJP's only ideological partner amidst several smaller allies. Despite its love–hate relationship with the BJP, not to forget the break-up at the state level in 2014, the Shiv Sena had continued to be a part of the NDA-led government at the Centre. This time, however, the BJP hadn't taken the Shiv Sena's overtures towards the Congress and NCP very kindly.

It was evident then that the Shiv Sena wasn't going to attend the NDA meeting the next day. Some in the Shiv Sena were annoyed with the falling out with the BJP, but some called it good riddance. Speaking to the media, Raut raised questions on the existence of the NDA. 'There is a lot of difference between the old NDA and today's NDA. Who is the convener of NDA today? Advaniji, who was one of its founders, has either left or is inactive,' Raut told ANI.

Shiv Sena's Arvind Sawant had already resigned as a minister from the Modi government. So, there was little role left for the Shiv Sena in the NDA meet. But was Sawant's resignation and the party's decision to not attend the NDA's meeting a sign of the Shiv Sena quitting the NDA?

Raj Bhavan, Malabar Hill

Regardless of the constant meetings that the three new allies were holding and the breakthrough between their top leadership, there was always an atmosphere of disbelief and mistrust among them. Some incidents, though minor in nature, were contributing to the confusion between them. This was one of them...

At around 2 p.m., mediapersons had started to gather at the gate of Raj Bhavan. The joint delegation of Shiv Sena, Congress and NCP was scheduled to meet the Governor over the farmers' issues. Shiv Sena leaders were getting ready for the meet, but with less than two hours to go, the Governor's office hadn't received the list of visiting leaders. In fact, the Shiv Sena too hadn't heard anything from its two allies. With less than an hour left for the meeting, the Congress and NCP informed the Shiv Sena that they will not be a part of the delegation. The Raj Bhavan was turning out to be not-so-lucky for the Shiv Sena—it was again set to be a scene of embarrassment for the party.

◆

For the session beginning on Monday, key players of the game were going to be in New Delhi. Pawar was scheduled to meet Congress President Sonia Gandhi to finalize the finer points of the alliance. But it wasn't just Sonia Gandhi that Pawar was going to meet in Delhi. There was someone else too, and this VVIP personality ended up adding a twist to the story...

DAY 25: SUNDAY, 17 NOVEMBER 2019

Thackeray Memorial, Shivaji Park

Shiv Sena workers began visiting Shivaji Park since early morning. The memorial of Shiv Sena founder Bal Thackeray was laden with magnolia (chafa/champa) flowers. Balasaheb really liked these flowers with a beautiful aroma.

Bal Thackeray had a special connect with Shivaji Park. It was here that his party was born. It was here that Keshav 'Prabodhankar' Thackeray, one of the greatest reformers in Maharashtra, had announced that he was offering his son for the service of Maharashtra, when the Shiv Sena was formed in 1966. The son was none other than Balasaheb Thackeray. On 17 November 2012, when Balasaheb breathed his last, millions had gathered in and around Shivaji Park to pay their respects and bid him adieu. And it was in Shivaji Park that he was cremated. The Congress government had then gone out of its way to offer a state funeral to the person it had once referred to as a rabble rouser.

Since then, every year on Balasaheb's death anniversary, Shivsainiks from across the state gathered in large numbers to pay their respects to the founder of the party.

On Sunday morning, Sharad Pawar was one the first among the top leaders to pay his tributes to the person who was once his political rival but also a very good friend. In his autobiography *On My Terms*, Pawar has shared several memories with Thackeray, but a particular anecdote reflects his amazing equation the best. In 2006, when Pawar's daughter Supriya contested the Rajya Sabha polls, Bal Thackeray himself called Pawar and assured that his party will not field a party candidate against 'daughter' Supriya... That wasn't all. Thackeray in his own trademark style also assured him that he would take care of 'Kamla Bai' (a reference to BJP, with its symbol being the lotus).

The equations between Uddhav and Sharad Pawar had taken a hit after 2014, when the latter had unconditionally supported the BJP government in the state. However, a lot had changed ever since. Many in the Shiv Sena and NCP felt that Pawar's move to lend support to a Shiv Sena-led government was not just political; it was also his way of returning the favour of his old friend Thackeray, for supporting Supriya in 2006.

♦

Political activity on this day was going to be centred on Bal Thackeray. While Pawar fondly remembered Thackeray, Devendra Fadnavis took the opportunity to take potshots at Shiv Sena. While offering a tribute, Fadnavis tweeted a video of Bal Thackeray and said, 'Respected Balasaheb gave us the message of self-respect!' The obvious taunt left the Shiv Sena red-faced.

Sanjay Raut left no time in hitting back at Fadnavis and said no one should teach Shiv Sena self-respect and reiterated that very soon Uddhav Thackeray would fulfil the promise given to his father of making a Shivsainik the Chief Minister of Maharashtra. Till this day, no prediction by Raut had gone wrong...

♦

This year the number of Congress and NCP leaders paying tributes to Bal Thackeray had multiplied. Uddhav arrived at the memorial at around 11.45 a.m. along with his wife Rashmi and their sons Aditya and Tejas. He spends a lot of time at the memorial on every death anniversary of Balasaheb's, but this year he hurriedly left. The reason for Uddhav's sudden exit was known in the next few minutes. He wanted to avoid a direct meeting with the person who would be arriving at the memorial soon.

Around 12.30 p.m., Fadnavis arrived with his party colleagues Vinod Tawde and Pankaja Munde. By now, his tweet on 'self respect' from earlier in the day had gone viral. Just as Fadnavis entered Shivaji Park, Shivsainiks burst into sloganeering. '*Sarkar Kunacha? Shiv Senacha!* (Who will form the government? Shiv Sena!)' Fadnavis tried to ignore the sloganeering, but even before he could do so, there was a fresh round of clamour that hit him, '*Mee punha yein, mee punha yein,*' the crowd started taunting Fadnavis.

A visibly upset Fadnavis left with his entourage in less than five minutes without reacting to the jeers.

Modi Baug, Pune

The angry crowd at Shivaji Park wasn't the only group poking fun at Fadnavis. In Pune that evening, a group of top NCP leaders from the state shared a few WhatsApp jokes and memes on Fadnavis and their Party President, usually a serious man, laughed heartily at the social media gags. This was no ordinary meeting at Modi Baug, Sharad Pawar's residence. Pawar and his key men met at his house before he left for Delhi for the Parliament session. After a series of serious meetings, this one was more relaxed.

Jitendra Awhad animatedly narrated a Tiktok video, where a man is seen walking towards his motorbike. He hears a voice from nowhere, '*Mee punha yein....*' He looks into the camera and says, 'Ok, bring me chuna (lime) when you come back...'[34]

Chhagan Bhujbal too did not lag behind. The politician who once

---

[34] The Tiktok video had gone viral.

flirted with acting read out a WhatsApp forward. Referring to the long-standing monsoons in the state, the meme said it was good that Fadnavis has gone, taking away the prolonged monsoons with him. Dhananjay Munde described how Marathi comedian Bhau Kadam in his recent stand-up act had cracked a joke on *'Mee punha yein'*.

Pawar was enjoying all the jokes.[35] The party top brass, which included Ajit Pawar, Supriya Sule, Sunil Tatkare, Nawab Malik and others, also joined in on the laugh riot.

New Delhi

As the political upmanship was playing up at Bal Thackeray Memorial, the national capital saw a development that many described as the last nail in the coffin of the Shiv Sena–BJP alliance.

Union Parliamentary Affairs Minister Pralhad Joshi announced in Delhi that Shiv Sena MPs will be allotted seats on the Opposition benches in both houses of parliament. Joshi explained that this was happening because Shiv Sena's lone minister had resigned and the party was working out an alliance with the Congress and NCP to form a government in Maharashtra. Shiv Sena had already announced that it would not attend a meeting of NDA constituents on the eve of the winter session of the Parliament. While the war of words had been going on between the two parties for quite some time, this was the official announcement of Shiv Sena and BJP snapping their ties of 25 years at the Centre. The actions that had been set off in Delhi were now to go on for the next few days…

DAY 26: MONDAY, 18 NOVEMBER 2019

While winter was slowly setting in, Delhi's weather was going to witness the heat of Maharashtra politics at least for the next few days. Except Uddhav Thackeray, most of the key players were going to be in Delhi. Shiv Sena had its eyes glued to the much-awaited meeting between Sonia Gandhi and Sharad Pawar. Even as the modalities of the common agenda were being worked upon, the

---

[35] The video of the meeting went viral and was widely reported by the TV media.

Congress hadn't made an official announcement yet. The delay from Congress was only adding to the anxiety in the Shiv Sena.

Parliament, New Delhi

The Parliament session began with a condolence motion offering tributes to the members and other prominent personalities who had passed away since the last session. As soon as Lok Sabha Speaker Om Birla completed the obituary references, Shiv Sena MPs started raising slogans demanding justice for farmers. The tone for the protests over farmers' issues had already been set earlier in the day in *Saamana*'s editorial, which had advocated for adequate compensation with no conditions attached. The sight of an NDA ally rising up against the BJP was soothing for some members of the Opposition and they too joined the Sena MPs for a brief time. Shiv Sena's Sindhudurg MP Vinayak Raut demanded compensation for the farmers affected by unseasonal rains. After making all the right noises to assert its present seating arrangement on the Opposition benches, Shiv Sena members staged a walkout from the House.

Meanwhile, in the Rajya Sabha, Prime Minister Narendra Modi was slated to address the 250th session of the upper house of the Parliament. Interestingly, the NDA was in power at the time of the 200th session of the Rajya Sabha. Known for his mastery in spinning surprises, the Prime Minister showered praises on Sharad Pawar's party in his speech. He lauded two parties—the NCP and Biju Janata Dal (BJD)—for their conduct in the house. But his praise for the NCP, especially in the volatile political situation in Maharashtra, was bound to raise eyebrows. Commending the NCP for adhering to parliamentary norms, Modi said, 'While effectively raising their points, NCP members have never gone into the well. Other parties, including mine, have a lot to learn from them.' The admiration came just a few hours before the scheduled meeting between Sonia Gandhi and Pawar.

Like Pawar, Modi is also known to hit many birds with one shot. This, however, wasn't the first time he had praised the Maratha strongman. Six months after the 2014 Lok Sabha polls, Modi in Baramati had very fondly narrated how Pawar helped him during his tenure as the Gujarat CM. This was the time Modi alleged that the UPA was trying to block schemes for the state. Modi said he has always looked up to Pawar for his guidance. Yet again, immediately after the most controversial decision of demonetization in 2016, Modi, in Pune, had announced that he has entered politics by holding onto Pawar's hand, referring to him as his political guru.

After the 2014 assembly elections in Maharashtra, NCP had announced its unconditional support to the BJP, when the BJP–Shiv Sena alliance was called off. The political equations between Modi and Pawar have always been a topic of curiosity not just in Maharashtra but also in the national political circles. It was against this backdrop that Pawar was going to meet Congress President Sonia Gandhi.

10, Janpath, New Delhi

Sharad Pawar and Sonia Gandhi met for 50 minutes. The issues to be included in the CMP were not the agenda of the meeting; it was about what the Shiv Sena had to exclude. Shiv Sena's hard-line Hindutva and the issues that the party had raised in line with its hard-line Right-wing agenda had to be dropped. Against the backdrop of the Ayodhya verdict, Uddhav Thackeray had announced that he will be visiting Ayodhya on 24 November. Sonia Gandhi expressed her strong reservations on this and it had to be communicated to Uddhav that his visit had to be called off.

After the meeting, Sharad Pawar, along with his party leader and MP Sunil Tatkare, addressed a press conference, where he dropped yet another bombshell. He informed the media that government-formation was not on the agenda of his meeting with the Congress President. 'I just had a meeting with the Congress President and along with her, A.K. Antony was there. We discussed in detail about Maharashtra's political situation. I have briefed her about the situation. After this briefing, we didn't discuss other issues,' Pawar said.

Pawar's total denial of any concrete discussions with the Shiv Sena in government-formation was surprising for the journalists present there. It was strange that leaders from the three parties had addressed a joint press conference just two days ago announcing the draft of a CMP. In fact, the meeting had taken place at senior NCP leader Chhagan Bhujbal's office in Bandra.

'BJP–Shiv Sena have fought together, we (NCP) and Congress fought together. They have to choose their path and we will do our politics,' Pawar further said, raising the suspense even more. In sharp contrast to what Pawar said, Congress Spokesperson Randeep Singh Surjewala said that NCP Chief Sharad Pawar met Sonia Gandhi to discuss the political situation in Maharashtra. Surjewala further elaborated that in the next couple of days the leaders of both the parties will hold a meeting in Delhi, where the current situation in Maharashtra will be discussed and a decision regarding the same would be taken.

Back in Maharashtra, Pawar's stand had disturbed a few Shiv Sena leaders. So much so that some of them yet again suggested that rather than trusting the NCP, it would be advisable for the party to patch up with the BJP as it was the 'known devil'. This wasn't, however, the end of the capricious turn of events in Delhi. Minutes after Pawar denied any political discussion on government-formation in Maharashtra with Sonia Gandhi and a contradictory statement from the Congress, Pawar had his usual visitor at his Delhi house—Sanjay Raut.

Raut added to the bewilderment when, after his meeting with Pawar, he said he had come to discuss the farmers' issue and not any political issues, but added that the party was positive about government-formation in Maharashtra.

Hours later, it was communicated that Shiv Sena President Uddhav Thackeray had called off his proposed visit to Ayodhya. The fluid political situation in the state was given as the reason.

Politics is a game of patience, and both Sonia Gandhi and Sharad Pawar are masters of the game. Uddhav's patience was put to test. After asking his minister to resign from the Modi cabinet, and subsequently walking out of the NDA, this was yet another waiver by the Shiv Sena—and certainly not the last...

Nagpur

In spite of all the confusion, the Shiv Sena, Congress and NCP were slowly inching closer to sealing the deal. However, the differences within the BJP were slowly coming out of the closet. The elections for the Mayor of Nagpur took place on the same day. In the house of 151, BJP had a comfortable majority of 108. The earlier two-and-half-year term had gone to Nanda Jichkar, a Gadkari loyalist. The Fadnavis camp had thought that the Mayor's post would be with them for the next two and a half years, but the Gadkari camp put their foot down. Right under the nose of Reshim Baug, which housed the RSS headquarters, the tug of war was being played out between two strong leaders of the state. Ultimately, a compromise formula was worked out. The term of two and a half years was further split into one year and three months each to the Fadnavis and Gadkari camp members. Sandeep Joshi, Fadnavis's Man Friday in Nagpur, became the Mayor and it was decided that Gadkari's man Dayashankar Tiwari would succeed Joshi.

This incident, though appearing to be local to Nagpur, wasn't. It broadly underlined the factionalism within the BJP, especially between the Fadnavis and Gadkari camps. At a time when the party was supposed to show a united face, frictions like these were impacting the morale of the party MLAs who were keenly awaiting the waving of some magic wand by the party leadership that would stop the situation from getting out of hand...

◆

Late in the evening, Maharashtra Congress leaders also arrived in the national capital to meet Party Chief Sonia Gandhi.

DAY 27: TUESDAY, 19 NOVEMBER 2019

'Who are you to remove Shiv Sena from the National Democratic Alliance (NDA)?' read the hard-hitting editorial on page 4 of

Saamana. Even as very few were still hoping that the Shiv Sena and BJP will come together at the last moment, this editorial dashed whatever little hopes they had. Sanjay Raut, though now in Delhi, continued lashing out at the BJP through his editorials. The latest trigger was the Shiv Sena's ouster from the NDA and the party being made to sit on the Opposition benches. The *Saamana* editorial pointed out that Balasaheb Thackeray had formed the NDA along with others at a time when no one was even talking about the issue of Hindutva, and that the very fact that Shiv Sena was removed from the NDA on the death anniversary of Balasaheb Thackeray was demeaning. 'There was a time when the BJP was untouchable for everyone. Nationalism and Hindutva were not even discussed. Shiv Sena had put oil in Jan Sangh's lamp. [BJP was earlier Jan Sangh.] Stalwarts like Balasaheb Thackeray, Atal Bihari Vajpayee, L.K. Advani, George Fernandes, Badals of Punjab had formed the NDA. People who are running NDA now were nowhere to be seen. Advani was the Chief of NDA while Fernandes was the convenor. Can they tell, who is the convenor of NDA now? In which meeting was the decision of Shiv Sena's ouster taken?' The editorial called the removal of Shiv Sena from NDA without giving it a hearing a dictatorial act. The party has also promised that it will end the existence of such 'egotistic people in Maharashtra'.

The Shiv Sena loves to use to anecdotes from Maratha history. During the 2014 assembly election campaign, Uddhav Thackeray had compared Amit Shah with Afzal Khan's army.[36] This time, the Shiv Sena compared the BJP with Muhammad Ghori, the Sultan of the Ghurid dynasty. Drawing parallels between the two, the *Saamana* editorial said, 'We made the same mistake as that of Prithviraj Chauhan, who let Ghori live even after defeating him

---

[36] Uddhav's assembly election speech in Tuljapur, Osmanabad, on 6 October 2014. Afzal Khan, a notorious general who served in the Adil Shahi dynasty, was sent on a mission to finish off Shivaji. But in the famous batle of Pratapgarh, Shivaji killed Afzal Khan. The epic historical incident is known in every Maharashtrian household.

17 times. But he got stronger and jailed Chauhan the 18th time.' It further went on to say, 'Did you ask us before carrying out "Nikaah" with Mehbooba Mufti's party who loves Pakistan? What right do you have to criticise us for growing close to Congress?' Calling the BJP betrayer, backstabber and ungrateful.' 'Maharashtra is the land of Shivaji and Sambhaji. If you want to charge on into us, come on... we are ready... Your countdown has begun,' the editorial warned.

If there were any hopes of a possible truce between the two parties, they were now washed away by the Shiv Sena's scathing attack on the BJP. The BJP too decided that enough was enough. A close aide of Fadnavis told some journalists in Malabar Hill that if the Shiv Sena was so adamant, they'd also see how it forms the government. When asked by a journalist how they'll stop the Shiv Sena–NCP–Congress alliance from forming the government, he responded with 'wait and watch', gesturing at his wristwatch[37]...

Nagpur

The bitter separation of the Hindutva parties that had been together through the thick and thin of things for over 25 years was painful for a few. The RSS had led the reconciliation between the two political parties after some petty and some serious fights in the past, but it wasn't seen taking an initiative this time. Fadnavis and Gadkari had separately met the RSS Chief Mohan Bhagwat in the last few days of the stalemate. The Thackerays too enjoyed a special place in the RSS scheme of things. Political observers are of the opinion that during the peak of the Ram Temple movement, the BJP did not have a mass base in Maharashtra as a political party. It was the Shiv Sena that had indirectly operated as the implementing arm of the RSS's agenda in Maharashtra at that time. The Sangh Pariwar was more than happy to let Shiv Sena occupy that space as it was in alliance with the BJP. The only reason for the stalemate in Maharashtra was that one assurance of 50:50 power sharing. Shiv

---

[37] The watch is the NCP's symbol.

Sena claimed it was promised by the BJP and BJP said it never gave that promise.

The BJP's national leadership was already conspicuous in its silence on the entire political drama even after 19 days. Everyone was keeping a close eye on what the RSS Chief had to say. At a function in Nagpur, the RSS Chief made a statement for the first time since the drama had unfolded. 'Everybody knows that selfishness is bad, but very few people leave away their own self-interests. You may look at nations or individuals, you'll find the same thing,' Bhagwat, a man of few words, said in an apparent reference to the political deadlock in Maharashtra.

The Sangh is known to never get directly involved in the political course of action, even in matters pertaining to the BJP. Breaking from the tradition, this statement in a way was the Sangh's message to the warring torchbearers of Hindutva to keep aside their selfish motives. Things, however, had by now gone beyond the point of no return....

10, Janpath, New Delhi

Barely 24 hours after NCP Chief Sharad Pawar claimed that he had not discussed government-formation in Maharashtra with Sonia Gandhi, senior Congress leaders went into a huddle with their interim President at 10, Janpath. Before officially coming out with its support to the tripartite alliance, the national leadership was also weighing in options. Like the BJP, there were also factions in the State Congress. The former Chief Ministers Ashok Chavan and Prithviraj Chavan never got along really well. A participation in the government would have also meant fanning the fire of factionalism even further. K.C. Venugopal, a close aide of Rahul Gandhi, was still of the opinion that the support should be extended from outside. Rajeev Satav felt otherwise.

The NCP, on the other hand, wasn't quite happy with the pace at which the Congress was moving. The dilemma of the Congress in being part of the government was adding to the anxiety levels of both the Shiv Sena and NCP. There was a feeling in the NCP camp that the Congress had to join in, if the government had to be stable.

◆

Like the NCP and Congress, there was unease in the Shiv Sena camp as well. Narendra Modi showering praises on Sharad Pawar had left many pondering on what exactly was cooking. The job was left to the man who was frequenting Sharad Pawar every now and then. Sanjay Raut tried hard to hold the fort for now. His reply was political: 'It needs 100 births to understand what Sharad Pawar says'—that was all he could say to defend Pawar's statements a day earlier.

After giving the number of MLAs supporting the government, Raut went on to announce the time of the formation of the tripartite government. 'By early-December, a Shiv Sena-led alliance government will be in power in Maharashtra and it will be a stable government,' he said.

◆

Meanwhile, the experiment of three ideologically disparate parties forming an alliance bore its first fruit in Western Maharashtra. In the Mayoral elections in the most important district of the region, Shiv Sena supported the Congress–NCP alliance candidate Surmanjiri Latkar, as she got elected as the Mayor of Kolhapur Municipal Corporation.

Kolhapur is the hometown of Maharashtra BJP President Chandrakant Patil. Interestingly, it was also the town of BJP National President Amit Shah's in-laws!

DAY 28: WEDNESDAY, 20 NOVEMBER 2019

Rajya Sabha

The NCP Chief was sitting in the front row in the Parliament session. Sanjay Raut, sitting in the fourth row, walked up to Sharad Pawar. They discussed something for close to five minutes, after which

Raut walked out of the house. A couple of minutes later, Pawar looked back at the bench of Raut, but he had already gone to inform his Party President about the development that was going to take place in the next couple of hours—a development that was going to cause tremors...

12.30 p.m., Prime Minister's Office, New Delhi

At around noon, Sharad Pawar walked towards the PMO in South Block, which overlooks the grandeur of the Rashtrapati Bhawan. Not just journalists covering the Parliament session, but also Congress leaders were on the qui vive. Sharad Pawar said he was meeting the Prime Minister over the issues being faced by the farmers in Maharashtra, especially the agrarian crisis due to unseasonal rainfall.

The news mills started buzzing with speculation over the meeting. Assumptions and theories of the possibility of the NCP going with BJP for government-formation were but natural, as the meeting between the duo was taking place within 24 hours of Modi praising the NCP for their discipline in Rajya Sabha.

Sharad Pawar presented a three-page memorandum to Prime Minister Modi. 'Due to President's Rule in the state, your urgent intervention is highly necessitated. I shall be grateful if you could take immediate steps to initiate massive relief measures to ameliorate distressed farmers,' Pawar said in the letter. Amidst the meeting, Prime Minister Modi also called Home Minister Amit Shah and Finance Minister Nirmala Sitharaman, who were present there for a few minutes.

After emerging out of the meeting, Pawar emphatically denied that the meeting had any political agenda. But then again, Pawar never means what he says.

According to reports, while the farmers' problems were discussed in the meeting for a few minutes, after the memorandum was presented, Narendra Modi directly put forward an offer to the NCP: 'Our views on several issues are similar... We think alike on many issues like development, industrialisation, agriculture. We should work together.' He further elaborated the proposal. According to the deal, the BJP and NCP would form the government in Maharashtra. BJP would have its Chief Minister while NCP will get the Deputy CM's post. That wasn't all—Pawar's daughter Supriya would also be given a plum portfolio in the Narendra Modi cabinet at the Centre. The offer was too good to refuse. Sharad Pawar thought for a few seconds before he replied.[38]

In those few seconds, his entire political career flashed in front of his eyes—from his debut in politics to becoming the youngest Chief Minister of Maharashtra at the age of 38. Whatever were the reasons behind his coup in 1978, Pawar's detractors always loved to label him as someone who can never be trusted. The imposed blot of being the backstabber never really left his back. In spite of a career spanning five decades and even 41 years after that infamous coup, Pawar has not been able to wash away the blot. Any adventure at the twilight of his political career would have tarnished his image more than ever. Moreover, Pawar was at the peak of his popularity. Over the last few days, social media was full of videos of Pawar campaigning day in and day out during the assembly elections. One of the highlights of the elections, in fact, had been the powerful image of a rain-drenched Pawar delivering a speech in Satara.

Pawar, almost getting up from the seat, replied politely, 'I would be happy to work with you... our personal relations are good and it would continue to be so...but the prospects of working together is not politically possible...' After coming out of the meeting, Pawar preferred not to talk about it.

In that room that day, there wasn't just one astute politician. There were two, and the other had already started working on Plan B...

◆

After his brief interaction with Sharad Pawar on his Rajya Sabha bench, Sanjay Raut had briefed his Party President about the impending meeting between Pawar and Modi and so Uddhav wasn't on edge.

---

[38] Pawar had confirmed this in several interviews to TV channels later.

But there was no dull moment in this entire saga... Even as Uddhav and his close aides were busy finalizing the modalities of the alliance, old videos of him slamming Rahul Gandhi resurfaced and went viral. Uddhav had attacked the then Congress President over the latter's remarks on V.D. Savarkar. The Shiv Sena chose not to react to the social media slur, but this wasn't the first or last time when the Shiv Sena would have to take a stand on the Savarkar issue...

◆

10, Janpath, New Delhi

Sonia Gandhi yet again met senior party leaders at the party headquarters in New Delhi ahead of the Congress–NCP meet. The path was more or less charted. It was decided that every small aspect of power-sharing should be worked out before they say 'I do'. Sonia Gandhi was herself not going to be present for the final talks. But her trusted aide and political advisor Ahmed Patel was going to lead the power talks. After all, the Congress was also aware that it was dealing with one of the most perceptive politicians...

6, Janpath, New Delhi (Sharad Pawar's Residence)

Media cameras were allowed for a photo op a few minutes into the joint meeting between the Congress and NCP. Sharad Pawar and Ahmed Patel sat in the front chairs. Mallikarjun Kharge and Praful Patel sat right opposite Pawar. Jairam Ramesh from the Congress was the new member in the dealing. His cameo was restricted to this meeting. He sat with a laptop, continuously jotting down the intricate details. Supriya Sule, Ajit Pawar, Jayant Patil, Chhagan Bhujbal, Sunil Tatkare and Nawab Malik from the NCP went into a huddle with K.C. Venugopal, Prithviraj Chavan, Balasaheb Thorat and Naseem Khan from the Congress.

After the meeting in MET in Mumbai, where the basic CMP was drafted, this was the biggest meeting involving all top leaders, including Sharad Pawar and Ahmed Patel. This was not just the most important joint meeting, but it also turned out to be the longest one.

Former Chief Minister Prithviraj Chavan and NCP spokesperson Nawab Malik addressed the media after the meeting. Malik said a government in Maharashtra cannot be formed without a Congress–NCP–Shiv Sena alliance. Chavan stated that the discussions were in the final phase and went on to announce the date for the final decision—Friday, 22 November. Sanjay Raut also claimed that Sonia Gandhi had given her nod for the tripartite alliance.

DAY 29: THURSDAY, 21 NOVEMBER 2019

15, Gurudwara Rakabganj Road, New Delhi

There was a feeling in the NCP and Shiv Sena camps that the Congress was dilly-dallying and unnecessarily delaying the government-formation process. The Congress was least bothered about the impediment, as it continued with brainstorming. An urgent meeting of Maharashtra leaders was convened at 15, Gurudwara Rakabganj Road. This place has a special significance for the Congress—it is known as the Party's war room. Maharashtra state in-charge Mallikarjun Kharge, K.C. Venugopal, State President Balasaheb Thorat, Vijay Wadettiwar, Naseem Khan, Ashok Chavan and Nitin Raut discussed the finer points of power sharing. This was going to be a crucial meeting before the final rounds of cross-table talks with the NCP later in the afternoon. Apart from the power-sharing formula, all leaders were to shown the newly drafted CMP.

This wasn't the first meeting of the day. Top leaders of the party had met at 10, Janpath earlier. Sonia Gandhi, A.K. Antony, Jyotiraditya Scindia, Ghulam Nabi Azad, Anand Sharma, Ambika Soni, Ahmed Patel and Adhir Ranjan Chowdhary were present in that meeting. The Congress was all set to take a historic and equally daring step while supporting the Shiv Sena-led government. The Congress and Shiv Sena, with their respective ideologies, had been like parallel lines that had never met in the past. Maharashtra leaders had their own set of logic behind going with the Shiv Sena, but it wasn't going to be easy to ram it down the throats of leaders from the other states. The Shiv Sena is seen in bad light in the Hindi-speaking belt, especially in Uttar Pradesh and Bihar, because of the party's anti-migrants stance.

But Sonia Gandhi had given her nod. The new alliance had her approval and the leaders sitting in the meeting had no option but to listen to the brief about the developments in Maharashtra.

◆

Immediately after the meeting, Ahmed Patel, Mallikarjun Kharge and Prithviraj Chavan reached Sharad Pawar's house. The primary discussions were over now. The action was going to shift from Delhi to Mumbai. Prithviraj Chavan was the point person in Delhi, convincing the Congress High Command for the new alliance. His not-so-good equation with the Pawars was one of the important reasons why he convinced the party leadership in going with the Shiv Sena. Prithviraj, who had once helmed the PMO, had put up a theory in party meetings that if the Congress didn't take a stand on going with the Shiv Sena, the NCP had the option of going with the BJP or the Shiv Sena in the future, which would isolate the Congress in the state. In order to give itself a shot in the arm, the Congress needed to go out of its way and join the government. In spite of his political differences with Pawar, Prithviraj was seen taking the lead in making important announcements. Pawar was also going to fly down to Mumbai for the final round of talks.

'Congress and NCP have completed the discussions on all important issues. There is a complete unanimity between us. We are moving to Mumbai tomorrow and also holding discussions with our other pre-poll alliance partners. Further we will hold move discussions with the Shiv Sena,' Prithviraj announced.

Mumbai

The *Saamana* headline pompously announced that the government in Maharashtra will be formed any moment. With this news, it also attached a photograph of the meeting between the Congress and

NCP leaders in Delhi.

The pace at which things had started to move after Pawar's refusal of Prime Minister Modi's offers was making BJP in Maharashtra restless. Till now, only a few in the party were aware of the offer made by Modi to Pawar. After seeing the confidence oozing from the *Saamana* article, the Fadnavis camp decided to make a final attempt to extend an olive branch to the Shiv Sena. A senior leader from the state BJP reached out to Milind Narvekar, Uddhav's close aide and personal assistant. In a little over two decades, the significance of this man had grown manyfold not just at Matoshri or in Shiv Sena, but also in the state's politics. Narvekar's rise in the Sena hierarchy from a *gata pramukh* (group head) from suburban Malad to the post of the Party Secretary has been phenomenal. In the last 20 years, Narvekar had grown close to Uddhav and was considered as his troubleshooter. Narvekar's proximity often infuriated the party top brass. When leaders like Narayan Rane and Bhaskar Jadhav had quit, they had narrated tales of how Uddhav operates on the directions of Narvekar.

They say the way to a man's heart is through his stomach. Similarly, it is believed in Shiv Sena that the route to Uddhav is through Narvekar. It wasn't just the Shiv Sena; even other political parties knew this well. No wonder then that Devendra Fadnavis never failed to visit Narvekar's home during Ganpati festival every year without fail.

The proposal sent to Shiv Sena had the BJP taking a step back. This was the first time the party was offering the CM's post to Shiv Sena for two and a half years. This, however, would be in the second half of the government's term, which even Narvekar knew was only a move to deviate the Shiv Sena's attention at this point. But this time, Uddhav's calls were not influenced by Narvekar. There was someone else who was involved in all his decisions.

This person had played a key role in Uddhav's political rise, especially during the major roadblocks he had faced—be it Narayan Rane's exit and the subsequent verbal attack questioning Uddhav's leadership abilities or Uddhav's cousin Raj Thackeray walking out from the party. Every time Uddhav's leadership was questioned, he not only received great moral support from this person but also advice. No wonder then that at such a critical juncture of his political career, this was the person Uddhav was relying on the most. This person was none other than his wife Rashmi. The graceful lady with a charming smile was equally well-versed in political astuteness.

Many eyebrows went up when Rashmi Thackeray was seen taking the centre stage in crucial meetings. Be it the decision to make Aditya contest the elections or turning down the BJP's earlier proposals, she stood by her husband as she was the first he had reached out to. No wonder then that the final proposal from the BJP too went out of the windows of Matoshri...

Uddhav became more suspicious of the BJP's motives after the recent proposal. He called for an urgent meeting at Matoshri on Friday at 10 a.m., where he was going to address his MLAs. This was also the day when the Congress legislative party had finally called for a meeting of its newly elected MLAs in Mumbai to elect their legislative party leader. Delhi leaders like Mallikarjun Kharge, K.C. Venugopal and Ahmed Patel were to attend the meeting as an observer.

◆

Leaders like Sanjay Nirupam continued to oppose the plan even as the alliance was looking almost evident. 'The Congress had committed a grave mistake by joining hands with the Bahujan Samaj Party in Uttar Pradesh. So much was the damage that the party is still not able to recover from it. It is committing the same mistake in Maharashtra,' Nirupam said in an attempt to thwart the possibility of the alliance. But his words were treated more like the rant of an insignificant character in the present situation.

While the three parties had decided to get into an alliance, the final announcement was still stuck over the power sharing. With Ahmed Patel's entry into the negotiations, the Congress wanted a large piece of the cake. The 4:1 ratio was proposed in the joint meeting. This meant that all three allies were to get one ministerial berth for every four seats won. This would translate into the Shiv Sena getting 16 ministerial berths (64 seats won, including eight for the independents), NCP would get 13/14 ministers (54 seats) and the Congress, 11 (44 seats).

A list of important ministries including Home, Revenue, Urban Development, Public Works Department (PWD), etc. was drawn. These ministries were divided equally amongst the three.

The Congress wanted equal distribution of portfolios between the three allies. In the backroom talks, Shiv Sena had strongly put its demand for Urban Development, PWD, Home, Education (Higher Technical, Medical and School) and Rural Development. The NCP wanted the Speaker's post, also Home, Finance, PWD, Water Resources and Rural Development. The Congress too laid its claim on the Speaker's post, Finance, Rural Development and Revenue.

Another major bone of contention was regarding who will lead the government as the CM. Both the Congress and NCP were averse to Eknath Shinde and Subhash Desai. Aditya was too young and inexperienced to take up the job and, more importantly, lead a coalition government that had stalwarts from the allies. The only name that appeared acceptable to all was of Uddhav Thackeray. In the rapid developments that had taken place over the last couple of days, Uddhav's name emerged as the frontrunner.

◆

The portfolios and details of power-sharing were not the only things on the minds of the leaders. The tripartite alliance needed a name. The media was already abuzz with the name of 'Maha Shiv Aghadi'. The Congress, NCP and other smaller parties in Maharashtra were together called Maha Aghadi. The addition of Shiv Sena to the Maha Aghadi prompted speculations of the new name. But adding the name of one party in the multi-party alliance would have not gone down well with other constituents of the alliance. The name of 'Shiv' would have also triggered politics giving leeway to the BJP to object to the use of Shivaji's name. To avoid any controversy, 'Maha

Vikas Aghadi' or the MVA, the grand alliance of development, was proposed as the name for this new alliance.

11.45 p.m., Silver Oak Estate

After wrapping up a series of meetings in Delhi, Sharad Pawar and Ajit Pawar landed in Mumbai at 9.45 p.m. The uncle–nephew duo headed straightaway to Silver Oak Estate where they were expecting some late-night visitors. At 11.45 p.m., Uddhav, Aditya and Sanjay Raut reached Pawar's residence. Pawar informed Uddhav of the allies' choice of name and that in such a scenario he should be ready to helm the affairs. Everything was almost in place. What now remained was the final meeting between all three parties on Friday, after which they would stake claim to form the government.

DAY 30: FRIDAY, 22 NOVEMBER 2019

Friday was going to be a crucial day for the alliance. The Congress had already announced that a final decision would be taken on this day. *Saamana* announced the alliance with the tone of finality early in the morning: 'Confirmed! Congress and NCP agree to the alliance unanimously. Talks with Sena leaders in Mumbai today'.

Uddhav Thackeray had already sent out a message to party MLAs for a meeting at Matoshri. This was going to be the last time when Uddhav would talk to his party colleagues on why it had become imperative for the Shiv Sena to go with the Congress and NCP.

11:15 a.m., Matoshri

All 56 MLAs of the Shiv Sena gathered at the Thackeray residence for the meeting.

'The talks of forming government with the Congress and NCP are almost finalized. Any moment you will be needed in Mumbai as we may have to present our full strength before the Governor. So stay back in Mumbai,' Uddhav informed his party MLAs. But Uddhav still sensed a feeling of scepticism in the minds of a few leaders. 'Why did we take this step? The BJP has practically coerced [us] into taking this step. Had they complied by their word, we wouldn't have had to take this step,' Uddhav explained.

Uddhav also went on to say that had the BJP's leadership taken some efforts to reach out, he could have thought otherwise. 'During the entire deadlock, neither Narendra Modi nor Amit Shah ever called me once,' Uddhav pointed, reflecting on the BJP's central leadership's lack of interest in Maharashtra.

While it had been decided earlier that Shiv Sena MLAs would be flown to Jaipur, with the rapid developments, they were shifted to Hotel Lalit near the International Airport instead.

11:30 a.m., Dhananjay Munde's Official Residence

Even though the talks had been almost finalized, there was one more formality that needed to be completed. The Congress and NCP had other smaller allies as part of their pre-poll alliance. Their opinion also mattered and so, all of them held a meeting at Dhananjay Munde's official residence. The People's Republican Party (PRP) led by Jogendra Kawade, Samajwadi Party, Peasants and Workers Party of India (PWP), and Raju Shetti's Swabhimani Shetkari Sanghatana, among others, had to be taken into confidence.

The USP of the new alliance that appealed to parties from such varied ideologies was that it was brought together to keep the BJP out of power. So, for leaders like Jogendra Kawade, a staunch Ambedkar follower, supporting a Shiv Sena-led government wasn't going to be a big issue. 'We are happy with the Shiv Sena's transformation. We are happy that Shiv Sena says they will work for the Constitution believing in the preamble,' Kawade said, welcoming the Shiv Sena into the new secular fold.

While Kawade was unconditional in his welcoming of Shiv Sena as part of the alliance, Samajwadi Party laid some conditions: 'Uddhav Thackeray will have to leave the topic of Mandir and Masjids... We welcome his gesture of supporting the cause of Muslim reservation... let's see how it works in the future...' Abu Azmi said while laying the condition.

The Congress was headed for its legislative party meeting after this, but it assured that there was no contention over the CM's post as the Shiv Sena will be getting that post. Congress's Manikrao Thakre said, 'There is no doubt that the Chief Minister will be from Shiv Sena. There has been no talk about rotational Chief Minister post... Every detail regarding power sharing has almost been finalized. Decision regarding staking claim and oath-taking ceremony is likely to be taken today,' he informed.

NCP's Jayant Patil also informed that the talks were positive. 'All our allies have decided to come together and keep BJP away from power. After our talks now, we will hold discussions with Shiv Sena later in the evening. Decision on staking claim will be taken after discussions with Shiv Sena,' he said.

Vidhan Bhavan, Nariman Point, Mumbai

Ahmed Patel, Mallikarjun Kharge, K.C. Venugopal and Avinash Pande landed in Mumbai for the Maharashtra Congress Legislative party meet where the MLAs were to elect CLP leader. It was Friday and after coming out of the airport in the afternoon, Ahmed Patel went to a masjid in Bandra to offer his daily prayers before heading for the CLP meet.

As is the norm in the party, the CLP meeting ended with a single-point resolution. The resolution authorizing Party President Sonia Gandhi to appoint a CLP leader was passed unanimously.

All three parties in the game were now headed to Nehru Centre for a decisive meeting. The politics of the state was not going to be the same after this meeting.

4.00 p.m., Nehru Centre, Worli, Mumbai

For the first time ever, topmost leaders from all three parties, including Uddhav Thackeray, Sharad Pawar and Ahmed Patel, among others, were sitting across the table for talks to give final touches to the arrangement.

Foremost on the agenda was to pick the Chief Minister candidate of the MVA. Both the parties had already made their choice clear. Sharad Pawar himself proposed in the meeting that Uddhav Thackeray should take up the role. Sanjay Raut from the

Shiv Sena seconded the proposal. Congress had no reason to take any exception. The decision was unanimous—Uddhav Balasaheb Thackeray was going to be the next Chief Minister of Maharashtra. This was the first time a person from the Thackeray clan was going to take up a public office. Uddhav's promise to his father of a Sena Chief Minister was finally coming true. While Uddhav had been hesitant so far, he knew he was left with little choice. Things had changed rapidly over the last few days and the usual options had disappeared at an equally high speed.

The unanimous decision of Uddhav Thackeray as the Chief Minister of MVA was welcomed with a loud applause. The only thing that now remained to be done was to meet the Governor and stake claim at forming the government.

While everything appeared to be falling into place, the issue of the Speaker's post cropped up. According to the initial talks, Shiv Sena was to get the CM's post for the entire tenure, while the Congress and NCP were to get one Deputy Chief Minister post each. Later, apart from asking for important portfolios like Revenue and PWD, the Congress had also demanded the Speaker's post. For the party, it was a way to placate two of its top leaders. In 2010, Prithviraj Chavan, who was the Minister of State in the then PM's cabinet, was sent to Maharashtra to replace Ashok Chavan as the state's CM. Prithviraj was not keen on being the Deputy Chief Minister or handling any portfolio as a minister. He was, however, keen to become the Speaker. The party saw this demand as a solution to accommodate one more name, but the NCP was not in favour of Prithviraj as Speaker. Prithviraj, also known as Baba in the political circles, has a history with Pawar. Chavan's father Anandrao and his mother Premalakaki never got along well with Pawar's mentor and former Deputy PM Yashwantrao Chavan.

The NCP President never had great liking for the belletrist Baba. The equations had soured, especially after Baba became the Chief Minister of Maharashtra. A large section of the NCP felt that Baba was working against the interests of their party. Files pertaining to NCP ministers were delayed. The NCP supremo himself had targeted Chavan, saying that the CM's hands suffer a paralytic attack when it comes to clearing files. Prithviraj Chavan too hit back, raising the pitch of the duel between the two. It was Baba who had called for a white paper on irrigation, indirectly pointing fingers at Ajit Pawar who was controlling the department.

Chavan had pointed out that in spite of spending over ₹66,000 crore on various irrigation schemes in the last 10 years, only 0.1 per cent land was brought under irrigation. The issue later snowballed into a great political controversy leading to the much-hyped irrigation scam. With an impending inquiry, Ajit Pawar resigned as the Deputy CM. The very thought of Prithviraj Chavan in the Speaker's chair left the NCP pondering on whether Baba would use it against the party.

The name wasn't discussed in the meeting so far, but Mallikarjun Kharge raised the issue. Deliberately or otherwise, Pawar chose to ignore it and moved ahead with other details. Everyone, including Uddhav Thackeray, realized that Pawar was not comfortable discussing the issue. After a few minutes, Kharge raised the issue of the Speaker's post again. It was again ignored. This time, however, digging in his heels further, Kharge reminded Pawar that he had promised that Congress would be given the Speaker's post. As he did so, Kharge's voice went up. (He usually speaks in a high octave.) Sharad Pawar was visibly offended at the tone and tenor, and the usually calm Pawar also gave it back in the same pitch. 'What are you trying to suggest? Are you trying to suggest that I'm lying? I'm not interested in talking any further if this is how the talks are going to be,' the sudden duel between the two stalwarts stunned the boardroom.

Pawar is rarely known to lose his temper, but when he does, he isn't known for anger management. Just as the duel continued, he started wrapping up the files and papers. His nephew Ajit Pawar jumped into the fight, as if waiting for the opportunity. He hit back at the language in which a leader like Pawar was being addressed.

Sharad Pawar left the meeting midway. On his way out, he broke the news to the media: 'Detailed discussion has taken place. The drafting process is going on. As far as Chief Minister post is concerned, there is no difference of opinion about that. Everybody has agreed that the government should be formed under the leadership of Uddhav Thackeray. Discussion on the rest of the programmes is going on. We will take a detailed press conference tomorrow and inform everyone,' he said sitting on the front seat as cameras almost mobbed his SUV.

A few moments later, Uddhav Thackeray emerged from the meeting. 'I don't want to share any half-baked information with you. We will discuss and finalize everything and won't leave one single point to be discussed. Some things are still left to be finalized, and are being discussed,' Uddhav told the reporters thronging him from all sides outside the lobby of Nehru Centre.

While Sharad Pawar asked his men to stay back and finalize the modalities, Ajit Pawar hurriedly left after his uncle. Other party leaders thought that the irate leaders left because of the heated exchange in the meeting. However, that wasn't the case.

Sharad Pawar left for Silver Oak Estate. Meanwhile, Uddhav Thackeray halted at the Mayor's Bungalow where the proposed Balasaheb Thackeray Memorial was shaping up and Sanjay Raut left for Bhandup. Later, Raut received a phone call from Pawar, asking him what had happened in the meeting after he left. Raut informed Pawar that Uddhav and he had left immediately after him. A curious Pawar inquired the whereabouts of his nephew Ajit. Raut informed him that Ajit too had left immediately after him.

Pawar immediately inquired about Ajit with Jayant Patil, who told him that the former had gone to his lawyer to discuss some important matter. Both Raut and Pawar immediately tried calling Ajit after this call. None of his staff or close aides knew where he was. He had gone incommunicado...

Undisclosed location, Mumbai

The BJP national secretary Bhupendra Yadav, who was in charge of the Maharashtra assembly polls, hurriedly reached Mumbai. Party President Amit Shah had sent him to oversee a mission. With the options of getting Shiv Sena back completely exhausted, the BJP was simultaneously working on Plan B. At an undisclosed location, Bhupendra Yadav and Devendra Fadnavis anxiously waited for a man. They were not sure whether the plan would unfold as expected, and they breathed a sigh of relief when the man arrived. They shook hands and started working towards the completion of the mission.

The night of 22 November to the dawn of 23 November was going to be one long stretch of time...

DAY 31: SATURDAY, 23 NOVEMBER 2019

8.00 a.m., Matoshri

An early morning phone call woke up Uddhav Thackeray. What the caller informed him pulled the carpet from under his feet and left him shocked and speechless.

As the state was sleeping, in an early morning development, Devendra Fadnavis was sworn in as the Chief Minister of Maharashtra. Even more shocking was the name of the Deputy Chief Minister sworn in with Fadnavis. The man was none other than Ajit Pawar, who was sitting in front of him in the meeting the previous evening. At 8.01 a.m., ANI tweeted about Fadnavis and Ajit Pawar taking the oath.

Sanjay Raut, who had recently undergone angioplasty, could feel his heart palpitating. It was he who had been coordinating with Sharad Pawar's NCP. He had assured his Party President that the NCP will not ditch the Shiv Sena. And now here he was, trying to gather the courage to speak to Uddhav. Raut picked up the phone, but dialled Sharad Pawar instead.

NCP's State President Jayant Patil had retired to bed late the previous night after binge-watching his favourite series, *Jack Ryan*, on Amazon Prime.[39] He woke up to a dozen missed calls on his phone, of which eight were from Uddhav Thackeray.

The news was too big to believe. Even before anyone could confirm or deny the development, the biggest confirmation came in from none other than Prime Minister Narendra Modi, who at

---

[39] Source-based information on condition of anonymity.

8.16 a.m. tweeted congratulations to the new Chief Minister and Deputy Chief Minister of Maharashtra.

The Shiv Sena and Congress camps were left devastated by the newsbreak, with both camps believing they had been backstabbed. For both of them, the man at the centre of suspicion was the same!

6.30 a.m., Silver Oak Estate

An early morning phone call woke up Sharad Pawar. It was an urgent call from a party MLA. The information given by the MLA left him shocked. He was informed that Ajit Pawar had been calling party MLAs since late last night and a few of them had gone with him to Raj Bhavan. 'Dada is taking oath with (Devendra) Fadnavis,' the MLA informed Pawar. Pawar looked at the watch, but it was too late to do anything. He knew he wouldn't be able to stop the inevitable. All he knew was that he had to stop any further damage.

Pawar started gathering information on who all had gone with Ajit. The previous night he had sensed that something was not right, as Ajit had disappeared suddenly after the meeting. Pawar now started to make calls to Ajit's close aides. Dhananjay Munde, Ajit's close confidante, had also gone incommunicado.

By this time, the news of Ajit Pawar's coup had spread like wildfire. The first thing Pawar had to do was to regain his allies' trust. He immediately called Uddhav and informed him that he had nothing to do with Ajit's move of going with the BJP. He also made a lightning call to Congress President Sonia Gandhi.

A senior Congress leader, Abhishek Manu Singhvi, had already taken to Twitter to attack Sharad Pawar, saying, '*Waah Pawar Sahab, Waah*!!' (This was deleted later.)

Uddhav Thackeray and Sharad Pawar decided to meet urgently. Meanwhile, Pawar started gathering information on what had happened till now...

11 p.m., 22 November

The game had begun almost two weeks ago. Friday's was the last nail. After excusing himself suddenly from the meeting at Nehru

Centre, Ajit Pawar had come out and changed his car. Bhupendra Yadav and Ajit Pawar met at an undisclosed location to finalize the swearing-in. Ajit had already consented to join hands with the BJP a few days ago. Immediately after Pawar's refusal to Narendra Modi, 'Mission Ajit Pawar' was expedited by the BJP. An NCP leader who was friends with a top state BJP leader had already tipped Fadnavis on how Ajit Pawar had once insisted on the possibility of thinking of BJP as an option in the initial days of the political logjam. The lines of communication with Ajit Pawar were opened from then and there. Bhupendra Yadav started working the deal with Ajit. During Ajit's visit to Delhi, a meeting was also organized between him and Amit Shah to give Ajit the confidence that the BJP's top leadership was closely involved in the developments. Ajit had since started to indentify MLAs who would join him in the coup. It was not going to be an easy rebellion. After all, it was going to be against one of the most astute politicians. Add to it that Ajit was rebelling against his own uncle and mentor Sharad Pawar. Like the BJP, Ajit too had his Plan B. He knew that as the leader of the Legislative Party, he had all the powers to issue the letter of support. He was sure that a big chunk of party MLAs would follow him in his move. He started making phone calls. First on his dialler list was Sindkhed Raja (Buldhana district) MLA Rajendra Shingne.[40] 'We have an important meeting tomorrow. Reach Dhananjay's (Munde) Bungalow before 5 a.m. And since this is top secret, keep this to yourself,' Ajit warned Shingne in his baritone voice. More such calls followed.

Raj Bhavan, Malabar Hill

The BJP, meanwhile, had already made all preparations for the overnight takeover. Governor Bhagat Singh Koshyari was scheduled to travel to Delhi for the two-day Governors' Conference. He cancelled his trip, as he was informed about 'an important development'. He was told late in the evening that he needed to

---

[40] Source-based information on condition of anonymity.

stay back in Mumbai. Fadnavis communicated to the Raj Bhavan that he intended to stake claim to form the next government. After receiving the intimation, the first step for the Governor was to seek the letters of support. He had to follow the procedure or at least show that it was being followed. Ajit Pawar then submitted the requisite letter, extending support for the Fadnavis-led government. The next step according to the rule book was to recommend to the Centre to lift the President's rule.

At around 12:30 a.m., Governor Koshyari sent a petition to the Centre for lifting the President's Rule in Maharashtra. The Centre was more than quick in obliging. At an unusual time of 1:30 a.m., the Central Government gave its nod to the petition and without wasting any time, it was forwarded to President Ramnath Kovind. The President's office acted on the petition without any delay.

At 5.47 a.m. the President's Rule in Maharashtra was revoked, paving the way for the swearing-in. The Governor's Office by that time had already informed Chief Secretary of Maharashtra, Ajoy Mehta, to arrange the swearing-in at 6.30 a.m.

◆

NCP MLAs started arriving at Dhananjay Munde's residence. When Rajendra Shingne reached, he saw a few MLAs sitting there already. They were made to sit together in a vehicle. Majority of them were told by Ajit Pawar's key aides that they had to reach Raj Bhavan. Some of them had started getting suspicious, but the key aide ferrying them whispered in Shingne's ear that this move has the blessings of 'Saheb'.

Around 5.30 a.m., Ajit Pawar and Devendra Fadnavis had already arrived at the Raj Bhavan.

◆

A team from ANI had got a message late last night that Devendra Fadnavis would be giving a sound byte early next morning. In the last few years, this had become a norm. Whenever Fadnavis wanted to issue a statement, he preferred speaking to the ANI. For the ANI team, this was a routine assignment till the team reached Varsha, where Fadnavis was still staying. The TV crew with their live source was ferried to Raj Bhavan. When they entered the Governor's office with their cameras, they were stunned to see Devendra Fadnavis and Ajit Pawar together. Just as they were gathering their thoughts, the national anthem started playing with the Governor's arrival. A permission was sought to start the proceedings.

At 7.45 a.m., the Governor began the swearing-in ceremony. The first name that was called was of Shri Devendra Gangadharrao Fadnavis.

'Mee Devendra Gangadharrao Fadnavis, ishwar saksh shapath gheto ki...,' Fadnavis started his oath as the CM.

After he completed his oath, the second name was called out— Shri Ajit Anantrao Pawar.

'Mee Ajit Anantrao Pawar, gambhirya purvak drudh kathan karto ki...'

NCP MLAs, who till now had any doubt left in their minds, now got a clear idea what they were part of. It was a coup!

◆

After the swearing-in, both Fadnavis and Pawar gave a small sound byte to the news agency. Ajit's claim to join the BJP-led government was as bizzare as the late-night development. 'After the results were announced [on] October 24, no party was able to form the government. Maharashtra was facing many problems, including farmers issues. So we have decided to form a stable government,' Ajit said.

Fadnavis's reaction after the swearing-in is worth mentioning. 'I extend my gratitude to Prime Minister Narendra Modi, BJP national president Amit Shah and working president J.P. Nadda for giving me the chance to serve Maharashtra as the Chief Minister again. People had given us a clear mandate, but Shiv Sena tried to ally with other parties after the results, after which President's rule was imposed. Maharashtra needed a stable government, not a "khichdi" government. Ajit Pawar backed the BJP and with the support of Independent MLAs and smaller parties, we have formed the government in Maharashtra,' Fadnavis told the news agency. Fadnavis's statement was noteworthy for two reasons: In spite of calling it a coalition government, he didn't mention Sharad Pawar in the list of gratitude. Secondly, the most striking thing that no one could miss was Fadnavis's body language. Known for his supreme confidence, the very USP of Fadnavis was missing. His body language was clearly suggestive of reluctance. His tone and tenor suggested that he was not keen on the formation of this government.

♦

1991

Like most of the politicians in the state, Ajit Pawar too made his debut in politics through the co-operatives by becoming the Chairman of the Pune District Central Co-operative Bank (PDCC). He had earlier taken baby steps in politics by being on the board of directors of a Sugar Co-operative in Baramati. Ajit's entry into politics was also not planned. His father Anantrao, Sharad Pawar's elder brother, was inclined towards making a career in the film industry. While Ajit was schooled at his maternal grandparents' home in Ahmednagar, his father worked as an Art Director with the legendary Bollywood director V. Shantaram. Shantaram is known to have produced and directed several Bollywood classics, including *Do Aankhen Barah Haath, Navrang, Geet Gaya Paththaron Ne, Jhanak Jhanak Payal Baje*, as well as several Marathi movies. After his father's untimely demise, Ajit gave up his studies and started working with his uncle Sharad Pawar, who had by now risen as a formidable figure in the state's politics. While staying with his super busy uncle, the person who took care of young Ajit was his Kaki (aunt), Sharad Pawar's wife Pratibha. Sharad Pawar, even in those times, had led by example with a small family, with just one child, a daughter. It is said that if there is one person in the entire Pawar clan whom Ajit Pawar greatly respects and who could even now hold him by his ears, it is his Pratibha Kaki.

The Pawars are a very close-knit family. Sharad Pawar's siblings include brothers Appasaheb, Anantrao, Prataprao and sister Saroj. Excluding Ajit Pawar, who had to give up education due to his father's death, the entire Pawar family is highly educated. Unlike other political families, the bonding in the Pawar family has always been a topic of curiosity for everyone. Every year during Diwali, dozens of Pawar clan members gather at Govind Baug, Sharad Pawar's house in Baramati. A grand family picture is mandatory.

With Pawar's daughter still young and not very inclined to follow in her father's footsteps, it was in Ajit that many saw Sharad Pawar's heir apparent. Soon after taking his first big step into politics as the PDCC Chairman, Ajit contested the Lok Sabha polls from the Baramati seat. He, however, had to vacate the seat for his uncle, who was inducted in erstwhile Prime Minister P.V. Narsimharao's Cabinet as the Defence Minister. Ajit then became a Minister of State in Sudhakarrao Naik's Cabinet in Maharashtra. He continued to be there even when uncle Pawar returned from Delhi to take over the mantle of the State's Chief Minister following the Mumbai riots. Since 1995, Ajit Pawar has contested the Baramati assembly seat and won.

After forming his party—the NCP—Sharad Pawar was building a strong second plank of leaders. But Pawar's choice were leaders who had emerged from scratch and had made it big in politics. An OBC face like Chhagan Bhujbal was given the role of the state's chief of the party, while other faces like the late R.R. Patil, Jayant Patil and Dilip Walse Patil were carefully groomed by Pawar. But in the party hierarchy, Ajit was still at the top, despite having no big position.

In 2004, when the United Progressive Alliance (UPA) led by Dr Manmohan Singh came to power at the Centre, Pawar was made the Union Agriculture Minister. Things in the party changed when Pawar shifted his base to Delhi. Political circles started buzzing when Pawar decided to launch his daughter Supriya into active politics. In 2006, Supriya Sule was elected to the upper house unopposed. This was the onset of speculations of Ajit being sidelined in the party.

The family, including both Ajit Pawar and Supriya Sule, denied the speculations on numerous occasions, but the political turnout of events in the next few years only added fuel to this theory.

Within two years of Supriya's entry into politics, in 2008 Ajit Pawar started showing the first signs of discomfort in the party. After the dreaded terror attacks of 26/11, heads rolled in Maharashtra. Chief Minister Vilasrao Deshmukh and Deputy Chief Minister R.R. Patil had to resign. While the Congress replaced Deshmukh with Ashok Chavan, Pawar brought back old hand Chhagan Bhujbal. This had annoyed Ajit Pawar, who had gone incommunicado for two days. Pawar himself had to persuade Ajit to return. In September 2012, following the announcement of the White Paper on Irrigation projects by erstwhile Chief Minister Prithviraj Chavan, Ajit had unexpectedly resigned. The move came as a surprise even for Sharad Pawar.

In April 2013, Ajit was embroiled in one of the biggest controversies of his life. While addressing a rally, Ajit, while referring to a hunger strike undertaken by a drought-affected farmer, had said: '[He] is sitting on a hunger strike for the last 55 days demanding water be released from the dam. But if there is no water there, what should we release? Should we urinate there?'[41] Ajit's crass sense of humour came under criticism from all quarters. He publicly apologized, calling it the biggest mistake of his life and took penance by observing a maun vrat (vow of silence) at the memorial of Yashwantrao Chavan in Karad.

Before the 2019 Lok Sabha elections, Ajit insisted for a ticket for his son Parth from the Maval Lok Sabha seat. Sharad Pawar was against it, and so were other leaders in the party. The young Parth was a complete greenhorn and Sharad Pawar wanted him to work in the party system first before taking the big leap. A ticket to Parth would also mean three members from the Pawar family getting tickets. Sharad Pawar tried to build the pressure by withdrawing

---

[41] https://www.indiatoday.in/india/south/story/ajit-pawar-on-maharashtra-drought-urinate-remark-158064-2013-04-07; last accessed 16 March 2020.

his decision to contest from the Madha Lok Sabha seat, and had to stick to it as Ajit had put his foot down. Parth eventually lost the election. The defeat left Ajit badly bruised.

Just ahead of the assembly elections, Sharad Pawar was named in the ED Enforcement Case Information Report (ECIR) in the Maharashtra State Co-operative Bank scam. The entire politics of the state was stirred when NCP workers across Maharashtra took to the streets after Sharad Pawar announced that he himself will visit the ED Office. The protests had come as a blessing in disguise for the party, which was marred by mass exodus. Just as Sharad Pawar had infused a lease of life into the party, the same evening Ajit dropped a bombshell by resigning as an MLA. Even this time, Sharad Pawar had no clue what Ajit was up to. But one thing that was sure was that Ajit Pawar was not following the party line.

While Sharad Pawar was planning a major political realignment by getting together parties like the Shiv Sena and Congress, Ajit was never convinced about the idea. He openly expressed his reservations in the party meeting. As the talks between the three parties were increasing in frequency, Ajit lost his cool. He also walked out of one of the meetings, informing journalists waiting at Silver Oak Estate that he was going to Baramati.

Amid the deadlock, the BJP sensed a weak link. Ajit was approached through a common friend of him and Devendra Fadnavis. After the initial talks, the big meeting with Bhupendra Yadav set things in motion.

On the morning of 23 November, Ajit Pawar stirred a hornet's nest, when he took oath with Fadnavis, the same man who once almost smashed his political career by raising the Irrigation Scam.

Ajit Pawar's coup was not just against the party. It was not about one leader from one party going to another to extend support. It was a rebellion by a family member of the party supremo. It was a coup led by the legislative party leader who was conferred all constitutional rights to take a decision on the party's behalf. It was also the breaking away of a nephew from an uncle. For the first time, after all his small and failed rebellions that had been considered 'tantrums' by the party, this was far more serious.

More than the party, it was shocking for the close-knit Pawar family. Never ever in the history of the family had any dispute gone public to such an extent. Ajit's decision wrecked the family, leaving every single member, including those not into politics, devastated.

As everyone in the family struggled for words to react, the first reaction came in from Supriya Sule. It wasn't a public statement, but her WhatsApp status read: 'Party and family split.' Within a few minutes of this status, a visibly hurt Supriya uploaded yet another message as her WhatsApp status: 'Who do you trust in life...never felt so cheated in my life...defended him, loved him, look what I get in return.'[42]

♦

With the state yet to come out of the shock, Supriya's emotional outburst was hinting at the clear division. Though in murmurs, the political circles were abuzz with conspiracy theories. The most prominent among these was that Ajit's coup had his uncle's blessings, and that Sharad Pawar too would soon follow the suit and join him in a couple of months. Many corroborated the theory with the recent Pawar–Modi meeting. Pawar's history of political shock therapy (or 'Dhakka-Tantra' as it is known as) was only working against him. The onus was now on Pawar to come clean. His silence would have been termed as the silence of conspiracy. At 9.27 a.m., Pawar finally issued his statement on Twitter. 'Ajit Pawar's decision to support the BJP to form the Maharashtra Government is his personal decision and not that of the Nationalist Congress Party (NCP). We place on record that we do not support or endorse this decision of his.' The smog was slowly clearing up.

♦

This sudden twist had caused Sanjay Raut much stress. After all, he was the one who was constantly hinging on to the alliance

---

[42] Part of author's ground reporting; also widely covered by TV and print media.

with NCP. Some in the party had already started to accuse him of leading the Shiv Sena to this situation. BJP leader and former Chief Minister of Madhya Pradesh, Shivraj Singh Chouhan, took a dig at the Shiv Sena in the same poetic style that Raut had made popular in the last few days. Speaking to reporters in MP, Chouhan said, '*Na Khuda mila, na Misal-e-sanam...Na idhar ke huye na udhar ke...*'

After a brief word with Uddhav Thackeray and Sharad Pawar, Raut came out with a statement in front of TV cameras. 'Ajit Pawar had stabbed us (Shiv Sena) in the back by joining hands with the BJP. The state will never forgive Ajit Pawar for this act. This is betrayal,' he said. He further asserted that Ajit Pawar's decision didn't have the approval of NCP Chief Sharad Pawar.

In Delhi, the Congress had also joined the chorus, calling the late-night developments as murder of democracy. 'Lust for power washes away principles and corruption,' tweeted Congress spokesperson Randeep Surjewala, attaching a grab of an old tweet by Devendra Fadnavis in which he had said that under no situation would the BJP ever ally with the NCP as it had 'exposed' the latter's corruption.

Silver Oak Estate

Apart from Rajendra Shingne, there were others who were present for the early morning swearing-in. By now, Sharad Pawar had gathered the list of all those who had gone with his nephew. The 'backstabber ghost' was here to haunt Pawar yet again. In this moment of crisis was an opportunity for him to come clean of the blot that has bothered him all through his political career. After leading the campaign from the front, Pawar padded himself up for another innings. There were only two options before him—accept what had happened and move on, or go ahead using all his political experience and quell the rebellion. Being true to his recent fighter image, Pawar chose the second option.

Pawar called for a joint meeting with Uddhav Thackeray and Ahmed Patel. In the meanwhile, Pawar's trusted men had already got hold of the first batch of rebels.

Y.B. Chavan Centre, Nariman Point, Mumbai

Immediately after the news broke, NCP workers started gathering outside the Yashwantrao Chavan Centre, where the NCP supremo usually holds party meetings. For last few days this place had become the centre of political activity. It was not just NCP workers who assembled there, the Shiv Sena and Congress workers too joined in.

In the next one and half hours, a noticeably perturbed Uddhav reached the Y.B. Chavan Centre accompanied by Aditya. By now, Sharad Pawar had already begun his mission to crush the revolt. A list of 'missing' MLAs was prepared. While some of them weren't 'missing', they were suspected to be in touch with Ajit. Pawar carefully went through the list. The names in the list didn't surprise him.

1. Dhananjay Munde, Parli
2. Rajendra Shingne, Shindkhed Raja
3. Sanjay Bansod, Udgir
4. Sunil Bhusara, Vikramgarh
5. Dilip Bankar, Niphad
6. Sunil Shelke, Maval
7. Manikrao Kokate, Sinnar
8. Sandeep Kshirsagar, Beed
9. Narhari Zirwal, Dindori
10. Daulat Daroda, Shahapur
11. Anil Patil, Amalner
12. Nitin Pawar, Kalwan
13. Babasaheb Patil, Ahmedpur
14. Datta Bharne, Indapur

Pawar carefully studied the list. Munde, Bansod, Bharne, Shelke and Balasaheb Patil were known members of the Ajit Pawar camp within the party. The others were unsuspecting MLAs who had no idea of what was happening. They were carefully chosen tribal MLAs— Bhusara, Zirwal, Daroda and Nitin Pawar. And then there were those who had been newly elected as MLAs or those who had made a comeback after staying out of political action for a long time. This included senior MLAs Kokate and Bankar on one hand and the likes of Kshirsagar and Shelke on the other.

The first step was to get these MLAs back. Sharad Pawar took the reins in his hands. With his phones constantly ringing, he was taking updates of the whereabouts of these MLAs while constantly giving instructions. Pawar's office in Y.B. Chavan Centre almost appeared like a war room.

Domestic Airport, Kalina, Mumbai

A private plane belonging to Reliance was set to fly out of Mumbai. According to the flight plan, this private jet had sought landing space at the Surat airport at 10 a.m. The passenger manifest submitted to Mumbai Airport mentioned nine names. These nine passengers were none other than Dilip Bankar, Sanjay Bansod, Daulat Daroda, Nitin Pawar, Narhari Zirwal, Anil Patil, Sunil Bhusara, Babasaheb Patil and Sunil Shelke. Devendra Fadnavis's key man, Prasad Lad, who runs the security and housekeeping agency Krystal at the airport, had arranged for the charter plane.[43]

In the mission to get back the missing MLAs, NCP and Shiv Sena immediately starting working in tandem since early morning. Mumbai's airports were the first place where Sena and NCP men were deployed to stop the MLAs from flying out of the city. The Shiv Sena has a strong presence in various workers unions at the Mumbai airport. Key men were asked to keep a close eye on the movements. Due to the strict vigil, the take-off of the charter plane was delayed.

◆

After the swearing-in, Ajit Pawar holed himself up at his brother Shriniwas Pawar's house at Nepean Sea road. The BJP camp wasn't expecting such immediate retaliation by the NCP. The plan was that two-thirds of the MLAs would follow Ajit Pawar, resulting in

---

[43] Source-based information on condition of anonymity.

a split in the party. With the NCP on a mission to bring back these MLAs by hook or by crook, the possibility of a split was hanging in a limbo. It was decided to take these MLAs to a safer place. In such politically charged situations, it is a thumb rule that politicians follow. They never keep all the eggs in one basket. The rebel camp was, hence, split into various groups.

12.30 p.m., Rangswar Auditorium, Y.B. Chavan Centre

The high-octane drama was only getting bigger with each passing moment. Amidst slogans of *'Shivsenecha wagh aala'*, Uddhav and Aditya Thackeray arrived at Y.B. Chavan Centre. NCP workers willingly joined the sloganeering. Congress leaders Ahmed Patel, Ashok Chavan and Balasaheb Thorat too arrived. After a brief meeting with Sharad Pawar, they left as the Congress was going to hold a separate meeting.

Sharad Pawar, accompanied by his daughter Supriya, had already reached. Supriya came down to receive Uddhav. On her way back, she was stopped by mediapersons to get her reaction on the developments. Supriya just stood before the cameras without uttering a single word. The lump in the throat was evident.

At 12.40 p.m. Sharad Pawar, Uddhav Thackeray, Aditya Thackeray, Sanjay Raut, Praful Patel, Eknath Shinde, Chhagan Bhujbal and other leaders arrived in the auditorium that was packed to its capacity. The tension in the air was evident. The auditorium buzzing with activity of mediapersons suddenly witnessed pin-drop silence as Pawar and Thackeray entered. All ears and camera lenses were focused on what the man at the centre of the controversy had to say.

'NCP, Congress and Shiv Sena had started talks on government formation as we had the support of around 169–170 MLAs including some independents. After yesterday's meeting, there were certain developments. I was informed by a party colleague in the morning that some of our MLAs were taken to Raj Bhavan. I was told that they went with Ajit Pawar and that Devendra Fadnavis and Ajit Pawar took oath. I would like to make it clear that Ajit's decision is completely against the interest of the Party; it's a breach of party discipline. No worker of the NCP would ever go with the BJP,' Pawar began by clearing doubts about his and his party's role. Then changing gears, he cautioned the rebels: 'All those have gone (with Ajit Pawar) and those who plan to go should remember that there is a strong anti-defection law, and they may lose their membership. If they resign and go and re-contest, the NCP, Congress and Shiv Sena will come together and do all that takes to defeat them.'

Pawar then played his first card: 'I have an information that around 10–12 MLAs have gone with Ajit Pawar. Some of them have already contacted us...' Pawar paused and said, 'Call him,' as he turned around.

A person in a grey kurta was handed over the mic. 'I am Dr Rajendra Shingne... I was contacted by Ajit Pawar late last night. I was told that there was an important meeting and I have to reach Dhananjay Munde's bungalow early in the morning we were taken to Raj Bhavan...we were clueless of what was happening till we reached Raj Bhavan...' Shingne narrated the entire story of how he was misguided and made to be a part of the rebellion.

Next to be paraded was a very boyish-looking MLA dressed in white. This was Sandeep Kshirsagar from Beed. He too recounted the same story. The only difference was that Sandeep's voice was shivering as he spoke. Both of them said that immediately after the Governor left, they contacted Sharad Pawar to inform him that they are with him. The third MLA on display was Sanjay Bhusara, who added that while witnessing the turn of events, his blood pressure had shot up.

Pawar himself called out the names of these MLAs and introduced them. After this, Pawar added that there were a few more MLAs who were on their way back.

'Every party has a list of its MLAs, a signed letter. I think that has been used and the Governor has been misguided,' Pawar said. Pawar just didn't stop at that. He announced that the newly sworn-in Chief Minister will not be able to prove the majority and then the NCP, Congress and Shiv Sena will stake claim.

Uddhav wasn't looking like he was in a mood to speak. All

throughout Pawar's address, he seemed to be restless. 'This is a new Hindutva... Rather than saying "I will come back," it would have been better if he (Fadnavis) had said that I will never go and stick himself to the chair with Fevicol. Shiv Sena never plays games in the dark. Come what may, we all will stay together...'

Before the press conference ended, Pawar and Uddhav said two things that perhaps underlined the way ahead and the strategy that was planned. Recounting how his 'Pu.Lo.Da' government was brought down when all his MLAs were hijacked, Pawar, like a pro, said, 'I have seen this all before.' It was this poise of Pawar that also pumped confidence in his party leaders as well as Shiv Sena leaders who were present there. Uddhav was asked what if his party MLAs are poached. 'Let them try that... Maharashtra is not sleeping,' he almost roared.

Though Pawar claimed that only 10–12 MLAs were with Ajit Pawar, the actual list of those suspected to be in contact with the rebel faction was around 15–16. Just as the press conference was getting over, Sunil Shelke, the MLA from Maval, too came back. Sharad Pawar glanced at the list and, adjusting his glasses, struck out four names. NCP workers were assigned a man-to-man mapping of these MLAs. A local team was stationed at every MLA's house to monitor their movements. In most cases, family members were surprised to know about the rebellion 'against Sharad Pawar'. A team of NCP leaders sat at the home of Ajit's close aide till the time he returned, leaving his old mother scared. Not just homes, a team led by youth wing workers even reached the college of the son of one of the MLAs to know the father's whereabouts. No stone was being left unturned.

Shahapur MLA Daulat Daroda was another one who had gone with Ajit Pawar and attended the swearing-in ceremony. But he was not contactable ever since. His son Karan was present at Sharad Pawar's press conference. Stopping just short of alleging the 'kidnapping' of his father, he contended that his father was forcibly taken to the swearing-in. Karan claimed, 'I had come with my father in the morning. But I was not allowed to sit in the car in which he was made to sit. I tried to follow the car till Raj Bhavan, but then onwards I was not allowed. I haven't been able to contact my father ever since,' he said, adding that he would soon be filing a missing person report with the police.

◆

Immediately after the press conference, as leaders started to come out of Y.B. Chavan Centre, noisy slogans surprised many. No one would have ever imagined that slogans of '*Ajit Pawar murdabad*' would ever reverberate in the campus of Y.B. Chavan Centre.

The duel between the uncle and nephew had begun. Sharad Pawar was hell-bent on winning back 'his MLAs' who had gone with Ajit.

B2 Bungalow

The Congress had slowly started to come to terms with the shock. The Party President Sonia Gandhi by now was sure that it was a rebel faction within the NCP and not the entire party that had let the Shiv Sena and Congress down. Pawar's clarification and assurance to the Congress that the rebellion will be crushed was the much-required assurance. But in spite of that, the Congress had its own separate meeting, which was chaired by top leaders, including Ahmed Patel, Mallikarjun Kharge and K.C. Venugopal, along with state leaders.

'The Chief Minister and Deputy Chief Minister were sworn in without any "band, baaja, baarat" in the wee hours... This event will be written in black ink in the country's history,' Ahmed Patel attacked. 'There was blatant violation of constitutional principles that crossed all levels of shamelessness,' he added. Patel announced that the Congress was still on board and will soon be formulating a joint strategy with the Shiv Sena and NCP to defeat the BJP in the confidence motion in the state assembly.

The Congress had emerged as the smartest player in the game in the last one month, as its leaders had earlier foreseen the inevitable danger of poaching and moved its MLAs to a resort. The Shiv Sena, too, guarded its MLAs. The NCP was the only player in the game that was slightly negligent and it had ended up paying the price for it. The Congress yet again decided to move its MLAs to a hotel in Mumbai.

Shivalay, Shiv Sena Party Office, Nariman Point, Mumbai

Just a few metres away from where the Congress meeting was taking place, Uddhav Thackeray, after meeting Sharad Pawar, reached the Shiv Sena Office 'Shivalay'. In spite of the assurance by Pawar and his subsequent mission to quell the rebellion in full swing, Uddhav was devastated with what had happened. He was feeling a mix of anger, frustration, betrayal and heartbreak. He had seen several ups and downs in his political career, but this time the feeling of being cheated was weighing down his heart. The moment he reached the party office, he went alone inside a room, strictly instructing the staff to not allow anyone in. He wanted to spend time with himself. After almost half an hour, Rashmi Thackeray and Milind Narvekar knocked on the door and spoke to him. Uddhav had calmed down by then. He came out more determined and with a stronger will to hit back. Uddhav then headed to Hotel Lalit where his party MLAs were already in a state of confusion since the morning.

Y.B. Chavan Centre, Nariman Point, Mumbai; NCP Meeting

Pawar's war room in the mission was working at a lightning pace. Contact had been established with most of the rebel MLAs, including Ajit Pawar.

Pawar was by now sure of the return of most of them. Some claimed being misguided and had returned. Some who had miscalculated, had by now realized what misadventure they were up to. Some who had spent reasonable time in the state's politics knew well that challenging Sharad Pawar is no child's play. The immediate effect of Pawar's mission was seen on MLAs who were supposed to fly out of Mumbai. Some of them developed cold feet and decided to stay back in Mumbai.

The rebel team was falling apart.

At 3 p.m., sensing that the team of rebels had become weak at the knees, Pawar decided to open communication links directly with the Commander. Three in the party were assigned the most important task of the day to speak to Ajit Pawar, who was almost in hiding at his brother's place—Ajit's close friend in the party Sunil Tatkare and Sharad Pawar's trusted lieutenants Dilip Walse-Patil and Hasan Mushrif. The brief given to the trio was simple—tell Ajit Pawar that everyone from his stable is on their way back. The party has decided that under no circumstances will it go with the BJP. On the day of the floor test, the party will stay together. It's Ajit Pawar who will have to take his call now. The party doors were still open for him...

3.00 p.m., Domestic Airport, Mumbai

The strategy was multi-pronged. Shashikant Shinde, who had lost the elections this time from his constituency in Satara, was keeping a close vigil at the airport. After spending some time in figuring out the locations, he was delighted to see a few known faces from the party walking towards the gate. But the number was far lesser than expected. These were only four of the missing MLAs heading with full security to board the private jet that was waiting to take off since the morning. Shinde tried to sneak past the security to stop the MLAs for a brief word, but the security personnel wouldn't budge. Shinde failed at stopping the MLAs and had to return empty handed. But he passed on the message that four MLAs have escaped and are flying out of the city for sure. These four MLAs were Daulat Daroda, Nitin Pawar, Narhari Zirwal and Anil Patil. But before leaving, he noted that Sanjay Bansod was missing in the camp that left.

The flight finally took off. The initial plan of taking them to Gujarat was changed, and the plane flew towards a different destination...

4.00 p.m., BJP State Headquarters, Nariman Point, Mumbai

Minutes after the flight took off, Devendra Fadnavis reached the BJP Office where celebrations had already begun. This was the second such celebration outside the party office within a span of one month. On 24 October, he would have never thought that he will return to power in such a dramatic manner. The newly sworn-in Chief Minister walked amid bursting of crackers and playing of dhols.

'All allies are with us except one,' Fadnavis started without naming the Shiv Sena. 'Ajit Pawar with his MLAs have supported us and we will provide a stable government in Maharashtra for the next five years, and will work for the betterment of farmers,' he announced. The confidence on his face was, however, still missing.

Fadnavis concluded by saying something that left many wondering: '*Modi hai toh mumkin hai* (Everything is possible when Modi is around)'. Fadnavis had to take oath with the person who he had been fighting against all throughout his political career. The secret swearing-in had already led to questions being raised about the biggest USP he had—his integrity. Fadnavis, who had became a poster boy of non-corrupt political leadership, was now accused of being power hungry. A person who could go to the extent of joining forces with the man he accused as the epitome of corruption... By going beyond just expressing gratitude, he was trying to send out a message that he was not alone in the scheme of things; his party bosses were involved as well.

Y.B. Chavan Centre, Nariman Point, Mumbai

The second round of the NCP meeting started under Pawar's direction. All MLAs from every corner of the state were summoned to Mumbai. Outside the Y.B. Chavan Centre, some or the other MLA was arriving every 30–40 minutes.

Counter-reaction was the only thing that was needed for course correction. A decision needed to be taken on Ajit Pawar for his 'anti-party activity'. Despite most of the MLAs now deciding to return to the party fold, Ajit's rebellion was still worrying because he was still the leader of the legislative party. He had submitted the letter of support in the same capacity. If Ajit continued in that capacity, things would be easier for him, as his letter would be considered authentic and all MLAs will have to follow the whip issued by him. If the MLAs defy the whip, it would have led to the disqualification of all these MLAs. It would have been a catch-22 situation!

Two big decisions regarding Ajit Pawar were on their way. The party was, however, waiting to hear from the three emissaries—Dilip Walse-Patil, Hasan Mushrif and Sunil Tatkare—who had gone to meet Ajit. But the only message they got from Ajit was, 'Let's see'. As the trio arrived at the Y.B. Chavan Centre, cameras mobbed them. There was another car that followed them to the meeting venue. The party workers were shocked, surprised and angry at once to see the person who got out of that car. It was none other than Dhananjay Munde, the man who was witness to the entire plot from the moment it started.

Known as a close aide of Ajit Pawar, it was Dhananjay's house that Ajit had chosen to carry out the deal. All MLAs had been brought to Dhananjay's house before being taken to Raj Bhavan for the swearing-in. Dhananjay was conspicuous by his absence since the previous night. Even as the drama unfolded after the swearing-in, he had preferred to stay out of reach. But after the three emissaries met Ajit at his brother's house, a message was also conveyed to Dhananjay.

As Dhananjay entered the Y.B. Chavan Centre, angry party workers started shouting slogans against him. Some even charged into him, shouting *'Gaddaar*! (traitor)'. Dhananjay went to the fifth floor to meet Sharad Pawar. Pawar stared straight into his eyes and asked him what misadventure he was up to. Dhananjay tried to explain the same story as other rebel MLAs. He had gone with Ajit, who had called him in the capacity of the leader of the legislative party, and that he had no option but to believe Ajit. Pawar heard him out, slightly in disbelief, but this wasn't the time to cross-question. All rebel MLAs had been welcomed back into the party fold unconditionally.

The moment the mission to get back Ajit started, other rebels started feeling the heat. Dilip Bankar, who was supposed to board the private jet, excused himself and at around 5 p.m., he tweeted his support to Sharad Pawar. 'I have full faith in the leadership of Sharad Pawar, I am with the party. I went to Raj Bhavan because Ajit Pawar asked me to. I had no clue of what was going to happen there.. I am not against the stand of the party...' Bankar tweeted. Manikrao Kokate too tweeted on similar lines. 'I am not against the party line. I went to Raj Bhavan on the orders of Ajit Pawar. I had to obey as he was the Legislative Party leader. I had no idea of what was going to happen. I am with the party and will not change my decision,' Kokate tagged Sharad Pawar and Supriya Sule in his tweet.

Within an hour, another close aide of Ajit Pawar, Datta (Mama) Bharne reached the meeting spot. The list of those developing cold feet was growing. Balasaheb Patil, too, contacted the party and pledged his loyalty. By now, Pawar had struck off nine of 14 names from the list; there were still five to be traced. If nine MLAs had returned on their own, bringing back the remaining five was going to be nothing less than a thriller.

4.30 p.m., Hotel Lalit, Andheri

Immediately after the swearing-in, Shiv Sena MLAs gathered at the hotel's cafeteria for breakfast at 9.30 a.m. Some MLAs had been vocal against going with the Congress and NCP. Prominent among them were Koregaon MLA Mahesh Shinde, Khanapur MLA Anil Babar, Guhagar MLA Bhaskar Jadhav, who had recently jumped from the NCP, and Shiv Sena's Shambhuraj Desai. They had, in fact, strongly batted for going with the BJP. You could see that these MLAs were tensed, as they could sense a big question mark staring at their political career.

A minister's PA, sipping his morning tea sitting on a table behind the MLAs, sensed the anxiety in the talk. A couple of them were blaming the situation on the decision to go with the Congress and the NCP. Some of them assertively proposed opening up communication lines with the BJP. The PA immediately came out and called his boss, alerting him about the discussion. A message was conveyed to Uddhav that he needed to step in and speak to the MLAs.

After his self-imposed solitary confinement, Uddhav arrived at Hotel Lalit at 4.30 p.m. to interact with his MLAs. They had been watching the drama on television and had also tried to get a sense of things on the ground from their sources. Any update was only adding to the already perplexed situation.

Uddhav Thackeray first asked his MLAs if they were afraid, to which they responded in the negative in chorus. 'Things have changed but it is not going to affect us at all. Our dream will come true. Just be calm. Pawar Sahab and Congress are with us,' Uddhav assured his MLAs.

Adversities bring people together. The Shiv Sena, known as a party of fighters, was looking more cohesive than ever. The solidarity was not just within the party. All three parties were working in tandem.

Sahar Hotel, Near the Domestic Airport

Meanwhile, just as Uddhav Thackeray and his team were on their way to Hotel Lalit, Eknath Shinde received a call from NCP leader Shashikant Shinde. Shashikant had been at the airport, tapping the movements of his party men who had joined the rebellion. He had got a tip off from his sources that one of the missing NCP MLAs, Sanjay Bansode, had been traced. He was kept at Hotel Sahar near the domestic airport. Shashikant told Eknath that around 100–150 men, which included BJP workers and some private security guards, were guarding the hotel. It wasn't going to be possible for Shashikant to get Bansode out of the citadel alone. Eknath immediately made a few phone calls and a few vehicles and 'core' Shivsainiks rushed to Hotel Sahar.

In what looked like a scene from a South Indian movie, a

convoy of Thane Shivsainiks made a grand entry into Hotel Sahar. Eknath, along with two armed bodyguards, entered the hotel lobby. A former autorickshaw driver and someone who was trained under the dreaded Shivsainik, the late Anand Dighe, confrontations like these were not new for Eknath. He, in fact, is referred to as 'Bhai' in his party circles, a term not just used for elder brother but also for someone who is feared.

Bhai confronted the BJP Youth Wing leader Mohit Bhartiya (Kambhoj) in the hotel lobby. Forgetting that he is a senior leader and a former minister, he snapped his fingers and charged into Kambhoj, uttering some typical Marathi abuses.[44] In the meantime, Shashikant went to Bansode's room and got him down. Bansode was almost stashed into the car, as Kambhoj and his men looked helplessly.

The convoy zoomed towards Hotel Lalit. Bansode was taken to the room Aditya Thackeray was in. Milind Narvekar then connected Bansode with Sharad Pawar on the phone line. An almost scared Bansode assured Sharad Pawar that he is with the party.[45]

With Bansode in the middle, escorted by Eknath Shinde on one side and Milind Narvekar on the other, and Shashikant Shinde in the front seat, the fleet entered Y.B. Chavan Centre and presented the rebel MLA in front of Sharad Pawar.

Hotel Lalit, Andheri

While the NCP and Shiv Sena were battling it out to bring back the rebel NCP MLAs, the BJP camp wasn't lagging behind either. They were now eyeing the independents supporting Shiv Sena. The initial response wasn't positive, but then they managed to hook Narendra Bhondekar, the independent MLA from Bhandara.

Devendra Fadnavis's close aide from Bhandara-Gondia, Parinay Fuke established links with Bhondekar. After a few phone calls, Bhondekar agreed to come out of Hotel Lalit. It was, however, not going to be easy to come out of the fortress guarded strongly

---

[44] Source-based information on condition of anonymity.
[45] Source-based information on condition of anonymity.

by Shivsainiks. In the hustle-bustle of the evening, Bhondekar got out of his hotel room. Speaking on his mobile phone, he walked towards the lobby and slowly started to move out. He was immediately stopped by Shivsainiks. Bhondekar informed that he was on a personal call with a family member. He then kept loitering around talking on the phone as his eyes kept a close watch on those guarding him. At an opportune moment, Bhondekar gave a slip to the Shiv Sena guards and came out to where a car was already waiting for him.

The moment Bhondekar got into the car, it rushed out of the hotel. A few moments later, the Shiv Sena leaders got to know about the escape and Eknath Shinde was left red-faced.

The BJP now had an additional MLA in its kitty.

Y.B. Chavan Centre, Nariman Point, Mumbai

With eight of the rebel MLAs present in the NCP meeting chaired by Sharad Pawar and two on their way, only four MLAs along with Ajit Pawar were still missing. The tables had been turned and the game was very much in Pawar's hand now. It was now time to quash the revolt on technical grounds. Ajit Pawar's appointment as the leader of the legislative party gave him some rights, including taking decisions on behalf of the party. The BJP camp had already started to hint at the constitutional role of the legislative party leader. Ajit was entitled to extend support, and it would be the Speaker's prerogative to accept it. The first thing that needed to be done was to remove Ajit from the post. A unanimous decision was taken to do so. A trusted lieutenant was needed to shoulder the responsibility. Jayant Patil was entrusted with the job.

Having being caught off guard, the NCP took another big decision. It decided to shift all its MLAs to a secure place. All the MLAs were be taken to Hotel Renaissance in Powai, Mumbai. Hotel Renaissance, incidentally, was the same hotel that, not very long ago, had witnessed the political drama of Karnataka.

8.00 p.m., Supreme Court, New Delhi

Till now, the battle was being fought in the mind and on the ground, but the tripartite alliance wanted to fight it legally as well. The decision was taken immediately after Uddhav met Sharad Pawar at Y.B. Chavan Centre. The matter was discussed with Ahmed Patel and Congress took the lead in pursuing the legal battle.

By evening, the writ petition demanding the quashing of the Maharashtra Governor B.S. Koshyari's decision to invite Devendra Fadnavis to form the government had been prepared. The petition also demanded further direction to invite the Shiv Sena, Congress and NCP coalition as they were the majority to form the next government.

The petition alleged that the 'Governor acted in a partisan manner and has made a mockery of the high office. He has belittled the constitutional office of the Governor and has allowed himself to be a pawn in the BJP's illegal usurpation of power.' There was no scope of waiting for another day, so the three parties sought an urgent hearing on their plea. Senior Supreme Court lawyer Devdutt Kamat reached the Registrar's office at the Supreme Court with the request. The Chief Justice of India, incidentally from Maharashtra, Sharad Bobade was not in Delhi; he had gone to Tirupati.

At around 8.25 p.m., the petition was accepted. In the meantime, Congress's Randeep Surjewala also reached the Supreme Court. Other senior leaders of the Congress and legal eagles like Kapil Sibal, who was in Jaipur, and Abhishek Manu Singhvi, who was in Ahmedabad, were asked to return to Delhi immediately.

The Supreme Court decided to hear the case on an urgent basis on Sunday. Surjewala informed the press that the petitioners had asked for an urgent floor test.

The bench for the hearing was decided. It was going to be Justice N.V. Ramana, Justice Ashok Bhushan and Justice Sanjiv Khanna. Maharashtra's political drama was now going to be played at Court no. 2 on Sunday.

Hotel Renaissance, Powai, Mumbai

At around 11.15 p.m., buses carrying NCP MLAs reached Hotel Renaissance. At around 1 a.m., the NCP MLA from Ahmednagar, Sangram Jagtap received a phone call. Hotel Renaissance is a huge property. As Jagtap was speaking on his phone, he slowly started strolling towards the gate. The group on guard found his movement to be suspicious and alerted the leaders present in the vicinity. Their doubt was right. The moment he came closer to the gate, Jagtap's movements gained momentum. The NCP team followed him. As he stepped out of the gate, a car started moving towards him. Just as he was about to open the doors of the car, he was intercepted. Jagtap informed them that he was only going out for some 'fresh air', to which one of the team members replied that there was enough fresh air inside. Sangram Jagtap was then taken inside the hotel. An attempt to hijack another MLA from the tripartite alliance was aborted.

Silver Oak Estate

Taking into account the MLAs who had returned to the party fold after the rebellion and those with whom a proper communication had been set up, the NCP's number was now standing at 49.

Sharad Pawar got a tip off in the afternoon about the whereabouts of the four MLAs who had been taken to Delhi. They had been kept in a tightly guarded hotel in Gurugram in NCR. To bring them back from another state was not going to be child's play.

Sharad Pawar wanted all his MLAs back by hook or by crook. But the biggest question was: Who will steer the mission? One thing that Pawar was sure about was that it had to be a local leader. The Shiv Sena had no presence in Gurugram and the Congress had no big name there to helm such a risk. Moreover, the entire operation had to be kept out of media glare.

Sonia Doohan's name was suggested for the daring mission. Knowing her courage and calibre, Sonia, National President of the NCP's Students Wing, was chosen for the tough job. The 27-year-old 'Jaatni' had to get back the last batch of MLAs from the claws of the BJP, at any cost.

♦

As everything was slowly settling down, the man who had been quiet the whole day now broke into action. Around midnight, Ajit Pawar came out in his car and started moving towards the suburbs. He gave the media cameras a slip and reached Vile Parle. As the political drama was now going to be fought in the courtroom, Ajit decided to seek legal opinion.

DAY 32: SUNDAY, 24 NOVEMBER 2019

9:00 a.m., Silver Oak Estate

NCP leaders Jayant Patil and Chhagan Bhujbal reached Sharad Pawar's residence. The situation had improved in the last 24 hours. The rebellion had been quelled by the evening and the only thing that remained to be done was to get the four MLAs and the commander of the mutiny to return. The NCP hadn't given up on Ajit Pawar yet.

Sharad Pawar had adopted a three-pronged strategy for tackling Ajit. First, get the MLAs back; second, get the legal points sorted and third, deal with Ajit as a family member and not as a politician. Supriya Sule, who had had an emotional outburst earlier, had calmed down by now. Some family members had already started approaching Ajit, appealing to him to return. Supriya's WhatsApp status read: 'power comes and goes, only relationships matter'. She also said that it was one of the toughest days of her life. Her tone now was more of burying the hatchet.

Rohit Pawar too, made an emotional appeal to uncle Ajit through a post on Facebook: 'Since my childhood, I have seen how Pawar Saheb looked after the family... After my grandfather Appasaheb Pawar passed away, it was Saheb who comforted my father Rajendra. I have also seen how, when Ajit Pawar lost his father it was Pawar Saheb who looked after him, showering father's love on him. Ajit Dada too reciprocated it by standing up for Pawar Saheb whenever he was in crisis'.

'Old times should remain like they were. Ajit dada should accept Pawar Saheb's decision and come back... Pawar Saheb never mixes politics with family and he never will... At a time when haughty rulers are trying to silence his voice, it's our duty to stand firm with Pawar Saheb...' Rohit further appealed in his post.

While the NCP leaders were busy getting back their party members, the Pawar family was now active in getting back its family member.

◆

The first thing that the NCP did was to send across the letter appointing Jayant Patil as the legislature party leader to the Governor. Immediately after intimating the Governor, a copy of the same was sent to the Supreme Court lawyers representing the party.

Dilip Walse-Patil reached Ajit Pawar's house at 10.45 a.m. for yet another round of persuasion. The message was yet again conveyed that there was no point in holding on to the rebellion. Walse-Patil was soon joined by Jayant Patil. Ajit was in no mood to relent. On the contrary, he advised the NCP that it was better to remain with the BJP. He said that in the present situation, the BJP was the only viable option for the NCP rather than hanging on to a government that had a bleak future.[46] Walse-Patil and Jayant Patil left Ajit's residence empty-handed.

TV crews were eager to know whether the meeting has resulted in any positive result for the NCP. Jayant Patil had no reactions to offer; he only said a few lines from the famous poetry by Sohanlal Dwivedi, 'Koshish karne walon ki haar nahi hoti... (Those who make the efforts never fail.)'

11.30 a.m., Room No. 2, Supreme Court, New Delhi

A battery of the country's top legal experts was going to appear for the petitioners in this case—Congress, NCP and Shiv Sena. Rarely has the apex court worked on a holiday. But the case was

---

[46] Source-based information on condition of anonymity.

such that not just Maharashtra but the entire nation was closely watching every development. One thing was certain—whatever the final outcome of this drama, the court would be playing the most crucial role.

Shiv Sena MP Gajanan Kirtikar arrived in court, closely followed by Prithviraj Chavan and Randeep Surjewala. Kapil Sibal was going to appear for the Shiv Sena, Abhishek Manu Singhvi for the NCP and Devdutt Kamat for the Congress. Mukul Rohatgi was going to appear for Devendra Fadnavis.

At 11.33 a.m., Kapil Sibal started the arguments. 'We apologize for troubling the court on a Sunday but we are not the only ones to blame,' he began with a jibe. Sibal then narrated the entire course of events from the election results to the break-up of the pre-poll alliance between the BJP and Shiv Sena.

'On 22 November, at 7 p.m., a press conference was held where we said Shiv Sena, NCP and Congress have agreed on a Common Minimum Programme and will stake claim to form the government...What happened after the announcement is bizarre. I have never seen anything like this. The Governor advises and [the] President Rule is revoked. There is no cabinet meeting, as if there is a national emergency... [At] 5 a.m. it's revoked. And 8 a.m. two people are sworn in. What happened is shrouded in mystery. What documents were given? What was the nature of the invitation? On the face of it, it's not just bizarre but it suggests that the Governor was acting under direct instructions. Otherwise such things are not done...' Sibal argued. 'If we have announced at 7 p.m. that we are going to stake the claim, how has someone else been invited? My first argument is that the act of the Governor smacks of bias, [and is] malafide. [It] [v]iolates all norms set out by judgments from time to time,' said Sibal. He further added, 'But what's needed now is that if they want to prove majority they should hold a floor test.'

A dialogue between the Bench and Kapil Sibal ensued. Sibal then referred to the Karnataka verdict of May 2018. 'Please see the Karnataka case. The order—what happened there. On 16th May 2018 there were certain communications addressed by the

Karnataka Governor to Yeddyurappa. We challenged them on 17th May, then on 18th May, and said [to] have the floor test on 19th May...In this case there is not even a letter from the Governor. The Maharashtra Governor has not given a letter to hold a floor test. We know nothing about this,' said Sibal.

Justice Ramana then asked the Solicitor General whether he was appearing for the Governor. He responded that he had been served with an advance copy as the Solicitor General and that he did not have any instruction from the Governor. He wasn't clear if the Governor was represented through him.

Mukul Rohatgi then came up with an intervention and informed that he was filing an intervention application. He began his argument: 'Political parties do not have any fundamental rights. They should have appeared before the High Court. There is already a government in place. There should not have been a hearing on a Sunday.' This was shot down by Justice Ramana, who said it was the discretion of the Chief Justice of India and that they had to hear the matter.

The Solicitor General too raised a point similar to the one raised by Rohatgi: 'Petitioners moved SC [Supreme Court] under Article 32. Political parties do not have fundamental rights. They should have gone to the HC [High Court]. Earlier orders were passed on pleas by individual persons.'

Kapil Sibal smiled at that argument. While appearing in a similar case of Karnataka, Sibal too had raised a similar point of political parties having no fundamental rights. Justice Khanna was quick to point out the irony of the matter: 'The irony is that this issue was raised in the Karnataka case by Mr Sibal. Now he is on the other side...'

Sibal then read out the Karnataka order of 2018. He also mentioned the Goa order to hold the floor test. 'All these orders are consistent. That you must hold a floor test... They are not holding a floor test because they want to do something else in the intervening period,' he said.

Abhishek Manu Singhvi then rose for arguments. He argued

that the Governor's role is to satisfy himself—through a physical document with signatures or a physical verification of the MLAs. 'How did the Governor take a decision overnight when the 7 p.m. press conference had said we are staking claim? Did he verify?' he questioned. 'What's the base for the Deputy Chief Minister and Chief Minister being sworn in? Ajit Pawar said that my MLAs have come with me. Yesterday there was an NCP meeting where 41 MLAs were present. When 41 MLAs signed and expelled Ajit Pawar, how are they claiming they have support?' he further questioned.

Presenting the letter submitted by Jayant Patil to the Governor earlier in the morning, Singhvi made further arguments. He quoted the Bommai judgment, saying that a floor test was best, adding that the idea was to prevent horse trading.

Singhvi also referred to the Anil Jha case, as well as the Jharkhand, Uttarakhand, Goa and Karnataka cases where he had appeared in similar situations. He stated how orders from the court were clear, important safeguards were created, a procedure was laid down and a pro tem Speaker was appointed in the Karnataka case. He then quoted the most important part from the case: 'The order clearly said that voting will not be by secret ballot. It will be open. There would be live telecast of the proceedings. [It was the same] In Goa case also. This is the most consistent thread of the SC to have a floor test immediately... Court can order floor test today or tomorrow—a composite floor test,' Singhvi said.

Rohatgi, appearing for BJP MLAs, came into the argument. 'The correct procedure is that notice should be issued, time should be given for reply. There is no tearing hurry to hear the matter...For 17 days you don't form the government. If you don't lift a finger and someone else stakes claim, the Governor will jolly well invite them to form the government. The choice of the Governor is not subject to judicial review...' he argued. He further stated that the Governor has some amount of discretion. Moreover, while the floor test was an option, the Court cannot direct a constitutional functionary to hold a floor test. He further added that it's the Governor's duty to choose a CM, and this is the Governor's individual discretion and is not guided by the cabinet. According to Rohatgi, the Governor's decision is immune from review.

To this, Justice Ramana responded, 'The Governor cannot just appoint anyone and it cannot be questioned. All that has been settled by judgments.'

'There's a prayer to direct the Governor to invite them. I've never seen such a plea,' said Rohatgi.

Justice Ramana responded, 'In this court, the sky is the limit for prayers. People come here saying "make me PM" also.'

Rohatgi further argued, 'Why did they file something in the middle of the night and disturb everyone? The Karnataka order is an order without a judgment on what the law is. If the court orders the Speaker to hold a floor test, it affects work inside the house...

'There is a reference made to a constitution bench on the issue of whether the SC can pass directions to a Speaker acting in a quasi-judicial authority. If that is under question, we are talking about the highest constitutional authority. We should get time to file a reply and we should be allowed to spend the rest of our Sunday in peace,' Rohatgi concluded.

After hearing everyone out, the Bench decided to issue notices to all the respondents—the Centre, the Maharashtra government, Devendra Fadnavis and Ajit Pawar. The Centre, though the Solicitor General, was asked to produce the Governor's decision letter and Fadnavis's claim letter the next day.

'The Interim Application to conduct a floor test has to be considered after perusing the order of the Governor and the letter of Fadnavis,' the Bench said, announcing that the matter would now be heard at 10.30 a.m. on Monday.

Hotel Renaissance, Powai

Manikrao Kokate, the NCP MLA who was with Ajit Pawar at the swearing-in the previous day, reached Hotel Renaissance. He, like several other MLAs, was returning to the party fold. He had already tweeted on Saturday evening that he was with the party.

After the Supreme Court proceedings felt like they were going the Karnataka way, the NCP started looking confident. Nawab Malik was the first to react to the developments in Supreme Court. 'We had 49 MLAs yesterday. Two more have got in touch since. We are even sure that Ajit Pawar will rectify his mistake and return...We have the numbers. We will defeat them on the floor of the house. But we also demand that Devendra Fadnavis should resign,' he said.

A relieved Sharad Pawar with daughter Supriya Sule left for Hotel Renaissance where all the MLAs were kept. After a short phone call with Pawar, it was decided that Uddhav Thackeray too will join Pawar and have a word with the NCP MLAs. After such dramatic developments, it was necessary for Pawar and Uddhav to show a united face.

Before holding talks with the MLAs, Pawar and Uddhav had a long discussion with Dhananjay Munde at the hotel. After all, he was privy to all the information of the coup and they wanted to gather as much information as they could.

It was a rare moment for NCP leaders—they were going to be addressed by the Shiv Sena President, whom they had criticized not very long ago. The politics of the state had changed radically in the last few days. Uddhav began with a question for the NCP MLAs: 'Are you afraid or under any stress?' Some of them admitted that they were being constantly approached by mystery names to switch over. Uddhav told the MLAs to not worry about his alliance with their party: 'It is not an alliance for short-term gains.... This alliance will last longer. We have the numbers and we will form a stable government,' he said. Sharad Pawar too boosted the morale of the MLAs and appealed to them to remain calm and patient.

After meeting the MLAs, Sharad Pawar and Uddhav Thackeray had a closed-door meeting. As suggested by the legal team, it was decided that all MLAs will sign and file an affidavit pledging support to the MVA government. The procedure began.

After spending four to five hours at the Hotel Renaissance, Uddhav moved towards Hotel Lalit to meet all the Shiv Sena MLAs.

Hotel Lalit, Andheri

The hotel had witnessed some drama before Uddhav's arrival. The Shiv Sena camp was extra vigilant while guarding the MLAs of all three parties. The BJP camp had not given up their attempts of winning over some more MLAs from Shiv Sena. The team assigned the task were zeroing in on weak links. Some close friends of the MLAs were also approached to mediate and bring them over to the other side. Shahaji Bapu Patil, an MLA from Sangola in Solapur district, was next on the BJP's radar. The person assigned the task was Vitthal Patil, a politician cum leader of a waarkari organization. Apart from delivering sermons (kirtan), Patil is often seen in the Mantralay for liaison-related works. The man on mission secretly sneaked into Hotel Lalit accompanied by a businessman. The duo managed to reach Shahaji Patil's room. But to Vitthal's bad luck, an official present there recognized the businessman, as he had once raided his premises. A message was immediately passed on to Shiv Sena leaders guarding the hotel and an SOS was sent to Munna Shaikh. Munna, a feeble-looking man, was in charge of the security of the MLA. Taking Munna at face value would be a mistake. A staunch Shiv Sena worker from Thane, stories about his daring adventures are well known. Munna immediately went into Shahaji Patil's room, and shooting expletives at Vitthal Patil and the businessman, he grabbed the duo by their necks and brought them before Shiv Sena leaders in the lobby.[47] Patil feigned ignorance and said that he was there to meet him casually. After issuing a warning to him, the duo was let off...

Vasant Smruti, Dadar

The BJP had called a meeting of its legislators at the party's Mumbai office to felicitate the newly sworn-in Chief Minister Devendra Fadnavis. As the meeting began, BJP leaders claimed that 118 MLAs were present for the meeting, a claim that wasn't proved. There

---

[47] Source-based information on condition of anonymity.

was a buzz that Ajit Pawar may attend the meeting, but it proved to be a rumour.

Instead, Ajit took to social media. Close to 36 hours after he took oath, Ajit Pawar updated his Twitter bio from 'former Deputy Chief Minister and MLA, Baramati' to 'Deputy Chief Minister of Maharashtra'.

As the BJP meeting was in progress, at 4 p.m., Ajit Pawar started responding to congratulatory tweets, starting with Prime Minister Narendra Modi. He replied to almost every tweet by BJP leaders. He didn't stop at that. He further dropped another bomb on the NCP as he tweeted from his verified handle, 'I am in the NCP and shall always be in the NCP and Sharad Pawar (@PawarSpeaks) Saheb is our leader. Our BJP–NCP alliance shall provide a stable Government in Maharashtra for the next five years which will work sincerely for the welfare of the State and its people. There is absolutely no need to worry, all is well. However a little patience is required. Thank you very much for all your support.'

This was a significant development—not for the statement but for the timing. This tweet came after his meeting with NCP leaders Dilip Walse-Patil and Jayant Patil. Their efforts to woo him back seem to have yeilded no results. On the contrary, Ajit seemed to be in a combative mood. His latest drub to the NCP gave the BJP that much-needed impetus. BJP leader Ashish Shelar emerged out of the meeting. 'We discussed the strategy to win the floor test. We also passed a motion to congratulate Devendra Fadnavis and Ajit Pawar. Ajit Pawar has mentioned on his twitter handle that he is the Deputy Chief Minister and the leader of the NCP. NCP leaders should now understand this that he is the legislative party leader and that he can issue a whip in that capacity,' Shelar said.

With the MLAs supporting Ajit Pawar having almost gone back to the party fold, the BJP was now relying on the role of Ajit Pawar as the leader of Legislative party, wherein he could issue a whip. But that wasn't the only trick the BJP was relying upon. Four men from the party were assigned the task of contacting MLAs from all the three parties.[48] These were not original BJP leaders. They were leaders who had shifted to the BJP from different parties and enjoyed a sizeable clout once... This was going to be BJP's 'operation lotus' in Maharashtra. Narayan Rane, a former Sena man, Radhkrishna Vikhe Patil, the former leader of the Opposition from the Congress, Navi Mumbai strongman Ganesh Naik, and former state president of the NCP Babanrao Pachpute were given responsibility of the operation.

◆

Ajit Pawar's tweet and his unabashed approach that he is still with the NCP was bound to send tremors in the NCP camp. Pawar was quick in rubbishing off his nephew's claim. 'There is no question of forming alliance with the BJP. NCP has unanimously decided to go with Shiv Sena and Congress to form the government. Sh. Ajit Pawar's statement is false, mischievous and misleading in order to spread wrong perception among the people,' Pawar's tweets set the record straight.

JW Marriott Hotel, Andheri

By now, the Congress had come to know of the BJP's attempt to poach its MLAs. An independent was taken away from the Shiv Sena's strong citadel under its nose. With the threat perception looming large, the Congress shifted 30 MLAs to JW Marriott Hotel, where none other than Ahmed Patel was monitoring all the moves.

Earlier in the morning, Patel himself had pumped up the morale of the party MLAs. 'We have come a long way, now let's stay together... we have to defeat the BJP... Central government and the Governor have challenged us, specially Modi and Amit Shah; let's defeat them. We have done lot of hard work. Let's stay united and win,' Patel had told the group of 30 MLAs, who were were slated to be joined by 14 others soon.

The tension in the air was perceptible. Ashok Chavan, who was

---

[48] Source-based information on condition of anonymity.

monitoring the situation, received complaints from some MLAs that they were receiving phone calls to switch sides. He alleged that the BJP was trying to do this: 'Our MLAs are being approached by BJP. They are getting calls. People associated with the BJP are booking rooms and staying in the hotel. Our MLAs are contacted by BJP, but let me assure you that our MLAs are intact. We are not worried about anything, we have the numbers. WE will prove the majority', Chavan told the reporters.

Hotel United 21, Thane

After the legal battle, top leaders from the Shiv Sena got stuck with other developments, slightly taking away their attention from guarding the MLAs. Independent MLAs were turning out to be the vulnerable lot. After one independent MLA was taken away by the BJP camp, extra precautions were taken to safeguard them. Rajkumar Patel, MLA of Bachchu Kadu's Prahaar Janshakti Party, was shifted slightly away to Hotel United 21 in Thane. Kadu had already pledged his party's support to the Shiv Sena. He was actively involved in the political developments. But his MLA needed to be guarded. At this point in time, every MLA mattered.

On Sunday, suddenly, some people barged into the hotel. They informed the staff that they were cops. But all of them were dressed in plain clothes. They demanded the guest register. There was always one person kept at these locations to tip off the higher-ups in the party. With the 'cops' still at the reception, a message was passed on to Rajkumar Patel. He was brought down from the service lift immediately and taken to Yeoor Hills. Rajkumar Patel's transfer from the hotel to Yeoor Hills happened literally in a flash.

Shiv Sena leaders at Hotel Lalit were immediately alerted on how some 'cops' in plain clothes had 'raided' Hotel United 21. Uddhav and the core team were fuming, but it couldn't be ascertained whether they were cops or not...

The development at Hotel Renaissance made them believe the 'cop theory'. A Shiv Sena worker spotted some suspicious movements of two men sitting in the hotel's lobby. The NCP leader Jitendra Awhad and Shiv Sena MP Shrikant Shinde were instantly informed about it. The duo along with other leaders walked towards the two men. Awhad asked them who they were and what they were doing there. One of them replied that they were police officials. Awhad sought their identity cards and they obliged. Awhad examined the ID cards carefully. A furious Awhad then again asked, 'What are you doing here?' One of them replied that they were just 'sitting there'.

'An officer of your rank is sitting here for no reason? Do you think we are fools?' Awhad raised his voice.

The NCP workers also shot a video on their mobile when the cops were intercepted and immediately made it viral. Jitendra Awhad alleged that the cops won't do any such thing unless and until they are instructed by those who are in government.

The atmosphere heated up. The cops were asked to leave the premises.

Hotel Lalit, Andheri

After giving a pep talk to all the NCP MLAs, Uddhav and Aditya left for Hotel Lalit to go into a huddle with their party MLAs. The times were delicate and every moment mattered.

Dressed in a smart formal sky-blue shirt, Uddhav started off by praising the MLAs for putting up a united face so far, even as the developments in the last two days had put everyone's tolerance to a severe test. He further disclosed to his MLAs that RSS leaders had contacted him, but he refused to entertain them as the time to reconsider an alliance with the BJP had already passed.

An independent MLA from Shirol in Kolhapur called to inform Eknath Shinde that a senior top cop of the state had called his brother and issued a warning to not indulge in any political adventure. He claimed that the top cop also threatened to 'open his files' if he supports the Shiv Sena. This needed to be dealt with immediately, but all three parties needed to hold the fort till there was some order from the Supreme Court.

With the incident of the cops 'allegedly spying' at Hotel

Renaissance fresh on his mind, Uddhav himself walked towards the lobby. He appealed to the Shivsainiks to not crowd the lobby area, as anyone could take advantage of the crowd and enter the hotel. He instructed them to be on alert at the inside gate.

Uddhav then had a word with the NCP supremo about the allegations. Earlier in the day, Ashok Chavan had also alleged that Congress MLAs were under threat from BJP. Taking the recent development seriously, the NCP decided to shift out its MLAs from Hotel Renaissance. Buses were immediately brought in, and at around 9.45 p.m. the NCP MLAs were ferried to Hotel Grand Hyatt in Kalina.

10.15 p.m., Varsha

After remaining indoors for the whole day, Ajit Pawar ventured out of his house in south Mumbai at 10 p.m. The newly sworn-in Deputy Chief Minister headed to the CM's residence, where the duo were going to have closed-door discussions. Interestingly, even though all his MLAs had gone back to the party, Ajit was sure that during the floor test, they will vote as per his wish. Fadnavis was slightly wary whether they will be able to stand the pressure, especially with Sharad Pawar himself now helming the political strategy. But Ajit was sure.

Hotel Oberoi, Gurugram

While all this was happening in Maharashtra, another high-voltage drama was playing out some 1,300 km away. Sonia Doohan was already in Gurugram on her mission.

Sharad Pawar's informant had told him that the still-missing MLAs were kept in a 5-star hotel called Oberoi somewhere on the outskirts of Delhi. Sonia and Dheeraj Sharma, the District President of the NCP, teamed up for the task. The first step was to find out the exact location. A couple of calls helped ascertain that the MLAs were kept at the Oberoi hotel in Udyog Vihar Phase 5, Gurugram.

Two teams were formed for accomplishing the task—one under Sonia herself and the other under Dheeraj. Sonia got some girls in her team. They reached Hotel Oberoi around early afternoon only to find it had been turned into a fortress. Sonia gauged the situation cautiously. As she walked towards the hotel lobby, a familiar face caught her attention. The presence of that man confirmed that it was a BJP mission to keep the NCP MLAs under supervision. The person Sonia saw was BJP's district President Bhupendra Singh Chauhan.[49] Sonia immediately hid herself from Bhupendra's sight. If he were to see her, her plan would fall apart.

The NCP team had booked a few rooms in the hotel. The mission had to be accomplished the same day. Sonia started taking a stroll in the hotel premises. Dheeraj Sharma knew some people in the staff. He informed that these MLAs were kept in room nos 5109, 5110 and 5111 on the 5th floor.

Sonia, by now, had done a complete recce of the hotel. Having got the confirmation of the MLAs' presence in the hotel, the details were communicated to the party bosses in Mumbai. Sonia and team got a go-ahead with a piece of advice—whatever happens should be without any fuss or fight.

By afternoon, Dheeraj Sharma brought in his first batch of 25 people inside the hotel. Another team was also kept outside the hotel with seven to eight vehicles on standby. By now, Sonia was successful in getting the information about all the escape routes in the hotel. The internal staff had tipped her off about the staff gate. This, she figured, was possibly the best exit route. There were no CCTV cameras there, plus it was at the back of the hotel. The additional advantage was that one could approach the gate through a staff or service lift. This was zeroed in as the escape route.

At around 5–5.30 p.m., Anil Patil excused himself from the room and managed to escape the hotel. The first team immediately whisked him away and took him to Delhi. As one MLA in their protection went missing, the guards became extra vigilant.

The task became even more difficult now. While she was closely watching every movement of those guarding the MLAs

---

[49] As reported by Sonia Doohan in her interviews with TV and print media.

since the morning, Sonia had realized one unique thing. These guards exchanged their places during lunch or tea time. She felt the exchange of duties was an opportune moment to strike. She kept waiting for it, until 9.30 p.m.

A team wanted to go out for dinner; the other team was about to come. The MLAs were asked to get ready and come out. Cars were ready at the back gate. The moment there was a change of guard, these MLAs started walking towards the pool side staff gate. They were guided by one of Sonia's team members. Sonia took over from there and she immediately rushed towards the exit gate. The MLAs sat in the car with Sonia. But by now, the guards had got an inkling and they started running towards the staff gate with clenched fists. Sonia and the MLAs had, however, driven past the gate. They too started to follow.

After a couple of kilometres, the car took a turn at a deserted location. The car that brought them here was handed over to another person who exchanged a white Fortuner with Sonia. Sonia took over the driver's seat. Being from Gurugram, she knew the city roads well. No wonder then the cars that were following her were given a slip. But this wasn't a moment to celebrate. They had realized that one MLA had been left behind at the hotel. Rather than leaving from the back gate, Narhari Zirwal, MLA from Dindori in Nashik, was taken from the front gate. The MLA who is always clad in a white kurta and loose pyjama with a white gandhi cap is recognizable from any corner.

With an alert sounded out about the escape of the other MLAs, Zirwal and Dhiraj Sharma's team were intercepted at the gate. Zirwal insisted on leaving the hotel. There was a verbal duel between those guarding and the NCP's team. Someone tried to manhandle Zirwal, which led to a scuffle between the two groups. In the pandemonium that followed, Zirwal managed to escape.

Sonia by now had reached 6, Janpath, the residence of her party chief Sharad Pawar. The team had dinner there. The accomplishment of the mission was communicated to the party in Mumbai amid cheers. The MLAs were booked on a 2.40 a.m. flight as there was no point in wasting anymore time. At 5.45 a.m. the next morning, the MLAs reached Mumbai.

Sonia Doohan, the feisty, bold and beautiful Haryanvi girl, had accomplished a near-impossible mission of whisking away MLAs from a well-guarded fortress. The only MLA now out of reach was Ajit Pawar.

DAY 33: MONDAY, 25 NOVEMBER 2019

8.30 a.m., Ajit Pawar's residence, Churchgate

All eyes were going to be on Delhi where the Supreme Court would be resuming the hearing on the Maharashtra political crisis. But before the drama at Supreme Court could begin, the NCP wanted to make yet another attempt at winning over Ajit Pawar. All the MLAs had returned to the party fold. A day after Walse-Patil and Jayant Patil made attempts at persuading Ajit, Chhagan Bhujbal was sent to Ajit's residence. The day was important for two reasons. One, an update was expected from the Supreme Court and two, Devendra Fadnavis was going to take charge as the CM. Ajit was also expected to join him. So, efforts were being made to dissuade him from taking charge.

Chhagan Bhujbal reached early morning with a message that Ajit should hold onto his horses for another day. In case the Supreme Court verdict went against Fadnavis and Ajit, the latter would be left with nowhere to go. At least if he held on and did not take charge, the doors of the NCP would remain open. Bhujbal realized that by now Ajit's confidence in the rebellion had started to crumble. Ajit assured him of thinking about it. The message was passed on to Sharad Pawar, who was in Karad to offer tributes to his political mentor (late) Yashwantrao Chavan.

Vidhan Bhavan, Nariman Point, Mumbai

As an annual ritual, the state's CM, along with other dignitaries, pays homage at the statue of Yashwantrao Chavan, the first Chief Minister of Maharashtra, in the Vidhan Bhavan premises. After taking oath, this would be the first official programme where the new Chief Minister and Deputy Chief Minister would be seen together. After meeting Bhujbal, Ajit Pawar immediately left for Vidhan Bhavan. Fadnavis and Ajit offered floral tributes at Chavan's statue. Other NCP leaders too had reached Vidhan Bhavan by now.

As per the BJP's strategy, Devendra Fadnavis and Ajit Pawar were to take charge in the first half of the day itself and, to diffuse the present political situation, announce a relief package to farmers. NCP had sensed the plan and hence planned a counter-strategy to keep Ajit busy in talks.

After the function, Fadnavis left while Ajit Pawar went inside the Vidhan Bhavan with Bhujbal, Tatkare and Walse-Patil.

Mantralay State Headquarters

At around 11 a.m., Fadnavis's convoy reached Mantralay. Fadnavis was going to take charge of the CM's office. A few BJP leaders and a few Ajit Pawar supporters had already reached there with flowers to welcome the new Chief Minister and Deputy CM. With his Principal Secretary Bhushan Gagrani by his side, Fadnavis took charge in the same office that he had quit not long ago. But his new Deputy was still not to be seen.

According to the initial plan, the Chief Minister and Deputy Chief Minister were going to hold a meeting, but the plan was dropped as there were no signs of Ajit Pawar coming to take charge. Fadnavis was now getting restless and he sent a message with Babanrao Pachpute, a former NCP leader who was now in BJP. Pachpute was once close to Ajit Pawar. He went to Vidhan Bhavan, but Bhujbal, Walse-Patil and Tatkare Pachpute allowed him to only give his greetings and then asked him to leave. With no positive indication coming from Ajit Pawar, Fadnavis decided to leave from Mantralay.

Sansad Bhawan, New Delhi

A major part of the action on Monday was going to take place in the national capital. After having being missed actively in the game, Congress leader Priyanka Gandhi made her entry in the Maharashtra political game through a tweet. Even before the courtroom drama or the Parliament was convened, she attacked the BJP over the Maharashtra crisis. 'TV channels are showing that the BJP is disregarding institutions and the constitution in Maharashtra to repeat the same game it played in Karnataka. Twelve thousand farmers in Maharashtra have committed suicide. BJP government did not help them. Have we reached the stage of open kidnapping of the mandate?' Priyanka's tweet was a precursor to what was going to happen in the Parliament through that day. The Leader of the Congress in the Lok Sabha, Adhir Ranjan Chowdhury, and Congress's Chief Whip in Lok Sabha, K. Suresh, submitted an adjournment motion notice in the House to discuss the Maharashtra issue. Apart from the Congress, the Indian Union Muslim League and Trinamool Congress also gave an adjournment motion notice in the Lok Sabha over the 'sabotage of democracy in Maharashtra'. As the Supreme Court hearing began, protests started in the Parliament premises near Mahatma Gandhi's statue. Congress President Sonia Gandhi too joined the protest.

The Lok Sabha witnessed noisy scenes over the issue and following the ruckus, it was adjourned till noon. A ruckus was also witnessed in the Rajya Sabha as opposition benches raised the issue of the Governor's role in Maharashtra. The opposition parties had submitted a notice seeking the setting aside of the business of the house to take up the issue in Maharashtra. But Chairman of the Rajya Sabha, Venkaiah Naidu, rejected the notice. Following commotion on the issue, the Rajya Sabha too was adjourned.

10.20 a.m., Raj Bhavan, Malabar Hill

Moments before the Supreme Court hearing began, leaders from all three parties went into an urgent huddle. Eknath Shinde of the Shiv Sena, Jayant Patil of the NCP, and Balasaheb Thorat and Ashok Chavan of the Congress held a joint meeting, immediately after which they, along with their MLAs, reached Raj Bhavan to submit a letter to the Governor staking claim to form the government.

Abu Azmi of the Samajwadi Party with two MLAs also reached the Governor's house with a letter to support the claim. While staking claim, the letter said,

> On 23/11/2019, Devendra Fadnavis took oath as the Chief Minister of Maharashtra. But earlier he had shown the inability to form the government for the lack of number. He will need to prove majority again.
>
> Even now he has no majority and will not be able to prove it. Hence we, Shiv Sena, are staking claim to form the government.
>
> We are also attaching herewith the list of MLAs from Congress, NCP, Independents and others supporting us. We have enough numbers to prove the majority and hence we should be invited to form the government.

After coming out of the Raj Bhavan, leaders from all the three parties addressed the media, claiming that they had the numbers. 'Our demand for a few more days was rejected earlier by Governor; this is against democracy. Our demand should be considered instantly. If they had the number, then they would have taken the oath in daylight. Fadnavis should resign,' demanded Eknath Shinde. Jayant Patil confidently claimed, 'We have informed the Governor that we have 162 MLAs...'

Hotel Lalit, Andheri

The problem with Hotel Lalit was that it had more than one gate. This was one of the major hurdles in keeping a watch on the movements of strangers. The party cadre was strictly warned against creating any nuisance for the tourists/patrons staying in the hotel. But given the volatile nature of the situation and recent incidents of poaching, the Sena was in no mood to take any chances. Moreover, the booking at Hotel Lalit was made at the last moment and was only for three days. A safe option needed to be found. One such place was zeroed in—Hotel Lemon Tree near Saki Naka in Andheri. The hotel had just one main entrance. The construction work outside the main gate had already put restrictions on the entry, making it very easy to track almost every small move. All Shiv Sena MLAs were shifted there.

Supreme Court, New Delhi

With the first hearing on the unprecented political crisis in Maharashtra held on a holiday, the hearing was set to resume on Monday. Shiv Sena leaders Anil Desai, Arvind Sawant and Gajanan Kirtikar were among the first to arrive. Randeep Surjewala and Prithviraj Chavan of Congress and Majeed Memon of NCP too reached the courtroom.

While Mukul Rohatgi was appearing for Devendra Fadnavis, Advocate Manindar Singh was going to appear for Ajit Pawar.

The Solicitor General Tushar Mehta submitted the letter of the Governor to the Court, saying the issue to be considered was whether the Court can substitute the decision taken by the Governor.

'After the declaration of poll results, what was in front of the Governor was that there was a pre-poll alliance. BJP was largest party in the house. Shiv Sena, which had pre-poll alliance with BJP, has 56 seats. NCP had 54 seats, Congress with 44 seats,' the Solicitor General said. 'The Court is being told about horse trading... but in this case the Governor thought maybe the whole stable has been stolen. [The] Governor waited for several days and gave opportunities to three parties to form the government. After their denial, he recommends President['s] [R]ule. The [O]pposition till date does not approach the Governor to form government [sic],' he added.

Rohatgi then showed the original copies of the Governor's order that included the BJP's letter to the Governor, informing that Fadnavis had been elected as the leader of the house. The letter was signed by all 105 BJP MLAs and some Independents. He also presented a letter of support given by Ajit Pawar, which had signatures of 54 MLAs.

Solicitor General Tushar Mehta then read out Ajit Pawar's letter of 22 November. 'All elected MLAs have unanimously elected me as CLP and have given rights to form the government to me,' Ajit's letter said.

The Solicitor General continued: 'The Governor having received these letters, with the suggestion that the largest party be invited to form the government. He requested the [P]resident to revoke the President's rule... [The] Governor noted that Fadnavis has the support of 170 MLAs. The [C]ourt should appreciate that the Governor in his wisdom invited the largest party to form the government. [The] Governor does not have to go into a fishing inquiry. He could not have any other information when the leader of a party has given a letter.'

The Supreme Court questioned who the first letter was from. To this, the Solicitor General responded that the first letter was by Fadnavis, staking claim.

'As far as the Governor is concerned, he has no reason to disprove of this... The Governor knows there is some sort of welding going on outside. So he says you form the government and prove it within the floor of the house. [T]here is no need for the litigant to come to court and say, "Hold the floor test within 24 hours or we will disperse"? [The] Governor wants to know how this is possible.'

Mukul Rohatgi appearing for Fadnavis and BJP then joined in.

[The] Position is now very clear. My pre-poll partner turning into a foe from a friend. [The] Governor waited for someone to form government. NCP CLP leader Ajit Pawar shows me signatures of 53 people and offers to join me. I go to Governor and say I have 170. No allegation that any of these documents are forged. [W]hatever is happening in Pawar family is not my concern. One Pawar is with me, one is in court today. They are not saying these signatures are forged. They are blaming us for horse trading. They are the ones indulging in horse trading. This is completely different from the Yeddyurappa case,' he said.

The Solicitor General stated that in a matter of this nature where legal and constitutional issues were involved, they should be given time to file a reply.

Rohatgi went on further, 'I want to put this on affidavit. When there is a letter with signatures involved, the Governor has no other choice. He's talking about 170 MLAs. It's not [the] Governor['s] job to ask people. He [would] had asked people had nobody came to form government. I'm sure they will say these signatures are meant for something else. But the signatures are before the Governor.'

The Bench clarified that they weren't saying anything about the Governor, and the issue was different.

Rohatgi said that the issue had been raised in the previous hearing where Singhvi had questioned how the Governor had accepted the signatures. '[Y]ou're talking about the past. Is anyone appearing for Mr Pawar? Yesterday there was an appearance on behalf of the NCP saying that we are not supporting [the Fadnavis government]. That's the situation before us... The suggestion is that the Chief Minister no longer enjoys support of the house. So shouldn't there be a floor test?' said Justice Khanna.

Rohatgi responded: 'I'm saying their attack on Governor is unfounded... Floor test is imperative. [The] Governor has said in his letter there should be floor test. Now that it's clear that there is no malafide in the [G]overnor['s] decision, should the [C]ourt act as an appellate court and say hold floor test in one day or 10 days? When there is no substance in the allegations, should the court interfere? Floor test can happen whenever. It is the discretion of the [S]peaker. Should this [C]ourt in judicial review pass orders? They say they have 54 today. I may have 54 tomorrow. [The] Governor has to act according to the Constitution. Appoint a pro tem Speaker and the speaker will hold a floor test. That's the procedure. Where is the role of the [C]ourt?'

To this the Solicitor General responded that it wouldn't be a question of horse trading but of the entire stable going to the other side, if the Governor decided to not hold a floor test today and let them work it out.

The Supreme Court Bench stated how in most of the cases that had been cited, the floor test was done in 24 hours.

'[T]hat's the Governor's decision. Can the [C]ourt decide what agenda will be taken in the [H]ouse? Constitutionally it is barred. Court can't monitor proceedings inside the [H]ouse. Court has to see what's the discretion of the Governor based on knowledge of the political scenario,' the Solicitor General argued. 'How can there be orders to a Governor to do something? It would have far reaching consequences,' he further argued.

Maninder Singh, appearing for Ajit Pawar, then joined in. '[T]he letter sent by me as CLP leader is [c]onstitutionally and legally correct. I have discretion. [The] Governor has taken decision... since someone has said NCP is there or here, I am NCP. I'm the leader. [W]hy should the court entertain this writ petition and permit leapfrogging? There is no allegation against this letter,' Singh said. He further questioned that with the Court having seen the documents, how can it entertain the plea.

'[M]aybe the Governor wants to avoid the 24-hour floor test. Maybe he wants to wait and see whether it can be worked out,' the Solicitor General said.

'[T]here [are] no grounds for interim order of the court. When issue of authority of the [S]peaker is referred to a Constitution bench, how can directions be issued to a Governor?' Rohatgi questioned.

Kapil Sibal, who till now was patiently hearing all the arguments, then rose to reply. He began by taking a jibe at Ajit Pawar. Taking a cue from the Solicitor General's comment on a 'stable being taken onto the other side', Sibal quipped that it wasn't the stable but the jockey who had run away, and that the horses were still there.

Sibal then continued with his arguments for the Shiv Sena: 'On 22nd November, the alliance (of Shiv Sena–Congress–NCP) was announced in a press conference at 7 p.m. See the conduct of the authorities. On the morning of the 23rd we would have staked claim. Why did the [P]resident['s] [R]ule get revoked overnight? The [G]overnor who waited for 20 days could[n't] wait for 24 hours?'

The Court responded, '[L]et's not go into that. The question is that they have given a letter of 54.'

'[T]hey have given the letter. There is no resolution of the Party! I can provide an affidavit of the MLAs saying "we don't support." What was the national emergency that the President's rule was revoked at 5 a.m. and oath taken? This is completely malafide. It's absurd… Has [the] Governor explained what was the emergency that '[P]resident['s] [R]ule [was] revoked at 5.17 a.m. and the oath [taken] at 8 a.m.? They said no one formed the government. I am appearing for the Shiv Sena. The pre-poll alliance fell out because BJP backed out of its promises to us. It had nothing to do with NCP or Congress. Normally all this is done after the cabinet approves of these things,' said Sibal.

The Solicitor General raised an objection to this, asking how allegations against the Centre could be raised in this manner.

Sibal said, [W]e are filing an application with the original affidavits from the MLAs, saying Ajit Pawar was not authorized to take a decision. Why are they objecting to a floor test? There are precedents. There should be an immediate floor test with the seniormost MLA being appointed as pro tem Speaker.'

It was now Abhishek Manu Singhvi's turn to argue on behalf of the NCP.

'When you try to cover up something, your fraud is exposed all the more. The entire argument on the other side is that the Governor acted wisely because he showed the letter. The case before the Court is a strange one. Both sides agree that the floor test is necessary but they say the floor test need not happen now. It's a fraud on democracy, of the worst kind. The Supreme Court asked a very simple question. Does even a single MLA say, "Mr Pawar, we agree to support the BJP?" Singhvi said. He further added, 'They've submitted a list of signatures with no covering letter. This is a fraud on democracy. One can't rely on signature[s] that were to elect Pawar as CLP leader to use the same letter as letter of support. There was no resolution. [The] Governor can't turn a blind eye [to the fact] that there is no covering letter or resolution.'

'I have affidavits from 48 NCP, 56 Shiv Sena and 44 Congress MLAs,' Singhvi added.

Rohatgi stood up with an objection and said that these signatures couldn't be filed before the Court.

The Supreme Court stated, 'The issue before us is very limited.

Both sides are expanding it so much. The moment you file these affidavits we will have to give time to the other side to reply.'

Singhvi said, '[W]hen I have 156 people signing affidavits, how can he claim he is the NCP?'

The Supreme Court directed for the issue of the floor test to be addressed.

Singhvi stated: 'The [C]ourt should order an immediate floor test… Appoint a pro tem Speaker with the sole agenda to hold a floor test…They are trying to circumvent and nullify the procedure… Safeguards for the floor test should be ordered. It should be by the pro tem Speaker. The only agenda should be swearing-in MLAs and an immediate floor test. They want to delay it. They say that after a pro tem Speaker is done, let a regular speaker be appointed. This will give Ajit Pawar time to issue a whip and try to disqualify MLAs.'

The Supreme Court asked, 'What do you say to their request for time to reply?'

Singhvi responded, 'You have a situation where, in principle, both sides agree to a floor test. Everything can be proved on the floor of the house. I'm happy to prove on the floor of the house.'

The Supreme Court asked about the conditions.

Singhvi responded that he was pointing to the 'core requirements' for a fair floor test. He then pointed out the precedent court orders. 'The [C]ourt should ask itself: Why do all these orders have a 24-hour period and not 48 hours?' Singhvi said.

'Only substantive or gross illegality can call for interference… the procedure is that pro tem Speaker calls the house and holds the oath. Then Speaker is elected. That's what the rules are. They want to do away with the office of the Speaker and let the pro tem person continue… if your Lordships hold that some order must be passed, I say it should not be passed, then the order should be pro tem, oath, Speaker, floor test. Process cannot be violated… there cannot be a floor test for at least seven days. Cannot order floor test tomorrow…' Rohatgi said.

Sibal counter-argued: 'The earlier orders of the [C]ourt did not allow for the [S]peaker to be elected. They were passed to ensure that the Chief Minister has confidence of the house.'

'Why is my friend saying—that there should be a Speaker? It's so that Ajit Pawar can issue a whip?' questioned Singhvi.

Rohatgi responded that the Speaker was needed because the Constitution and rules of procedure say so.

After hearing all the arguments, the Supreme Court decided to pass the final orders at 10.30 a.m. the next day.

Vidhan Bhavan, Nariman Point, Mumbai

For close to four hours, the NCP leaders did not leave Ajit Pawar. Fadnavis, who was anxiously waiting for Ajit to take charge of the office alongside him, had to leave within minutes. The anxiety in the BJP camp was growing and the NCP was getting confident as they were slowly moving towards success in convincing Ajit Pawar. The message given to Ajit in these four hours was simple. He was told that he will be defeated on the floor of the house, but everyone in the party wants that the Pawar family shouldn't break, as that will be disastrous for the party as well, and hence he should return to the party.

After spending four hours with his now 'former' colleagues, Ajit headed to his residence near Churchgate.

Ajit Pawar's Residence, Churchgate

Just after Ajit reached his home, a shocking news came in. A letter was circulated by a young Shiv Sena leader on social media, which showed that the Maharashtra Anti-Corruption Bureau (ACB) had given a clean chit to Deputy Chief Minister Ajit Pawar in the ₹70,000 crore irrigation scam. The scam that had almost ended Ajit's political career was the result of a probe orderd by the earlier Devendra Fadnavis government. During his election campaign of 2014, Fadnavis had gone to the extent of saying that Ajit would be sent behind bars if the BJP was voted to power. But politics makes strange bedfellows, they say—Ajit having now joined hands with Fadnavis was a testimony to that.

The news of the clean chit spread like wildfire. The Congress immediately attacked the BJP for working out a deal, alleging that Ajit Pawar had been 'exonerated' in lieu of his support to the BJP in forming a government.

The ACB then had to issue a clarification that it has closed the probe into alleged irregularities 'only in nine irrigation projects' in Maharashtra and that none of these were linked to Deputy Chief Minister Ajit Pawar. But even after the clarification from top officials, one question kept haunting everyone's mind: Was this development a mere coincidence?

◆

There was no end to the fast-paced developments that had been unfolding from the lanes of Mumbai to Delhi. In Mumbai, Sanjay Raut made a major announcement on his Twitter handle: 'We are all one and together, watch our 162 together for the first time at [G]rand Hyatt at 7 pm, come and watch yourself' the tweet said, tagging Governor B.S. Koshyari.

Varsha

With Ajit Pawar's chair next to him lying vacant, Devendra Fadnavis chaired his first meeting in the Committee Hall of Varsha. The initial plan of getting Ajit to attend the meeting to make a big announcement had fallen apart.

Fadnavis went ahead alone and announced a relief of ₹5,380 crore from the Maharashtra Contingency Fund to farmers affected by unseasonal rainfall. He also chaired a meeting to discuss the proposed 'Climate Resilience Improvement and Flood & Drought Management Programme' with representatives from the World Bank.

Fadnavis chaired the meet, but the empty chair next to him kept distracting his attention.

Hotel Grand Hyatt, Kalina

After staking claim to form the government, top leaders from all the three parties met at the MCA. Sanjay Raut from the Shiv Sena, Jitendra Awhad of the NCP and Balasaheb Thorat, Mallikarjun

Kharge and Naseem Khan of the Congress discussed a new plan to show the united strength.

Initially, the parties were of the opinion that all the MLAs from three parties should be taken to Raj Bhavan and paraded before the Governor, but that could be done only if the Governor asked for it. Moreover, the time was ripe to show all the MLAs not to the Governor but the people at large, to send across a message that the MVA had the numbers. The Supreme Court had reserved its orders till the next morning. The order could go anyone's way, but this show of unison would make all the right political noises. After the decision was made, Raut announced it on Twitter.

Preparations began on a war footing at the banquet hall of Grand Hyatt. Big banners and standies reading 'AMHI 162 (We are 162)' were placed inside the hall lit with blue and purple lights. A huge cut-out of the Constitution of India was put up inside the hall.

The buses carrying Congress and Shiv Sena MLAs arrived at Grand Hyatt. NCP MLAs were already staying in the same hotel. Supriya Sule almost took on the role of the host, welcoming all leaders and MLAs who entered the hall. She kept animatedly chatting with the younger lot of MLAs, clicking selfies at times.

At around 7.15 p.m., Uddhav and Aditya Thackeray entered the hall amidst sloganeering. After a few minutes, Mallikarjun Kharge walked in with Congress leader Ashok Chavan. Kharge and Uddhav happily posed for a picture. The hall witnessed the loudest cheers and sloganeering when the grand old man, who had by now checkmated the BJP on all fronts, entered the hall. Sharad Pawar looked far more confident and relaxed than he had appeared in the last two days.

This was a picture-perfect moment. The MLAs of all three parties were seated together. After the Congress leaders spoke, everyone was all ears for Uddhav's speech. The glow on Uddhav's face couldn't be missed. 'We aren't lusting for power. This is Satyamev Jayate..!' he started. 'If they watch this, and still don't open their eyes, then we will ensure that light seeps through them... You want to know what Shiv Sena is? We will show you how it is... Our alliance is not just for five years....we are here for the entire multiplication table... 5, 10, 15, 20..' Uddhav said with utmost conviction.

All eyes were now on Pawar. This was going to be his first such public interaction after the rebellion was quelled. 'The decision that we've taken is in the interest of the state... We saw how government was formed here without a majority... Those who are in power at the Centre, have done this in many other states...they did it in Karnataka, then in Goa, Manipur... They don't believe in democratic procedure. Power is being misused; BJP has shown this in the country's history... Now it's Maharashtra's turn,' Pawar started with an attack on the BJP.

But Pawar understood that the most important thing at this juncture was to reassure the MLAs. 'I heard new legislators are being misled. We elected Ajit Pawar as Legislative Party Leader and he decided to join hands with BJP. The party has taken action against him. He was the leader, and he decided to use the whip.... New MLAs were told that if you don't follow the whip, action will be taken. I want to tell you after we've taken the decision to remove him; he can't take any decision on behalf of the party... We've spoken to experts. Someone suspended from the party can't take any decision. I'm saying this with great responsibility. It's my own personal responsibility if anything of that sort happens. Don't believe anything,' Pawar said in an affirmative tone.

'I am sure that the Governor will have to call you. This is not Goa or Manipur... This is Maharashtra!' Pawar said to a thumping applause. 'Whoever tries to defeat us, we will defeat them. Now even Shiv Sena is with us! Of course I needn't say more about that,' Pawar made a tongue-in-cheek remark.

The highlight of the show of strength was not just the congregation of all the MLAs. Jitendra Awhad had planned a common pledge for all the MLAs. After the speeches, Awhad himself administered the pledge. Before starting the oath, he reminded the lawmakers that 26 November, the next day, was the 70th Constitution Day. He then appealed to the MLAs to stand up and repeat the oath: 'I (name of MLA) staying at (name of constituency) belonging to (name of party) party have contested and won the elections. In the name of the Constitution of India, I swear that under the leadership of Sharad Pawar, Uddhav Thackeray and Sonia Gandhi, I will stay loyal and honest with my party. I won't get lured by anything. I will not work against the interest of my voters. I will not betray my party and will follow the orders of my party leaders.'

Slogans were raised in the names of Dr Babasaheb Ambedkar and Chhatrapati Shivaji Maharaj. The grand show of unity 'WE ARE 162' had made a great impact.

DAY 34: TUESDAY, 26 NOVEMBER 2019

10, Janpath, New Delhi

Bal Thackeray was known for his fiery speeches, often laced with a crude sense of humour. Thackeray's uniqueness lay in the fact that during his blistering speeches, he never raised his voice. One of the highlights of his speeches used to be his near-perfect mimicry of top politicians. Though Thackeray openly admired Indira Gandhi and had even gone on to support her decision of imposing the Emergency, he never spared Sonia Gandhi in his speeches. Thackeray would often use his shawl as a prop to mimic Sonia Gandhi's style of an accented speech.[50]

But the politics of state was set to undergo a sea change. On Tuesday morning, the Constitution Day or 'Sanvidhan Divas' was to be observed in Parliament. Against the backdrop of the pandemonium over allegations of the murder of democracy in Maharashtra, the Opposition had decided to not participate in the programme. A delegation of the Shiv Sena MPs reached 10, Janpath early in the morning to meet Sonia Gandhi to inform her that Shiv Sena has decided not to participate in the Sanvidhan Divas celebrations. Shiv Sena MPs alleged that the government under BJP was bruising, abusing, misusing and insulting the sanctity of the Constitution of India every day. Instead, it was decided

---

[50] Thackeray's old videos attest to this. Also, Balasaheb Keshav Thackeray vs State of Maharashtra and Anr. (17 October 2002) made a mention of this. See https://indiankanoon.org/doc/1089248/; last accessed 16 March 2020.

that all the parties in Opposition will pay tribute to Bharat Ratna Dr Babasaheb Ambedkar by flowering the Constitution copy at his statue in the Parliament premises. A picture of Shiv Sena MPs with Sonia Gandhi went viral without any delay…

26/11 Memorial, Marine Drive, Mumbai

It was not just the Constitution Day. The nation was also remembering the most dreaded terror attacks seen in the history of the country. Every year, the Governor, Chief Minister, top state police officials and other state dignitaries offer tributes at the memorial building near the Police Gymkhana on Marine Drive.

As per the schedule, the Chief Minister and Deputy Chief Minister were supposed to reach together for the event. Fadnavis had reached and his staff was constantly keeping an eye on the watch. Ajit Pawar, the Deputy CM, was expected, as per protocal, to reach the venue before the Governor. That, however, didn't happen. The Governor's convoy reached the memorial. The Governor and the Chief Minister offered their tributes at the memorial sans the Deputy CM.

Ajit Pawar's actions over the last two days had puzzled Fadnavis and the BJP. The picture was going to get clear in the next couple of hours at the Supreme Court, but Ajit preferred to stay out of the event in the Deputy CM's role. Perhaps this was a sign of what was going on in his mind…

Ajit had left his house early in the morning, but rather than coming to the 26/11 memorial, he had gone somewhere else to meet someone important—someone he couldn't say 'no' to…

Hotel Trident, Nariman Point, Mumbai

After leaving his house, Ajit started towards Nariman Point. The media cameras followed him, expecting him to head towards the 26/11 memorial. But his car, rather than taking a right towards Girgaum Chowpatty, took a left turn towards the end of Nariman Point. He straightaway headed into the hotel, where someone was waiting for him.

The moment Ajit saw the person, he bent forward and touched the person's feet. There had never been such an awkward moment between him and his Kaki in the past. There was a long silence as Pratibha Pawar, Sharad Pawar's wife, saw Ajit for the first time since the coup. Pratibha Pawar had seen how the events had distressed her daughter. She was now sitting with the man at the centre of the coup—the nephew who she has always treated like her son. Caught in the silence was Supriya Sule's husband, Sadanand, who also shared an excellent bond with Ajit. Pratibha Pawar wasn't the first person from the Pawar family to speak to Ajit. Several other family members had approached him with a single line message: Family first, politics later!

People who know the Pawar family really well say that the Pawar clan, unlike other political families, is known for its values and a great sense of bonding. Everyone in the family has excelled in their respective fields. The value that is imbibed in the Pawars is to respect the opinions of others. There could have been differences of opinion in the family, but they were never discussed in public. No doubt that Ajit's rebellion had not only hit the party hard, but it had hurt the family immensely.

The meeting between Ajit Pawar and his aunt wasn't a very long one. Very few words were spoken, but a long message was conveyed. No politics was discussed between Ajit and his Kaki; there were no requests or deals. It was just an uncomfortable hush that communicated a thousand words…

While leaving, there was a positive smile on Ajit Pawar's face. He left with a renewed poise…

Urvashi Apartments, Malabar Hill (Praful Patel's Residence)

While coming out of the hotel, Ajit's original car and his security left, giving the media a slip. He left in a different car, all alone. A team of NCP leaders was going to meet at Praful Patel's house at Malabar Hill. Apart from Patel, Chhagan Bhujbal, Sunil Tatkare and Dilip Walse-Patil were already there. They were waiting for Ajit to join them. This was the first time that Ajit Pawar was coming to meet them in three days.

The hearing at the Supreme Court was about to begin. The NCP team wasn't sure if Ajit would come but just as the judges were about to arrive, he reached Praful Patel's house.[51]

Courtroom No. 2, Supreme Court, New Delhi

The noisy scenes at Courtroom No. 2 of the Apex court witnessed sudden silence as the judges arrived. The room was completely packed to its capacity. Leaders from Congress and Shiv Sena were present in the courtroom. It was not just those sitting in the courtroom who were eagerly waiting for the orders. The entire Maharashtra was glued to their TV screens to know what orders the Supreme Court would pass. At Matoshri, Silver Oak, 10, Janpath and Varsha, the orders were awaited with bated breath....

Breaking the pin-drop silence, the bench started reading out the much-awaited orders:

> There is no gainsay that boundaries between the court and parliamentary jurisdiction have been contested for a long time... There is need to recognise constitutional probity. This case pertains to one such situation where the court is being called to adjudicate. In this context, it is necessary and expedient to conduct the floor test as soon as possible to determine whether the Chief Minister, who was administered the oath of office, has the support of the majority or not.
>
> Court is called upon to adjudicate and maintain democratic values and facilitate the fostering of the citizens' right of good governance. In such emergent facts and circumstances, to curtail unlawful practices such as horse trading, to avoid uncertainty and to effectuate smooth running of democracy by ensuring a stable Government, we are of the considered opinion that it is necessary to pass certain interim directions in this case.

---

[51] This was a highly secretive meeting. However, based on an input by a strong source, the India Today TV team managed to reach and capture Ajit Pawar on camera.

The court relied on Harish Rawat case and the SR Bommai case.

Oath has not been administered to the elected MLAs even though one month has passed. And hence it is necessary to pass interim directions. It is necessary to conduct floor test as soon [as] possible... Detailed hearing on constitutional issues to be held after 6 weeks.

Pro tem speaker to administer oath to all MLAs. Floor test by 5 PM on 27th.

The following procedure is to be followed for conducting the floor test:

a. Pro tem Speaker shall be solely appointed for the aforesaid agenda immediately.
b. All the elected members shall take oath on 27.11.2019, which exercise should be and the entire procedure shall be completed before 5:00 p.m.
c. Immediately thereafter, the Pro tem Speaker shall conduct the floor test in order to ascertain whether the Respondent No. 3 has the majority, and these proceedings shall be conducted in accordance with law. The floor test will not be conducted by secret ballot.
d. The proceedings have to be live telecast, and appropriate arrangements are to be made to ensure the same.

The results brought beaming smiles on the faces of the Congress, NCP and Shiv Sena leaders present in the courtroom. The Court had asked Fadnavis to prove majority by 5 p.m. next day without secret ballot and telecasting it live. The major thing that the BJP and Ajit Pawar were relying on had fallen apart. The BJP camp earlier claimed that Ajit Pawar's men, though seen to have returned to the party voluntarily, would vote for the Fadnavis–Ajit Pawar government through a secret ballot.

The Supreme Court orders came as a big shot in the arm for the MVA. Crackers were already being burst in Maharashtra...

Varsha

Media teams were posted at Fadnavis's house already since early morning. First it was Ajit Pawar's gradual retreat of sorts and now the Supreme Court orders. Things had become tougher for Fadnavis.

It was BJP State President Chandrakant Patil who came out to give the first reaction on the Supreme Court orders: 'We respect the apex court's decision. We are ready for the floor test....and we will prove our majority on the floor of the house,' Patil said, with no idea of what was next in store.

Urvashi Apartments, Malabar Hill

As the Supreme Court orders were all set to be read out, Ajit Pawar reached Praful Patel's house. This was the last effort NCP was going to make to get Ajit back. 'Look, after the Supreme Court orders there is little left as an option for you. If you were to become the Deputy Chief Minister with the BJP, you were anyways going to get it here as well... If you stick with the BJP after the Supreme Court orders and the floor tests fail... There will be nothing left with you...But if you come back, that offer still stays... plus the family and party stay intact...' the offer was put across the table yet again in a more assertive manner. 'Save yourself the embarrassment by resigning before the floor test,' one of the leaders proposed. 'As it is, you have got a clean chit now,' quipped a senior leader, evoking impromptu laughter.

The meeting ended on a positive note, as hands were shook and hugs were exchanged between Tatkare and Ajit Pawar.

Ajit straightaway headed to Varsha, which was a stone's throw away from the meeting spot. Fadnavis and other top leaders were present there and Fadnavis was expecting Ajit. By now, he had an inkling of what his Deputy Chief Minister was up to. Fadnavis had sensed the inevitable. Both excused themselves from the other leaders.

'I have decided I cannot continue like this. I will be resigning. Things haven't worked as I wanted them to,' Ajit informed Fadnavis. 'If that's your final decision, then I have no problem. But we could still work out something. Think and let me know, no hurry...'

Fadnavis told Ajit Pawar.[52] Ajit then left Varsha, without talking to anyone else present there.

Other leaders present there were completely unaware of what was going on. A few moments ago, Chandrakant Patil had boasted in front of TV cameras that the BJP will win the floor test, but looking at Ajit's exit and Fadnavis's body language, he too realized that the game was slipping out of their hand...

◆

If there was anyone who was excited about the Supreme Court orders, it was Supriya Sule. The last three days had been of great emotional turmoil for her. From standing by her father, family and party in the turbulent times to political manoeuvering, sometimes leading from the front and sometimes following the leaders' directions, Supriya had played a pivotal role. Most importantly, she also kept reassuring the allies that things will fall in place. After the court orders, she was quick to tweet: 'On constitution day this is the best gift for the people of Maharashtra. Democratic and Constitutional values take precedence over politics. May the truth prevail. Jai Hind! Jai Maharashtra! #WeAre162'.

1.30 p.m.

Congress President Sonia Gandhi, who had been unanimously given all rights to appoint someone as the leader of the Legislature party, appointed Balasaheb Thorat on the expected lines.

Sofitel Hotel, Bandra Kurla Complex, Mumbai

Immediately after the Supreme Court's orders, Sharad Pawar and Supriya Sule left Silver Oak Estate to meet Uddhav Thackeray and other leaders at Sofitel Hotel. The strategy for the floor test, if the BJP went ahead with a confidence motion the next day, had to be decided.

Sharad Pawar, Supriya Sule, Uddhav Thackeray, Aditya Thackeray,

---

[52] Source-based information on condition of anonymity.

Praful Patel, Sanjay Raut, Jayant Patil and Chhagan Bhujbal went into a huddle. However, the discussion was interrupted by a news.

2.00 p.m.

Ajit Pawar had already made up his mind. Family ties prevailed over politics. At around 2 p.m., he resigned and his final decision was communicated to Fadnavis.

The fate of the Fadnavis government now hung in limbo, as they had been able to form the government only because of Ajit and the breakaway faction. The days of the 80 odd hours-old government seemed to be numbered. Fadnavis called for an urgent press conference at Sahyadri Guest House at 3.30 p.m.

The MVA had got the message, and the tripartite alliance also called for a joint briefing at 5 p.m.

3.30 p.m., Sahyadri Guest House, Malabar Hill, Mumbai

A sombre-looking Fadnavis reached the packed hall. Dozens of cameras stared at him as he began addressing the media amid a live telecast on all regional and national news channels. All eyes were on Fadnavis as he started speaking.

> We had got the mandate for the Maha Yuti before after the polls results... I am thankful to the people of Maharashtra for that. The mandate was also for BJP... because BJP contested and won 67-70 per cent seats while the Shiv Sena contested and won only 44 per cent. This mandate was for BJP. Unfortunately the number game was such that the Shiv Sena senses a bargaining opportunity...demanding the CM's post, they started talks with other parties... Shiv Sena even went on to make claims about a promise of 2.5 years of CM's post that was never made... Amit Shah made it very clear that no such promise was made. We were willing to fulfill promises that were made... But rather than discussing that with us, Shiv Sena started discussions with Congress and NCP...we all saw what happened next...

BJP was called to form the government, we informed that we don't have numbers. The Shiv Sena was invited. They went to form government but their claims were hollow and turned out to be a joke...NCP had no numbers... So President's rule was imposed... These three parties kept discussing for 10 days and couldn't even formulate a Common Minimum Program... The only Common Maximum Program they had was to keep BJP away and grab power... They are way different ideologically... Shiv Sena calls itself a Hindutvawadi party. It's a different case that they have now offered it on the feet of Sonia Gandhi.... We saw how their MLAs swore in the name of Sonia Gandhi yesterday... While all this was happening, Ajit Pawar contacted us and informed that he wants to support our government... So we formed the government together... However, he met me today and informed that he cannot remain part of our government ... Due to his resignation, we don't have numbers and we have decided not to form the government and resign... After this press conference, I will meet the Governor and submit my resignation...

Fadnavis announced his resignation barely three days after he was sworn in.

'We have already clarified that we will not indulge in horse trading... Interestingly, those who were alleging horse trading have bought the entire stable... The three parties that are planning to form the government will buckle under pressure and the three-wheeled vehicle will run in different directions... We will sit in opposition and work as an active opposition to become the voice of the deprived and farmers....' Fadnavis concluded before heading to Raj Bhavan to submit his resignation.

Things had changed drastically over the period of a month. The only man after Vasantrao Naik to have completed a full term as Maharashtra's Chief Minister was ironically now also the man who had become the state's Chief Minister for the shortest tenure of 80 odd hours!

Raj Bhavan, Malabar Hill

The tug of war wasn't over yet. All eyes were on who will be the pro tem Speaker of the Legislative Assembly. As per the set tradition, the seniormost member is usually appointed in this capacity and so, Congress's Balasaheb Thorat and BJP's Kalidar Kolambar were the frontrunners. Thorat and Kolambkar were eight-time MLAs from Sangamner and Wadala constituencies respectively.

Even though the Chief Minister and Depury Chief Minister had resigned, there was still uncertainty over Ajit Pawar's role. The pro tem Speaker's role hence was going to be very vital in the current drama....The pro tem Speaker enjoys all the powers that a permanent speaker enjoys as per the Constitution. The pro tem Speaker has the powers to determine the legislature party leader and consider whips issues by him.

Though the story was almost fading for the BJP, no one wanted to take any risk, given the last-minute surprises that had come up in the last few days...

By late afternoon, Kalidas Kolambkar got an urgent call from the Raj Bhavan to reach the Governor's office. He was appointed as the pro tem Speaker and was administered the oath. His appointment raised eyebrows, as he was known as a very close aide of Narayan Rane—the person who, two days ago, had been assigned the task of Operation Lotus in Maharashtra. The MVA wasn't happy with the appointment...

Immediately after administering oath to the Pro tem Speaker, the Governor under Article 174(1) of the Constitution called the assembly session on 27 November at 8 a.m.

Hotel Trident, Bandra Kurla Complex, Mumbai

The bus carrying NCP MLAs left from Grand Hyatt in Kalina. The MLAs flashed broad smiles and showed victory signs. These were perhaps the first truly relaxing moments in days. At around 6.25 p.m., the bus carrying Congress MLAs also reached Hotel Trident. Fifteen minutes later, the bus with Shiv Sena MLAs also arrived.

Party workers had already started to crowd outside the Hotel Trident gates. Amidst sloganeering in favour of the three parties, some NCP workers held posters that caught everyone's attention. They read: 'We Love Ajit Pawar!' This immediately fanned speculations that Ajit Pawar was back in the NCP fold.

At around 8 p.m., the joint meeting between the three parties started. A copy of the Preamble was read out in the meeting. This was going to be the foundation of the alliance, it was told. But as speeches began, Chhagan Bhujbal made an interesting statement: 'Now that we have get all our MLAs back, I think Pawar Saheb should bring back Ajit dada as well... He should forgive him for whatever that happened... Let bygones be bygones...let us welcome him back with open arms...' The proposal was welcomed with applause.

The first proposal on the agenda was to christen the alliance officially. Eknath Shinde, Shiv Sena's Legislative Party leader, proposed the name 'Maha Vikas Aghadi' for the alliance. The proposal was seconded by Raju Shetty of the Swabhimani Shetkari Sanghatana, Abu Asim Azmi of the Samajwadi Party, Bachchu Kadu of the Prahaar Janshakti Party and Kapil Patil of the Lok Bharati.

It was now the turn of announcing the leader of the MVA, who will be the next Chief Minister of Maharashtra. NCP's Jayant Patil rose to propose the name. 'I propose the name of Shri Uddhav Balasaheb Thackeray as the leader of Maharashtra Vikas Aghadi and the Chief Minister of Maharashtra,' Jayant Patil proposed. The proposal was welcomed with thunderous applause.

With Sharad Pawar, the architect of alliance, by his side, Uddhav stood up and thanked the MLAs with folded hands. Leaders of all the allies and elected MLAs supported the resolution and it was unanimously passed.

It was an emotional moment for Uddhav Thackeray, especially to watch the Congress and NCP MLAs cheering for him. 'The ones with whom we had an alliance of decades did not trust me, while the ones we fought against for long have trusted me with leadership.' Uddhav started with thanking Sharad Pawar and

Congress President Sonia Gandhi. 'This is not a government, this is one family... Every common man should feel that this is his government. I never even thought in my dreams that I will become the Chief Minister someday... Like my father, I wanted to carry forward the legacy of my grandfather of serving people and fighting for them... This fight is not against anyone... Try and understand, why did I have to take the extreme step of breaking the alliance... I was pained and hurt when they lied... Supporting someone who lies and goes back on their words is not my Hindutva...' Uddhav said. He didn't forget to hit back at the BJP: 'They came to us when they needed us, and dumped us when not needed... Even today they repeated that nothing was decided between the Shiv Sena and BJP...it is painful... Shiv Sena was not formed to carry your palanquins,' he warned the BJP. He also mentioned that he would go and meet 'mota bhai' (elder brother) in Delhi soon. This was a direct reference to Prime Minister Modi, who during his election rallies, called Uddhav his younger brother.

'I will need your support to run the government and make the common man and farmers happy... I am not the Chief Minister alone, you all are the Chief Ministers,' he concluded.

Sharad Pawar remembered his once political rival yet good friend Bal Thackeray in his speech. 'Balasaheb should have been alive today to witness this moment... He gave opportunities to political workers from the downtrodden and today I'm sure Uddhav Thackeray will carry forward the rich legacy,' Pawar said.

As the leaders came out of the hotel, party workers who were already celebrating, burst into loud cheers.

Matoshri

Bal Thackeray's room has been preserved in its original condition by the Thackeray family. All his things, including his bed, pillows, glasses, etc. have been kept intact. He may have been the dreadful leader who could bring the financial capital to a grinding halt at the snap of his fingers—one 'aadesh' from Matoshri would bring thousands on road—but inside Matoshri, he was a doting father—

Pilga, as he was called by his sons. Uddhav, the youngest, was called 'Dinga' by the family members. He was not only the youngest but the most submissive and obedient among the children. The first thing that Uddhav did after reaching Matoshri after being selected as the Chief Minister candidate was to go to his father's room. He knelt down in front of his father's portrait, ran his hand over the bed and with a big lump in his throat, said, *'Pilga, tujha Dinga Mukhyamantri zala...* (Pilga, your Dinga has become the Chief Minister).'

Raj Bhavan, Malabar Hill

After anointing Uddhav Thackeray as the leader, the legislative party leaders immediately headed to Raj Bhavan to stake claim to form the government. A joint statement was submitted to Governor B.S. Koshyari. The leaders submitted the letters of support of 166 MLAs, four more than the earlier day's claim of 162! Governor Koshyari, in a letter addressed to Uddhav Thackeray, asked him to submit a 'list' of 'majority support in the Assembly' by 3 December. It further said that since Uddhav is not a member of the Maharashtra legislature, he will have to become a member within six months after taking oath as the CM.

With everything in place now, the big announcement of the big day was made. An official message was circulated to the media by the Shiv Sena: Uddhav Balasaheb Thackeray will take oath as Maharashtra Chief Minister at 6.40 p.m. on 28 November 2019 at the party's favourite location, Shivaji Park.

9.10 p.m., Napean Sea Road

Amidst the rapid political developments, Ajit Pawar kept himself detached for the day. His decision had saved the party from a big embarrassment. But most importantly, his decision had saved the family from a permanent damage. Family members were happy and thanked Ajit for the mature move. While announcing his decision to family members in the morning, Ajit had said that he would like to quit politics.

His car started from his brother's house and headed towards Priyadarshini Park. Media vans started following him amidst the traffic. His car then took a left turn towards Breach Candy Hospital road. Towards the end of this road is Silver Oak Estate.

Sitting on the back seat, Ajit was engrossed in his mobile or at least was pretending to do so to avoid the media glare. As Ajit crossed the park ahead of Breach Candy Hospital, his car took a U-turn and then a right from the barricaded gates of Silver Oak Estate. Ajit hurriedly got out of the car and headed to the front gate. He turned around as someone called him from behind: '*Mama, ikde..!* (Uncle, this way!)'

Supriya Sule's daughter Revati asked her maternal uncle to enter from the rear gate. Ajit ran up the stairs and entered the house, with the door swiftly closed behind him.

After an 80-hour rebellion, Ajit Pawar was back home.

DAY 35: WEDNESDAY, 27 NOVEMBER 2019

The Supreme Court orders had asked the Fadnavis government to face the floor test by 5 p.m., but with the resignation the need for that didn't arise. The agenda for the day was only to administer the oath to the newly elected members of the house. This time the Maharashtra assembly had 97 first-time MLAs. For these MLAs, taking oath as MLAs for the first time was going to be a memorable event, but they wouldn't have known on the day of the election results that they will have to wait for more than a month for this moment.

7.30 a.m., Vidhan Bhavan, Nariman Point, Mumbai

Shiv Sena buses left from Hotel Lemon Tree at sharp 7 a.m. And so did other buses carrying NCP and Congress MLAs. They were excited as the big day was finally here. Congress leader Ashok Chavan was among the first to reach the assembly. Pro tem Speaker Kalidas Kolambkar too reached early.

But Supriya Sule was already at the Vidhan Bhavan entrance, welcoming MLAs and leaders with folded hands and an exuberant smile. At 7.55 a.m. Ajit Pawar reached the Vidhan Bhavan. All eyes and cameras turned towards him. Supriya welcomed her brother with a warm hug. After all, blood is always thicker than water...

♦

The oath was administered as per the seniority of the members. When Ajit Pawar walked towards the podium to take the oath, he was greeted with a thunderous applause as members thumped benches to welcome him. Inspite of the rebellion, Ajit's popularity in the party was intact. As Ajit walked out of Vidhan Bhavan that day, he told mediapersons: 'I changed my decision after the Supreme Court orders. My party will decide my role ahead.' Devendra Fadnavis, on the other hand, left quietly without speaking to the media. Just as the MLAs were being administered the oath, Uddhav Thackeray, with wife Rashmi, called upon Governor Koshyari over breakfast.

Shivaji Park, Dadar

Preparations for the grand swearing-in had begun at Shivaji Park—or Shiv-teerth as Shivsainiks called it. The stage was set close to Bal Thackeray's samadhi (memorial). Meanwhile, Maharashtra DGP Subodh Jaiswal, Chief Secretary Alok Mehta and Mumabi Police Commissioner Sanjay Barve met Uddhav to apprise him about the security and other preparations.

The ground of Shivaji Park has a special relation with the party. The party was born here on Shivaji Park in 1966. The innumerable rallies of the party, including its annual Dussera rally, happens here every year. When the Shiv Sena first came to power in 1995, Shiv Sena's first Chief Minister Manohar Joshi was also sworn in here. Not just that, when Bal Thackeray's nephew quit the party and formed his own outfit, the Maharashtra Navnirman Sena, it was also here at the same Shivaji Park. And yes, Bal Thackeray himself was cremated at Shivaji Park.

There could have been no more apt a venue for the swearing-in than this.

Y.B. Chavan Centre, Nariman Point, Mumbai

After taking oath, the NCP MLAs straightaway headed to the party meeting at Y.B. Chavan Centre. After all the strategy meetings that had taken place, this one was going to be less tedious. There was a surprise speaker who was going to give 'tips' on the way ahead for the new MLAs—ironically, it was Ajit Pawar.

A meeting of MVA leaders was planned to decide the number and names of ministers who would be sworn in with Chief Minister Uddhav Thackeray. An initial formula was worked out, which Praful Patel announced to the media: 'We had a meeting over preparations, Ministry distribution, and other aspects for the MVA Government. Other issues like distribution of the Legislative Council seats were also decided. One or two ministers each from the three parties will be sworn in tomorrow,' Patel announced, saying that the oath ceremony at Shivaji Park will not be an elaborate one. 'We have time till 3rd of December to prove majority on the floor of the house... Cabinet expansion will take place after that... Names will be decided by late tonight and will be sent to Chief Minister designate Uddhav Thackeray.'

But the big announcement was yet to come...

Contrary to the speculations, there would be only one Deputy CM—from the NCP. The Congress settled for the Speaker's post. This came as a respite for party higher-ups because there were several claimants to the Deputy Chief Minister post from the Congress and the decision would have been difficult.

10, Janpath, New Delhi

Decades ago, after the Emergency, Shiv Sena founder Bal Thackeray had met Indira Gandhi. Thackeray was a self-proclaimed admirer of Indira. Years later, two Thackerays had knocked on the doors of the Gandhis within a span of a few months. Bal Thackeray's nephew Raj had met Sonia Gandhi to discuss the issue of EVMs some months ago and now Aditya Thackeray, accompanied by Milind Narvekar, visited to invite Sonia Gandhi for the swearing-in the next day. After inviting Sonia Gandhi, Aditya and Milind went to former Prime Minister Dr Manmohan Singh's house to invite him.

While the invites were personally handed out to Congress leaders, a letter was faxed/emailed to Prime Minister Narendra Modi. Around 10.00 p.m., Uddhav received an unexpected call from Narendra Modi congratulating him. The Prime Minister informed Uddhav that he will not be able to attend the ceremony due to a prescheduled programme, but Devendra Fadnavis was going to attend the grand ceremony.

DAY 36: THURSDAY, 27 NOVEMBER 2019

Shivaji Park was all set to witness history. From kingmaker, a Thackeray was to be crowned as the king himself. Shiv Sena workers from every nook and corner of the state were going to attend the grand ceremony. A seating arrangement for 70,000 guests had been made. The grand stage—a replica of Fort Raigad, the capital of Maratha warrior-king Chhatrapati Shivaji Maharaj—was being erected by Bollywood art director Nitin Desai.

The passage of power from the BJP to the Shiv Sena via Congress and NCP and from Manohar Joshi to Uddhav Thackeray via Narayan Rane was not easy. Uddhav's political journey has always amused everyone who has watched his slow and steady ascendance. From being written off on his debut to rising to the most powerful seat of power in the state, Uddhav's journey has been no less than that of a Bollywood potboiler. Many consider Uddhav's entry into politics as accidental, but those who have watched him closely say his is a well-planned and excellently executed political journey.

During the Shiv Sena's heydays in the 1990s, no one would have expected the shy Uddhav to reach these heights in politics. Uddhav, who completed his diploma from the Sir JJ School of Arts, was always inclined towards photography, especially wildlife. At some point, he owned a display advertising business. Moreover, while Balasaheb's other sons, Bindumadhav and Jaidev, were seen in the public domain, they were not actively into politics. With his three sons relatively detached from active politics, it was Bal Thackeray's brother Shrikant's son Raj who stepped into his uncle's footsteps.

Raj had picked up his uncle's mannerisms, language and demeanor. The nephew saw himself as Thackeray's heir apparent in politics. In spite of the fact that the Shiv Sena was already an organization of the youth, a special students' wing was formed by Raj Thackeray. It was called the Bhartiya Vidyarthi Sena and Raj was the Founder President. The abbreviation of the organization would come down to Bha.Vi.Sena and Raj loved to be called as 'Bha.Vi.Senapramukh', which spelt together translated as the future/would-be Shiv Sena supremo. Raj's ambitions in the party were never a secret.

Till the time Shiv Sena came to power in 1995, Uddhav was rarely seen on the party platform. His presence in the mammoth rallies of his father was confined to clicking pictures of the rally. When the Shiv Sena came to power, Balasaheb often said that the remote control of the government was with him. But on the ground, apart from Shiv Sena Chief Minister Manohar Joshi, there were several other power centres other than the supremo. Suddenly, Smita Thackeray, Balasaheb's daughter-in-law, had also become powerful.

This was also the time when Raj was embroiled in one of the worst controversies of his life. His name was linked to the mysterious death of Ramesh Kini.[53] It was alleged that Kini was murdered after a property dispute and with some close friends of Raj named in the case. The needle of suspicion was also pointing towards his role. While Raj was given a clean chit in the case, the allegations had badly dented his prospects by then. Incidentally, this coincided with Uddhav taking interest in the party's political affairs. Uddhav, in contrast to his father, spoke little and lacked the aggression in speech, but in his calm composure and pragmatism, his father saw the streaks of an astute politician.

By the time Raj was back and active in the party, Uddhav had made up his mind to make politics as his base. During the 1999 elections, Uddhav was seen actively participating with his father in rallies, planning and strategizing. His advances were making Raj

---

[53] https://www.outlookindia.com/magazine/story/body-blow-to-the-sena/ 202264; last accessed 16 March 2020.

uncomfortable in the party. This was when the seeds of his rebellion against the party were sown. He, however, wasn't the only one. Former Chief Minister Narayan Rane was also feeling the heat of sharing powers with yet another Thackeray. However, some had started to adapt themselves to the new Shiv Sena. Those directly or indirectly hurt by Raj's rabble-rousing ways found solace in the soft-spoken Uddhav.

To say that Uddhav was a reluctant politician would be widely off the mark. He was as ambitious as Raj, but he was never flamboyant about his ambitions. He knew his shortcomings very well. He knew he was seen as the complete opposite of the extroverted Balasaheb, but he very intelligently built his political brand and image around the same soft-spoken image. Uddhav's uncomplicated, middle-class Marathi manoos image and the stamp of a complete family man always gave him an upper edge.

The twist in the tale came in 2003. After the Election Commission of India's directives, it was imperative for the monolithic party to choose its President. Uddhav was chosen by Balasaheb as the new head of the party at the Party's State Executive meeting in Mahabaleshwar. After this, there was no looking back for the mild-mannered Thackeray. Just over a year after Uddhav's anointment, Balasaheb's favorite Shivsainik raised the banner of revolt against Uddhav. Former Chief Minister Narayan Rane alleged that Balasaheb was blinded by the love for his son just like Dhritarashtra was for Duryodhan. Rane used the choicest of language to poke fun at Uddhav and his leadership qualities. Rane, who was expelled from the party, took away 11 Shiv Sena MLAs with him.

Even before the party could recuperate from the shock, it was hit by the biggest shock in its history. This time it was Raj Thackeray who caused tremors in the party and family. Alleging that his 'deity' Balasaheb was surrounded by a coterie, in 2005 Raj quit the party and formed his own outfit—the Maharashtra Navnirman Sena (MNS). In the 2007 municipal elections, Raj's party could not make an impact, but later, Raj aggressively took up the hard-line Marathi agenda, alleging that north Indian migrants, especially from Uttar Pradesh, and those from Bihar were snatching away job opportunities of the 'sons of the soil'. The agitation by his partymen turned violent and several migrant labourers were attacked.[54] Raj was arrested for provocative speeches and spreading animosity between communities. Maharashtra witnessed violent protests and shutdown in some areas after Raj's arrest.

Raj's popularity was soaring in the state. Call it political nuisance value or the relevance of his issues, Raj Thackeray was discussed in the Parliament on several occasions. The direct impact of Raj's popularity was seen in the 2009 Lok Sabha elections, where MNS made a strong dent into the Shiv Sena and BJP votes. The assembly polls that followed saw the emergence of MNS as one of the prominent parties of the state, winning 13 seats and eating into the Shiv Sena–BJP alliance's vote share. Raj's rise was seen by many as being directly proportional to the decline of the Sena's popularity.

The comparison between Uddhav and Raj was evident. Senior Thackeray himself wanted the cousins to patch up, but things had gone way beyond control. This also coincided with Narendra Modi gearing up for his big role in national politics. He was looking out for potential new allies and personal friends across the country that would suit his politics. With Bal Thackeray around, Modi, in spite of his strong saffron credentials, would not be seen as the Hindu Hriday Samrat. Modi saw the potential in Raj.

At the peak of his political popularity, Raj was invited by the then Gujarat Chief Minister Narendra Modi as a Special State Guest. Raj toured the state and came back impressed. In almost every rally, he pitched for the name of Narendra Modi as the most suitable and deserving candidate to become the Prime Minister of the country. The growing closeness of BJP's mascot to Raj hurt Uddhav badly. His close aides say that then and there he had arrived at a conclusion that the BJP could go to any extent to get power. He had since

---

[54] https://in.reuters.com/article/idINIndia-36069020081021; last accessed 16 March 2020.

harboured that resentment against the BJP.

Unfortunately for Raj, the lack of organizational structure and inter-party feuds had peaked. Party cadres had started to feel alienated with the rise of some mediocre leaders who were close to Raj. Ironically, his coterie accusation against the Shiv Sena was coming true for his own party. When his party was formed, Raj chose the 'right of the centre' path by including blue and green in his flag. Raj's stage always had the portrait of his grandfather Prabodhankar Thackeray, who was known for his prolific writings and fight against caste hierarchy. With his new stand, analysts went on to call him as his social reformer grandfather's heir. This was also why Raj's popularity among Dalit youths was sizeable. But some statements made by junior and immature colleagues against the proposed Ambedkar Memorial at Indu Mill and Raj legitimizing these leaders and their stance hit his popularity. In the 2012 BMC elections, MNS's vote percentage went down. In November 2012, Bal Thackeray passed away following a prolonged illness.

In all these years between the mass exodus of the party and the demise of his father, Uddhav had very smartly built a network of leaders in the party who owed their allegiance and loyalty only towards him. In the meantime, Uddhav had also undergone angioplasty, but inspite of his health issues, he had managed to keep singular control of the party. There was no factionalism now and no scope for harbouring top ambitions. While Raj was mostly concentrating on urban areas like Mumbai, Nashik and Pune, Uddhav took serious efforts to build his party in Marathwada and Vidarbha, mostly rural areas. The Shiv Sena was a far more organized and disciplined party under Uddhav's regime. Many poked fun at the corporate ways of functioning, but Uddhav didn't pay heed to his detractors.

The BJP by then had sensed the decline in the MNS vote share and immediately went back to its tried and tested ally, the Shiv

Sena. The Narendra Modi tsunami took the country in its stride in 2014 and the BJP won with a thumping majority, but after the victory, the BJP ignored Shiv Sena.

Uddhav had without any qualms played second fiddle to the BJP. In 2014, before the assembly elections, the Shiv Sena and BJP parted ways bitterly. In spite of this, Uddhav's party managed to win 63 seats. But the biggest loser in the Sena vs BJP battle turned out to be Raj Thackeray, whose party's numbers came down to one seat from 13. Devendra Fadnavis had formed a minority government with unconditional support from the NCP, but soon the BJP and Shiv Sena realized that it was realistic for the saffron siblings to kiss and make up again.

Even though the two ruled together, Uddhav had never forgiven the BJP for 'insulting' his party. Shiv Sena was not used to being treated like a younger brother in the state's politics. Uddhav was watching and waiting for an opportune moment to strike back. Through Modi's first term, Uddhav stayed in power with the BJP, but continued to attack the government on its policies and decisions like the demonetization and GST.

In January 2018, Uddhav announced that his party will not fight the forthcoming elections in alliance with the BJP. However, 13 months later, a tie-up with the BJP was announced in a press conference. Some thought of it as a complete surrender by the Shiv Sena, but Uddhav was playing his cards close to his chest...

♦

28 November 2019, Rangsharda Auditorium, Bandra

The only formality that was left was to announce the alliance's CMP. A joint press conference was announced for this by the top leaders from the Shiv Sena, Congress and NCP.

The key points of the CMP arrived at after discussions over several days were going to be farmers' issues, unemployment and social justice, apart from education, urban development and women's issues. The CMP was released barely a couple of hours before the swearing-in.

♦

28 September 2019, Rangsharda Auditorium

Exactly two months ago, a routine rally of Uddhav Thackeray at the same auditorium had proved to be prophetic. A day before the Navratri celebrations were to begin, Uddhav had called for a meeting of his party office bearers. The talks over seat-sharing with BJP were still on, but Uddhav Thackeray had by now scanned the list of aspirants from all 288 seats, including in Fadnavis's constituency. Till the very last moment, the Shiv Sena did not want to take any chances. In 2014, when the BJP suddenly snapped its ties with the Shiv Sena, it was not in a position to field candidates in most of the constituencies. This time, there was a Plan B in place.

While addressing the office bearers, Uddhav was in a nostalgic mood. The only reason behind calling this sudden meet was to pump confidence in his party cadres and keep them war-ready in case of any last-moment treachery. Uddhav shared an emotional memory of his father. But this wasn't just a recollection of a close moment: 'During the last days of my father, I took his hand and promised him that one day I will make a Shivsainik the Chief Minister... And for that, I am willing to go to any extent,' Uddhav had revealed in the rally.

The day had come to fulfil the promise...

♦

Shivaji Park/Shiv Teerth

Shivaji Park was almost packed to its capacity. The roads leading to it were decked up with Shiv Sena, Congress and NCP flags together—a very rare sight. Farmers from remote Maharashtra, the dabbahwala and representatives of the Warkaris sect were special invitees. Women wearing saffron turbans and men playing and dancing to the reverberating sounds of dhols and taasha were all around the ground. Balasaheb's memorial was decorated with yellow flowers. Noted marathi singer Nandesh Umap was enthralling the audience with his folk songs—the powadas...

The dignitaries started arriving on the stage. Two ministers from each party—Ekanth Shide and Subhash Desai from Shiv Sena, Chhagan Bhujbal and Jayant Patil from NCP, and Balasaheb Thorat and Nitin Raut from Congress—were to be sworn in with Uddhav. Supriya Sule was seen happily clicking selfies with leaders on the stage.

The entry of one person in a dark blue kurta received a thunderous applause. It was Raj Thackeray. In spite of his political differences, this was the moment to cheer for his cousin. He came and sat in one corner of the stage. NCP leader Nawab Malik noticed this and held Raj by his hand and brought him to the first chair close to the family.

On the other side of the stage were former Chief Minister Devendra Fadnavis with industrialist Mukesh Ambani, his wife Neeta and son Anant Ambani.

Watching the crowd and the proceedings very tranquilly was Sharad Pawar, the man behind the alliance, the architect of a battle that trumped the most powerful duo of Modi and Shah.

Uddhav, dressed in a saffron kurta, stood up to take the oath as the crowd went hysteric. *'Mee Uddhav Balasaheb Thackeray ishwar saksh shapath gheto ki...'* As Uddhav completed his oath, the crowd, not just at Shivaji Park but every shakha in Mumbai, celebrated with music and fireworks. A poignant Uddhav bowed to the crowd, touching his hands and head on the floor to express his gratitude to Shivasainiks and others who were present to witness his rise to the post.

As the dust on Shivaji Park settled, it was curtains for an unprecedented political turmoil in the history of the state...

◆

A few days later, on 30 November, Uddhav Thackeray effortlessly passed the floor test with 169 votes in favour, after the BJP and its allies walked out from the Assembly. On 1 December 2019, Congress's Nana Patole was elected unopposed as the Speaker of the Lower House as the BJP withdrew its candidate. On 30 December, the cabinet was expanded with Ajit Pawar taking oath as the Deputy Chief Minister (yet again!). Interestingly, Rajendra Shingne, Balasaheb Patil, Datta Bharne, Sanjay Bansod, MLAs who had joined the rebellion, found place among the 16 members from the NCP quota.

Aditya Thackeray was also sworn in as a Cabinet Minister with his father as the CM, a first in the history of Maharashtra politics.

12 January 2020, Pimpri Chinchwad

Someone in the BJP camp believes the battle is still not over. According to him, the three-legged race will not go on for long.

Devendra Fadnavis, when being interviewed at the Morya Youth festival, concluded yet again with his catchphrase: *'Mee punha yein...'* Someone close to him immediately snapped their fingers, saying, 'Operation Kamal is not over yet...'

ACKNOWLEDGEMENTS

The first book is always special to an author. It's like first love—every little bit of progress makes you happy. The entire process of starting the first word of the book and completing the last page remains firmly etched on the author's mind forever. This book has been more than just first love...

This book wouldn't have been possible without the support of some special people and I would like to express my gratitude towards them.

First and foremost, my wife Nikita, without whose support this wouldn't be possible at all. The three months of political activity and then the next two months of writing the book kept me away from the house and kids, in spite of being physically present. The writing work kept me occupied day in and day out. I did not even move a glass of water in the meantime. This was also the time when my elder son was appearing for his Class X boards. My wife had to play both father and mother to three kids—our two children and me, the last the most difficult to handle.

A special apology and thanks to my children: my elder son Orion, who had to compromise on his weekend outings and TV viewing times and adapt to forced silence whenever I was writing. From insisting on designing the cover page to making some awesome masala chai during my long writing spells, Orion stepped into his mother's shoes on many occasions.

My younger son Arhaan had been excited about the book from day one. He had already started writing his own stories long ago, and with me starting this book, he even alleged that Baba had copied his idea of becoming a 'writer'—indeed, my child!

My elder brother and friend Mohan inculcated the habit of reading in me by handing over my first story book to me when I was a child. Till date he remains the person whom I can fall back upon in times of crisis.

My nephew Parth chipped in to help me collate the daywise research when I got busy with my fellowship preparations.

Apart from family, there are people without whom this book would have never seen the light of the day—especially my friend and colleague from *India Today* magazine, Kiran Tare, who encouraged me from day one and from the first thought ever of writing the book—from patiently hearing out my ideas to giving valuable suggestions, reading the first draft and giving me much-required moral support during some real turbulent times in the period... My teacher Asha Deshmukh, who always encouraged me as a child and taught me to believe in myself.

The India Today Group, Mr Aroon Purie and Ms Kalli Purie, for providing endless opportunities.

Rahul Kanwal, whose infinite praises for me during the 36-day political drama amidst the breaking news scenario led to the germination of this book.

Rajdeep Sardesai, for inspiring me from my early days of journalism and giving me the impetus to work as a TV journalist.

Narendra Dubey for lending his laptop for months without a second thought.

All my cameramen from India Today group, who were part of the 24x7 grind during the 36-day drama.

My fellow journalists from TV and print media who shared the anxious moments on field.

To all the politicians who are part of the book: Sharad Pawar, Uddhav Thackeray, Sonia Gandhi, Sanjay Raut, Devendra Fadnavis, Prithviraj Chavan, Ashok Chavan, Supriya Sule, Aditya Thackeray, Ashish Shelar, Nawab Malik, Eknath Shinde, and others—you are the collective soul of this book.

This book was completed alongside my routine office work. Several friends helped me at various points: Rajendra Aklekar, Paulomi Saha, Ramraje Shinde, Mangesh Chiwate, Uday Jadhav, Sahil Joshi, Prachi Jatania, Priyamvatha P. You all have directly and indirectly contributed to this book.

Most importantly, Mr Kapish Mehra and the team at Rupa Publications, for believing in the idea of the book from our first ever interaction.

Finally, the politics of Maharashtra—astute, insightful, yet mature...

INDEX

6, Krishna Menon Marg, 62
10, Janpath, 38, 46, 48, 60, 76, 84, 91, 92, 108, 121, 126, 130, 131, 198, 201, 213

Aditya Sanvad, 6
Advani, Lal Krishna, 8
Ayodhya, 2, 23, 66, 82, 83, 84, 121, 122

Barve, Sanjay, 10, 26, 30, 32, 33, 36, 37, 41, 43, 46, 47, 51, 52, 54, 55, 58, 59, 61, 63, 65, 69, 70, 77, 78, 81, 87, 88, 90, 91, 92, 95, 103, 106, 112, 113, 117, 122, 124, 127, 129, 131, 134, 136, 138, 141, 142, 151, 153, 154, 155, 156, 160, 164, 195, 205, 212, 222, 224
Bharatiya Janata Party (BJP), xi, 1-9, 12-77, 79-81, 84-91, 95, 96, 98-100, 103, 104, 106, 107, 109-115, 117, 119-129, 132-138, 141, 143, 144, 146, 150-152, 154, 156, 158, 160, 161, 163-167, 169-171, 173, 176-182, 185, 186, 188, 189, 192, 194-199, 202-207, 209, 214, 217-220, 222
Bhima Koregaon, 7
Bhosale, Shivendra Raje, 9
Bhosale, Udayanraje, 9
Bhujbal, Chhagan, 10, 52, 95, 101, 103, 107, 108, 118, 122, 130, 148, 149, 155, 169, 184, 200, 205, 208, 221
Biju Janata Dal (BJD), 120
BJP Headquarters, Nariman Point, 17

BJP–Shiv Sena alliance, 3, 13, 17, 121
Chautala, Ajay, 26
Chautala, Dushyant, 26, 29, 33, 64, 81
Chavan, Ashok, 45, 46, 48, 49, 52, 67, 81, 101-103, 126, 131, 139, 149, 155, 178, 181, 186, 196, 211, 224
Chavan, Prithviraj, 29, 38, 40, 45, 46, 48, 52, 66, 67, 81, 102, 103, 108, 124, 126, 130-132, 139, 140, 149, 171, 188, 224
Chouhan, Shivraj Singh, 6, 152

Election Commission of India (ECI), 13

Facebook, 169
Fadnavis, Devendra, xi, 1, 2, 5, 7, 9, 10, 13, 14, 19, 20, 21, 24, 25, 30, 32, 35, 39, 40, 41, 43, 50-54, 59-62, 64, 65, 70, 73, 78, 80, 84, 104, 105, 109, 112, 114, 117, 133, 142, 143, 145, 146, 150, 152, 154, 155, 161, 165, 167, 171, 174, 175, 176, 177, 184, 185, 187, 188, 194, 195, 212, 214, 219, 221, 222, 224

Gadakh, Shankarrao, 34
Gandhi, Rahul, 13, 40, 46, 48, 67, 92, 126, 130
Gandhi, Sonia, 12, 40, 46, 48, 53, 58, 60, 61, 68, 76, 88, 90, 92, 93, 94, 97, 100, 104, 107, 108, 116, 119-123, 126, 130-132, 138, 143, 158, 168, 181-184, 186, 198, 199, 204, 206, 209, 213, 214, 224
Gandhi Vadra, Priyanka, 12
Ghar wapsi, 107

INDEX • 227

Hindu Hriday Samrat, 83, 217

India Today, 8, 77, 102, 103, 201, 224

Jal Yukta Shivar, 7
Jammu and Kashmir (J&K), 4, 81, 99
Jan Ashirwad Yatra, 5, 6

Kharge, Mallikarjun, 40, 48, 85, 88, 97, 130, 131, 132, 134, 138, 140, 158, 195, 196
Khattar, Manoharlal, 26, 29
Kolhapur, 9, 15, 127, 180
Koshyari, Bhagat Singh, 31, 61, 74, 79, 84, 86, 89, 92, 95, 96, 97, 105, 144, 145, 167, 195, 210, 212

Lok Janshakti Party (LJP), 3

Maatoshri, 91
Maha Janadesh Yatra, 6, 7, 8, 9
Mahajan, Girish, 9, 38, 62, 64, 73, 88, 110
Maha Shiv Aghadi, 135
Maha Yuti, 17, 18, 24, 39, 40, 79, 88, 205
Marathi manoos, 14, 83, 216
Modi, Narendra, 3, 6, 12, 13, 19, 24, 29, 39, 54, 56, 63, 84, 85, 96, 106, 120, 127, 128, 129, 137, 142, 144, 146, 165, 177, 214, 217, 219, 224
Mukherjee, Shyama Prasad, 4

National Democratic Alliance (NDA), 3, 55, 56, 67, 85, 89, 91, 115, 119, 120, 123, 124
Nationalist Congress Party (NCP), xi, 3, 8,-13, 18-21, 26, 28, 33, 34, 36, 38, 40-42, 45-47, 49, 5-53, 55-60, 64, 66, 69, 71-73, 75, 76, 81-105, 107, 108, 110, 112-123, 125-140, 142, 144-146, 148, 150-159, 161, 163-171, 173, 174, 175, 177-196, 200-203, 205-208, 211, 213, 214, 219, 220-222

Operation Kamal, 222

Patel, Praful, 21, 89, 130, 155, 200, 201, 203, 205, 213
Patil, Chandrakant, 19, 22, 24, 39, 64, 65, 73, 88, 89, 111, 114, 127, 203, 204
Patil, Rana Jagjit Singh, 9
Pawar, Ajit, 7, 9, 11, 33, 41, 42, 56, 58, 59, 91, 94-96, 101-103, 119, 130, 136, 140-163, 166, 169, 170, 173-175, 177, 178, 181, 184, 185, 188, 189, 191-195, 197, 199-208, 210-213, 222
Pawar, Anantrao, 41, 146
Pawar, Pratibha, 200
Pawar, Sharad, xi, 8-12, 18, 20, 21, 23, 28, 33, 34, 41, 46, 47, 49, 51, 52, 53, 55, 56, 58, 59-61, 65, 67, 69, 75, 87, 89, 9-95, 97, 98, 101, 102, 104-109, 112-114, 117-122, 126-132, 136, 138, 140-144, 147-160, 162, 163, 165-169, 175, 177, 181, 183, 184, 196, 198, 200, 204, 208, 209, 221, 224
Pichad, Madhukar, 9
Punyanagari, 67

Raje, Vasundhara, 6, 9
Ramana, N.V., 167, 172, 174
Ram Mandir, 2, 93
Rane, Nitish, 19, 100
Rashtriya Swayamsevak Sangh (RSS), 4, 31, 62, 65, 66, 75, 105, 123, 125, 126, 180
Raut, Sanjay, 26, 30, 32, 33, 36, 37, 41, 43, 46, 47, 51, 52, 54, 55, 58, 59, 61, 63, 65, 69, 70, 77, 78, 81, 88, 90, 91, 92, 95, 103, 106, 112, 113, 117, 122, 124, 127, 129, 131, 136, 138, 141, 142, 151, 155, 195, 205, 224
Reddy, Y.S. Jaganmohan (YSR), 6

Republican Party of India (Athawale) (RPI [A]), 3
Rohatgi, Mukul, 171, 172, 188, 189

Saamana, 18, 24, 26, 30, 33, 35, 36, 37, 43, 50, 52, 55, 57, 58, 59, 74, 83, 88, 106, 120, 124, 132, 133, 136
Samajwadi Party, 137, 187, 208
Sardesai, Rajdeep, 8, 224
Sattar, Abdul, 13, 72
Sawant, Satish, 19
Shah, Amit, 1, 8, 13, 25, 26, 27, 39, 48, 54, 59, 62, 63, 64, 66, 67, 70, 79, 80, 81, 104-107, 110, 124, 127, 128, 137, 141, 144, 146, 178, 205
Shinde, Eknath, 27, 44, 51, 72, 77, 85, 87, 90, 93, 108, 135, 155, 164, 165, 166, 180, 186, 187, 208, 224
Shiromani Akali Dal (SAD), 3
Shivaji, 1, 9, 10, 22, 25, 39, 52, 71, 102, 108, 116, 118, 124, 125, 135, 198, 210, 212, 213, 214, 220, 221
Shiv Sena, xi, xii, 1-5, 7, 8, 10, 13-15, 17-30, 32-61, 63-108, 112-125, 127, 130-133, 135-139, 141-143, 146, 150, 152,-159, 161, 163-168, 170, 171, 175, 176, 178-180, 186-188, 191, 192, 194-199, 201, 202, 205-221
Sholay, 21, 30, 41
Sibal, Kapil, 167, 171, 172, 191
Silver Oak Estate, 10, 20, 45, 46, 51, 67, 81, 89, 136, 141, 143, 150, 152, 168, 169, 204, 211
Singh, Dr Manmohan, 148, 214
Sule, Supriya, 41, 55, 91, 119, 130, 148, 149, 151, 163, 169, 175, 196, 200, 204, 211, 221, 224

Thackeray, Aditya, 1, 5, 6, 14, 22, 25, 28, 30, 42, 44, 45, 53, 57, 59, 75, 80, 86, 87, 91, 93, 94, 98, 99, 118, 134, 135, 136, 153, 155, 165, 180, 196, 204, 213, 214, 222, 224
Thackeray, Bal, 4, 19, 22, 27, 32, 33, 53, 76, 83, 84, 100, 103, 116, 117, 118, 119, 198, 209, 212, 213, 214, 217, 218
Thackeray, Balasaheb, xi, 1, 28, 34, 45, 46, 48, 77, 81, 94, 101, 103, 106, 107, 116, 117, 118, 124, 130, 131, 139, 141, 153, 155, 163, 186, 195, 198, 204, 207, 208, 209, 210, 214, 215, 216, 221, 222
Thackeray, Raj, 133, 215, 216, 217, 219, 221
Thackeray, Uddhav, xi, xii, 1, 4, 5, 14, 15, 20, 22, 23, 24, 25, 27, 28, 29, 30, 32, 33, 35, 36, 38, 39, 43-45, 47, 51, 54, 55, 57-61, 64-66, 68, 71-75, 77-81, 83-87, 89-93, 95, 98-101, 106-109, 112, 113, 117-119, 121, 122, 124, 129, 130, 133, 134, 135-143, 152, 153, 155-157, 159, 164, 167, 175, 176, 179, 180, 181, 196, 197, 198, 204, 208, 209, 210, 212-222, 224
Thorat, Balasaheb, 28, 29, 45, 46, 48, 94, 101, 103, 130, 131, 155, 186, 195, 204, 207, 221
Tihar jail, 26
Tiktok, 118
Twitter, 47, 97, 99, 111, 143, 151, 177, 195, 196

United Progressive Alliance (UPA), 121, 148

Vajpayee, Atal Bihari, 1, 4, 8, 33, 56, 77, 84, 124

Wagh, Chitra, 10
World Economic Forum, 2

Yashwantrao Chavan Centre, 41, 90, 91, 97, 153
Y.B. Chavan Centre 10, 40, 42, 58, 69, 70, 94, 96, 97, 153-167, 213
Yuva Sena, 1, 5, 53, 75

www.ingramcontent.com/pod-product-compliance
Lightning Source LLC
Chambersburg PA
CBHW020328170426
43200CB00006B/315